Visualize This

Visualize This

The FlowingData Guide to Design, Visualization, and Statistics

Nathan Yau

Wiley Publishing, Inc.

Visualize This: The FlowingData Guide to Design, Visualization, and Statistics

Published by
Wiley Publishing, Inc.
10475 Crosspoint Boulevard
Indianapolis, IN 46256
www.wiley.com

Copyright © 2011 by Nathan Yau

Published by Wiley Publishing, Inc., Indianapolis, Indiana

Published simultaneously in Canada

ISBN: 978-0-470-94488-2
ISBN: 978-1-118-14024-6 (ebk)
ISBN: 978-1-118-14026-0 (ebk)
ISBN: 978-1-118-14025-3 (ebk)

Manufactured in the United States of America

10 9 8 7 6 5 4 3 2

For general information on our other products and services please contact our Customer Care Department within the United States at (877) 762-2974, outside the United States at (317) 572-3993 or fax (317) 572-4002.

Wiley also publishes its books in a variety of electronic formats and by print-on-demand. Not all content that is available in standard print versions of this book may appear or be packaged in all book formats. If you have purchased a version of this book that did not include media that is referenced by or accompanies a standard print version, you may request this media by visiting http://booksupport.wiley.com. For more information about Wiley products, visit us at www.wiley.com.

Library of Congress Control Number: 2011928441

To my loving wife, Bea

About the Author

Since 2007, NATHAN YAU has written and created graphics for FlowingData, a site on visualization, statistics, and design. Working with groups such as *The New York Times*, CNN, Mozilla, and SyFy, Yau believes that data and information graphics, while great for analysis, are also perfect for telling stories with data.

Yau has a master's degree in statistics from the University of California, Los Angeles, and is currently a Ph.D. candidate with a focus on visualization and personal data.

About the Technical Editor

KIM REES is co-founder of Periscopic, a socially conscious information visualization firm. A prominent individual in the visualization community, Kim has over seventeen years of experience in the interactive industry. She has published papers in the *Parsons Journal of Information Mapping* and the InfoVIS 2010 Proceedings, and has spoken at the O'Reilly Strata Conference, WebVisions, AIGA Shift, and Portland Data Visualization. Kim received her bachelor of arts in Computer Science from New York University. Periscopic has been recognized in CommArts Insights, Adobe Success Stories, and awarded by the VAST Challenge, CommArts Web Picks, and the *Communication Arts Interactive Annual*. Recently, Periscopic's body of work was nominated for the Cooper-Hewitt National Design Awards.

Credits

Acknowledgments

THIS BOOK would not be possible without the work by the data scientists before me who developed and continue to create useful and open tools for everyone to use. The software from these generous developers makes my life much easier, and I am sure they will keep innovating.

My many thanks to FlowingData readers who helped me reach more people than I ever imagined. They are one of the main reasons why this book was written.

Thank you to Wiley Publishing, who let me write the book that I wanted to, and to Kim Rees for helping me produce something worth reading.

Finally, thank you to my wife for supporting me and to my parents who always encouraged me to find what makes me happy.

Contents

Introduction

Data is nothing new. People have been quantifying and tabulating things for centuries. However, while writing for FlowingData, my website on design, visualization, and statistics, I've seen a huge boom in just these past few years, and it keeps getting better. Improvements in technology have made it extremely easy to collect and store data, and the web lets you access it whenever you want. This wealth in data can, in the right hands, provide a wealth of information to help improve decision making, communicate ideas more clearly, and provide a more objective window looking in at how you look at the world and yourself.

A significant shift in release of government data came in mid-2009, with the United States' launch of Data.gov. It's a comprehensive catalog of data provided by federal agencies and represents transparency and accountability of groups and officials. The thought here is that you should know how the government spends tax dollars. Whereas before, the government felt more like a black box. A lot of the data on Data.gov was already available on agency sites scattered across the web, but now a lot of it is all in one place and better formatted for analysis and visualization. The United Nations has something similar with UNdata; the United Kingdom launched Data.gov.uk soon after, and cities around the world such as New York, San Francisco, and London have also taken part in big releases of data.

The collective web has also grown to be more open with thousands of Application Programming Interfaces (API) to encourage and entice developers to do something with all the available data. Applications such as Twitter and Flickr provide comprehensive APIs that enable completely different user interfaces from the actual sites. API-cataloging site ProgrammableWeb reports more than 2,000 APIs. New applications, such as Infochimps and Factual, also launched fairly recently and were specifically developed to provide structured data.

At the individual level, you can update friends on Facebook, share your location on Foursquare, or tweet what you're doing on Twitter, all with a few clicks on a mouse or taps on a keyboard. More specialized applications enable you to log what you eat, how much you weigh, your mood, and plenty of other things. If you want to track something about yourself, there is probably an application to help you do it.

With all this data sitting around in stores, warehouses, and databases, the field is ripe for people to make sense of it. The data itself isn't all that interesting (to most people). It's the information that comes out of the data. People want to know what their data says, and if you can help them, you're going to be in high demand. There's a reason that Hal Varian, Google's chief economist, says that statistician is the sexy job of the next 10 years, and it's not just because statisticians are beautiful people. (Although we are quite nice to look at in that geek chic sort of way.)

Visualization

One of the best ways to explore and try to understand a large dataset is with visualization. Place the numbers into a visual space and let your brain or your readers' brains find the patterns. We're good at that. You can often find stories that you might never have found with just formal statistical methods.

John Tukey, my favorite statistician and the father of exploratory data analysis, was well versed in statistical methods and properties but believed that graphical techniques also had a place. He was a strong believer in discovering the unexpected through pictures. You can find out a lot about data just by visualizing it, and a lot of the time this is all you need to make an informed decision or to tell a story.

For example, in 2009, the United States experienced a significant increase in its unemployment rate. In 2007, the national average was 4.6 percent. In 2008, it had risen to 5.8 percent. By September 2009, however, it was 9.8 percent. These national averages tell only part of the story though. It's generalizing over an entire country. Were there any regions that had higher unemployment rates than others? Were there any regions that seemed to be unaffected?

The maps in Figure I-1 tell a more complete story, and you can answer the preceding questions after a glance. Darker-colored counties are areas that had relatively higher unemployment rates, whereas the lighter-colored counties had relatively lower rates. In 2009, you see a lot of regions with rates greater than 10 percent in the west and most areas in the east. Areas in the Midwest were not hit as hard (Figure I-2).

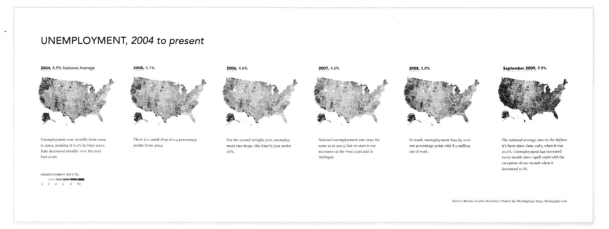

FIGURE I-1 Maps of unemployment in the United States from 2004 to 2009

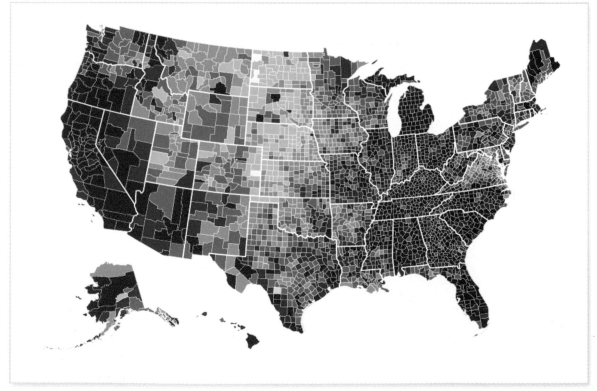

FIGURE I-2 Map of unemployment for 2009

You couldn't find these geographic and temporal patterns so quickly with just a spreadsheet, and definitely not with just the national averages. Also, although the county-level data is more complex, most people can still interpret the maps. These maps could in turn help policy makers decide where to allocate relief funds or other types of support.

The great thing about this is that the data used to produce these maps is all free and publicly available from the Bureau of Labor Statistics. Albeit the data was not incredibly easy to find from an outdated data browser, but the numbers are there at your disposal, and there is a lot sitting around waiting for some visual treatment.

The Statistical Abstract of the United States, for instance, exists as hundreds of tables of data (Figure I-3), but no graphs. That's an opportunity to provide a comprehensive picture of a country. Really interesting stuff. I graphed some of the tables a while back as a proof of concept, as shown in Figure I-4, and you get marriage and divorce rates, postal rates, electricity usage, and a few others. The former is hard to read and you don't get anything out of it other than individual values. In the graphical view, you can find trends and patterns easily and make comparisons at a glance.

News outlets, such as *The New York Times* and *The Washington Post* do a great job at making data more accessible and visual. They have probably made the best use of this available data, as related stories have come and passed. Sometimes data graphics are used to enhance a story with a different point of view, whereas other times the graphics tell the entire story.

Graphics have become even more prevalent with the shift to online media. There are now departments within news organizations that deal only with interactives or only graphics or only maps. *The New York Times*, for example, even has a news desk specifically dedicated to what it calls computer-assisted reporting. These are reporters who focus on telling the news with numbers. *The New York Times* graphics desk is also comfortable dealing with large amounts of data.

Visualization has also found its way into pop culture. Stamen Design, a visualization firm well known for its online interactives, has provided a Twitter tracker for the MTV Video Music Awards the past few years. Each year Stamen designs something different, but at its core, it shows what people are talking about on Twitter in real-time. When Kanye West had his little outburst during Taylor Swift's acceptance speech in 2009, it was obvious what people thought of him via the tracker.

Table 126. **Marriages and Divorces—Number and Rate by State: 1990 to 2007**

[2,443.5 represents 2,443,500. By place of occurence. See Appendix III]

State	Marriages [1] Number (1,000)			Marriages Rate per 1,000 population [2]			Divorces [3] Number (1,000)			Divorces Rate per 1,000 population [2]		
	1990	2000	2007	1990	2000	2007	1990	2000	2007	1990	2000	2007
U.S. [4]	2,443.5	2,329.0	2,204.6	9.8	8.3	7.3	1,182.0	(NA)	(NA)	4.7	4.1	3.6
Alabama	43.1	45.0	42.4	10.6	10.3	9.2	25.3	23.5	19.8	6.1	5.4	4.3
Alaska	5.7	5.6	5.8	10.2	8.9	8.4	2.9	2.7	3.0	5.5	4.4	4.3
Arizona [5]	36.8	38.7	39.5	10.0	7.9	6.2	25.1	21.6	24.5	6.9	4.4	3.9
Arkansas.	36.0	41.1	33.7	15.3	16.0	11.9	16.8	17.9	16.8	6.9	6.9	5.9
California.	237.1	196.9	225.8	7.9	5.9	6.2	128.0	(NA)	(NA)	4.3	(NA)	(NA)
Colorado	32.4	35.6	29.2	9.8	8.6	6.0	18.4	(NA)	21.2	5.5	(NA)	4.4
Connecticut	26.0	19.4	17.3	7.9	5.9	4.9	10.3	6.5	10.7	3.2	2.0	3.1
Delaware.	5.6	5.1	4.7	8.4	6.7	5.5	3.0	3.2	3.9	4.4	4.2	4.5
District of Columbia.	5.0	2.8	2.1	8.2	5.4	3.6	2.7	1.5	1.0	4.5	3.0	1.6
Florida	141.8	141.9	157.6	10.9	9.3	8.6	81.7	81.9	86.4	6.3	5.3	4.7
Georgia	66.8	56.0	64.0	10.3	7.1	6.7	35.7	30.7	(NA)	5.5	3.9	(NA)
Hawaii	18.3	25.0	27.3	16.4	21.2	21.3	5.2	4.6	(NA)	4.6	3.9	(NA)
Idaho	14.1	14.0	15.4	13.9	11.0	10.3	6.6	6.9	7.4	6.5	5.4	4.9
Illinois.	100.6	85.5	75.3	8.8	7.0	5.9	44.3	39.1	32.8	3.8	3.2	2.6
Indiana	53.2	34.5	51.2	9.6	5.8	8.1	(NA)	(NA)	(NA)	(NA)	(NA)	(NA)
Iowa	24.9	20.3	20.1	9.0	7.0	6.7	11.1	9.4	7.8	3.9	3.3	2.6
Kansas	22.7	22.2	18.6	9.2	8.3	6.7	12.6	10.6	9.2	5.0	4.0	3.3
Kentucky.	49.8	39.7	33.6	13.5	10.0	7.9	21.8	21.6	19.7	5.8	5.4	4.6
Louisiana	40.4	40.5	32.8	9.6	9.3	7.6	(NA)	(NA)	(NA)	(NA)	(NA)	(NA)
Maine	11.9	10.5	10.1	9.7	8.3	7.7	5.3	5.8	5.9	4.3	4.6	4.5
Maryland	46.3	40.0	35.5	9.7	7.7	6.3	16.1	17.0	17.4	3.4	3.3	3.1
Massachusetts . . .	47.7	37.0	38.4	7.9	6.0	6.0	16.8	18.6	14.5	2.8	3.0	2.2
Michigan	76.1	66.4	59.1	8.2	6.7	5.9	40.2	39.4	35.5	4.3	4.0	3.5
Minnesota	33.7	33.4	29.8	7.7	6.9	5.7	15.4	14.8	(NA)	3.5	3.1	(NA)
Mississippi.	24.3	19.7	15.7	9.4	7.1	5.4	14.4	14.4	14.2	5.5	5.2	4.9
Missouri	49.1	43.7	39.4	9.6	7.9	6.7	26.4	26.5	22.4	5.1	4.8	3.8
Montana	6.9	6.6	7.1	8.6	7.4	7.4	4.1	2.1	3.6	5.1	2.4	3.7
Nebraska	12.6	13.0	12.4	8.0	7.8	7.0	6.5	6.4	5.5	4.0	3.8	3.1
Nevada	120.6	144.3	126.4	99.0	76.7	49.3	13.3	18.1	16.6	11.4	9.6	6.5
New Hampshire . .	10.5	11.6	9.4	9.5	9.5	7.1	5.3	7.1	5.1	4.7	5.8	3.9
New Jersey	58.7	50.4	45.4	7.6	6.1	5.2	23.6	25.6	25.7	3.0	3.1	3.0
New Mexico [5] . . .	13.3	14.5	11.2	8.8	8.3	5.7	7.7	9.2	8.4	4.9	5.3	4.3
New York [5]	154.8	162.0	130.6	8.6	8.9	6.8	57.9	62.8	55.9	3.2	3.4	2.9
North Carolina . . .	51.9	65.6	68.1	7.8	8.5	7.5	34.0	36.9	37.4	5.1	4.8	4.1
North Dakota	4.8	4.6	4.2	7.5	7.3	6.6	2.3	2.0	1.5	3.6	3.2	2.4
Ohio.	98.1	88.5	70.9	9.0	7.9	6.2	51.0	49.3	37.9	4.7	4.4	3.3
Oklahoma	33.2	15.6	26.2	10.6	4.6	7.3	24.9	12.4	18.8	7.7	3.7	5.2
Oregon	25.3	26.0	29.4	8.9	7.8	7.8	15.9	16.7	14.8	5.5	5.0	4.0
Pennsylvania	84.9	73.2	71.1	7.1	6.1	5.7	40.1	37.9	35.3	3.3	3.2	2.8
Rhode Island	8.1	8.0	6.8	8.1	8.0	6.4	3.8	3.1	3.0	3.7	3.1	2.8
South Carolina . . .	55.8	42.7	31.4	15.9	10.9	7.1	16.1	14.4	14.4	4.5	3.7	3.3
South Dakota	7.7	7.1	6.2	11.1	9.6	7.7	2.6	2.7	2.4	3.7	3.6	3.1
Tennessee.	68.0	88.2	65.6	13.9	15.9	10.6	32.3	33.8	29.9	6.5	6.1	4.9
Texas	178.6	196.4	179.9	10.5	9.6	7.5	94.0	85.2	79.5	5.5	4.2	3.3
Utah.	19.4	24.1	22.6	11.2	11.1	8.6	8.8	9.7	8.9	5.1	4.5	3.4
Vermont	6.1	6.1	5.3	10.9	10.2	8.6	2.6	5.1	2.4	4.5	8.6	3.8
Virginia	71.0	62.4	58.0	11.4	9.0	7.5	27.3	30.2	29.5	4.4	4.3	3.8
Washington	46.6	40.9	41.8	9.5	7.0	6.5	28.8	27.2	28.9	5.9	4.7	4.5
West Virginia	13.0	15.7	13.0	7.2	8.7	7.2	9.7	9.3	9.0	5.3	5.2	5.0
Wisconsin	38.9	36.1	32.2	7.9	6.8	5.8	17.8	17.6	16.1	3.6	3.3	2.9
Wyoming.	4.9	4.9	4.8	10.7	10.3	9.3	3.1	2.8	2.9	6.6	5.9	5.5

NA Not available.   [1] Data are counts of marriages performed, except as noted.   [2] Based on total population residing in area; population enumerated as of April 1 for 1990 and 2000; estimated as of July 1 for all other years.   [3] Includes annulments.   [4] U.S. total for the number of divorces is an estimate which includes states not reporting. Beginning 2000, divorce rates based solely on the combined counts and populations for reporting states and the District of Columbia. The collection of detailed data of marriages and divorces was suspended in January 1996.   [5] Some figures for marriages are marriage licenses issued.

Source: U.S. National Center for Health Statistics, National Vital Statistics Reports (NVSR), *Births, Marriages, Divorces, and Deaths: Provisional Data for 2007*, Vol. 56, No. 21, July 14, 2008 and prior reports.

FIGURE I-3 Table from the Statistical Abstract of the United States

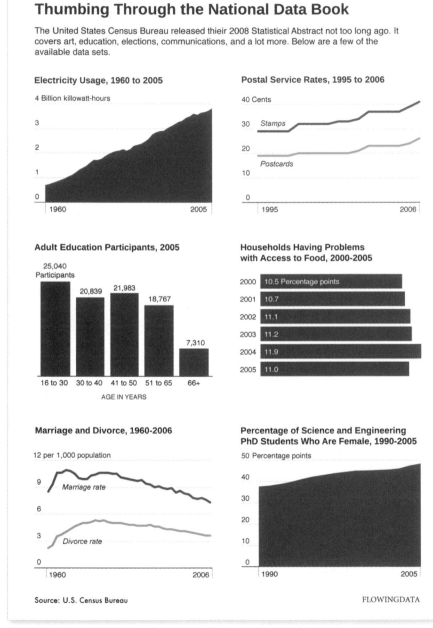

Thumbing Through the National Data Book

The United States Census Bureau released thieir 2008 Statistical Abstract not too long ago. It covers art, education, elections, communications, and a lot more. Below are a few of the available data sets.

Electricity Usage, 1960 to 2005

4 Billion killowatt-hours

3

2

1

0

1960 — 2005

Postal Service Rates, 1995 to 2006

40 Cents

30 Stamps

20

Postcards

10

0

1995 — 2006

Adult Education Participants, 2005

25,040 Participants

20,839 — 21,983 — 18,767

7,310

16 to 30 | 30 to 40 | 41 to 50 | 51 to 65 | 66+

AGE IN YEARS

Households Having Problems with Access to Food, 2000-2005

2000 | 10.5 Percentage points
2001 | 10.7
2002 | 11.1
2003 | 11.2
2004 | 11.9
2005 | 11.0

Marriage and Divorce, 1960-2006

12 per 1,000 population

9 Marriage rate

6

3 Divorce rate

0

1960 — 2006

Percentage of Science and Engineering PhD Students Who Are Female, 1990-2005

50 Percentage points

40

30

20

10

0

1990 — 2005

Source: U.S. Census Bureau

FLOWINGDATA

FIGURE I-4 A graphical view of data from the Statistical Abstract of the United States

At this point, you enter a realm of visualization less analytical and more about feeling. The definition of visualization starts to get kind of fuzzy. For a long time, visualization was about quantitative facts. You should recognize patterns with your tools, and they should aid your analysis in some way. Visualization isn't just about getting the cold hard facts. Like in the case of Stamen's tracker, it's almost more about the entertainment factor. It's a way for viewers to watch the awards show and interact with others in the process. Jonathan Harris' work is another great example. Harris designs his work, such as *We Feel Fine* and *Whale Hunt*, around stories rather than analytical insight, and those stories revolve around human emotion over the numbers and analytics.

Charts and graphs have also evolved into not just tools but also as vehicles to communicate ideas—and even tell jokes. Sites such as GraphJam and Indexed use Venn diagrams, pie charts, and the like to represent pop songs or show that a combination of red, black, and white equals a Communist newspaper or a panda murder. Data Underload, a data comic of sorts that I post on FlowingData, is my own take on the genre. I take everyday observations and put it in chart form. The chart in Figure I-5 shows famous movie quotes listed by the American Film Institute. It's totally ridiculous but amusing (to me, at least).

So what is visualization? Well, it depends on who you talk to. Some people say it's strictly traditional graphs and charts. Others have a more liberal view where anything that displays data is visualization, whether it is data art or a spreadsheet in Microsoft Excel. I tend to sway more toward the latter, but sometimes find myself in the former group, too. In the end, it doesn't actually matter all that much. Just make something that works for your purpose.

► Find more Data Underload on FlowingData at http://datafl .ws/underload

Whatever you decide visualization is, whether you're making charts for your presentation, analyzing a large dataset, or reporting the news with data, you're ultimately looking for truth. At some point in time, lies and statistics became almost synonymous, but it's not that the numbers lie. It's the people who use the numbers who lie. Sometimes it's on purpose to serve an agenda, but most of the time it's inadvertent. When you don't know how to create a graph properly or communicate with data in an unbiased way, false junk is likely to sprout. However, if you learn proper visualization techniques and how to work with data, you can state your points confidently and feel good about your findings.

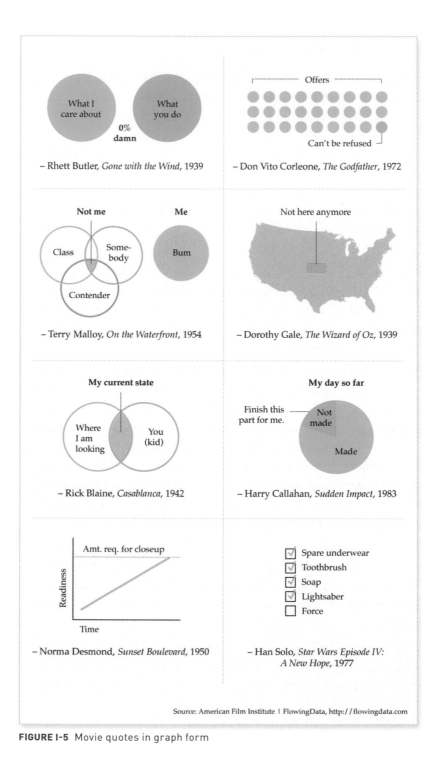

FIGURE I-5 Movie quotes in graph form

Learning Data

I got my start in statistics during my freshman year in college. It was a required introductory course toward my unrelated electrical engineering degree. Unlike some of the horror stories I've heard, my professor was extremely enthusiastic about his teaching and clearly enjoyed the topic. He quickly walked up and down the stairs of the lecture hall as he taught. He waved his hands wildly as he spoke and got students involved as he walked by. To this day, I don't think I've ever had such an excited teacher or professor, and it's undoubtedly something that drew me into the area of data and eventually what led to graduate school in statistics four years later.

Through all my undergraduate studies, statistics was data analysis, distributions, and hypothesis testing, and I enjoyed it. It was fun looking at a dataset and finding trends, patterns, and correlations. When I started graduate school though, my views changed, and things got even more interesting.

Statistics wasn't just about hypothesis testing (which turns out isn't all that useful in a lot of cases) and pattern-finding anymore. Well, no, I take that back. Statistics was still about those things, but there was a different feel to it. Statistics is about storytelling with data. You get a bunch of data, which represents the physical world, and then you analyze that data to find not just correlations, but also what's going on around you. These stories can then help you solve real-world problems, such as decreasing crime, improving healthcare, and moving traffic on the freeway, or it can simply help you stay more informed.

A lot of people don't make that connection between data and real life. I think that's why so many people tell me they "hated that course in college" when I tell them I'm in graduate school for statistics. I know you won't make that same mistake though, right? I mean, you're reading this book after all.

How do you learn the necessary skills to make use of data? You can get it through courses like I did, but you can also learn on your own through experience. That's what you do during a large portion of graduate school anyway.

It's the same way with visualization and information graphics. You don't have to be a graphic designer to make great graphics. You don't need a statistics PhD either. You just need to be eager to learn, and like almost everything in life, you have to practice to get better.

I think the first data graphics I made were in the fourth grade. They were for my science fair project. My project partner and I pondered (very deeply I am sure) what surface snails move on the fastest. We put snails on rough and smooth surfaces and timed them to see how long it took them to go a specific distance. So the data at hand was the times for different surfaces, and I made a bar graph. I can't remember if I had the insight to sort from least to greatest, but I do remember struggling with Excel. The next year though when we studied what cereal red flour beetles preferred, the graphs were a snap. After you learn the basic functionality and your way around the software, the rest is quite easy to pick up. If that isn't a great example of learning from experience, then I don't know what is. Oh, and by the way, the snails moved fastest on glass, and the red flour beetles preferred Grape Nuts, in case you were wondering.

This is basic stuff we're talking about here, but it's essentially the same process with any software or programming language you learn. If you've never written a line of code, R, many statisticians' computing environment of choice, can seem intimidating, but after you work through some examples, you start to quickly get the hang of things. This book can help you with that.

I say this because that's how I learned. I remember when I first got into more of the design aspects of visualization. It was the summer after my second year in graduate school, and I had just gotten the great news that I was going to be a graphics editor intern at *The New York Times*. Up until then, graphics had always been a tool for analysis (with the occasional science fair bar graph) to me, and aesthetics and design didn't matter so much, if at all. Data and its role in journalism didn't occur to me.

So to prepare, I read all the design books I could and went through a guide on Adobe Illustrator because I knew that's what *The New York Times* used. It wasn't until I actually started making graphics though when I truly started learning. When you learn by doing, you're forced to pick up what is necessary, and your skills evolve as you deal with more data and design more graphics.

How to Read This Book

This book is example-driven and written to give you the skills to take a graphic from start to finish. You can read it cover to cover, or you can pick your spots if you already have a dataset or visualization in mind. The chapters are organized so that the examples are self-contained. If you're new to data, the early chapters should be especially useful to you. They cover how to approach your data, what you should look for, and the tools available to you. You can see where to find data and how to format and prepare it for visualization. After that, the visualization techniques are split by data type and what type of story you're looking for. Remember, always let the data do the talking.

Whatever way you decide to read this book, I highly recommend reading the book with a computer in front of you, so that you can work through examples step-by-step and check out sources referred to in notes and references. You can also download code and data files and interact with working demos at www.wiley.com/visualizethis and http://book.flowingdata.com.

Just to make things completely clear, here's a flowchart in Figure I-6 to help you figure what spots to pick. Have fun!

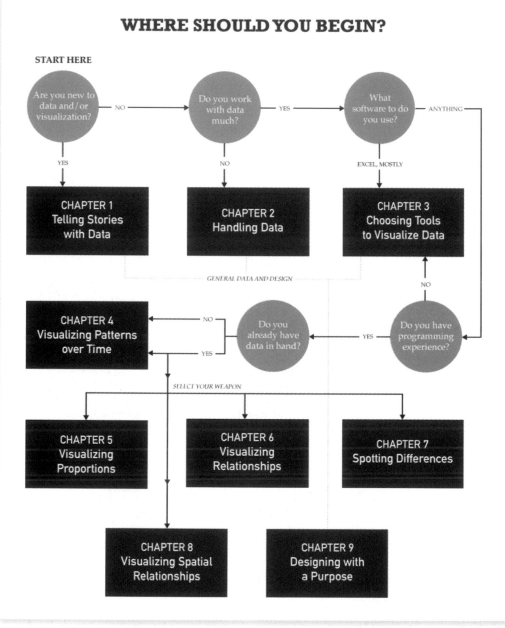

FIGURE I-6 Where to start reading this book

Telling Stories
with Data

1

Think of all the popular data visualization works out there—the ones that you always hear in lectures or read about in blogs, and the ones that popped into your head as you were reading this sentence. What do they all have in common? They all tell an interesting story. Maybe the story was to convince you of something. Maybe it was to compel you to action, enlighten you with new information, or force you to question your own preconceived notions of reality. Whatever it is, the best data visualization, big or small, for art or a slide presentation, helps you see what the data have to say.

More Than Numbers

Face it. Data can be boring if you don't know what you're looking for or don't know that there's something to look for in the first place. It's just a mix of numbers and words that mean nothing other than their raw values. The great thing about statistics and visualization is that they help you look beyond that. Remember, data is a representation of real life. It's not just a bucket of numbers. There are stories in that bucket. There's meaning, truth, and beauty. And just like real life, sometimes the stories are simple and straightforward; and other times they're complex and roundabout. Some stories belong in a textbook. Others come in novel form. It's up to you, the statistician, programmer, designer, or data scientist to decide how to tell the story.

This was one of the first things I learned as a statistics graduate student. I have to admit that before entering the program, I thought of statistics as pure analysis, and I thought of data as the output of a mechanical process. This is actually the case a lot of the time. I mean, I did major in electrical engineering, so it's not all that surprising I saw data in that light.

Don't get me wrong. That's not necessarily a bad thing, but what I've learned over the years is that data, while objective, often has a human dimension to it.

For example, look at unemployment again. It's easy to spout state averages, but as you've seen, it can vary a lot within the state. It can vary a lot by neighborhood. Probably someone you know lost a job over the past few years, and as the saying goes, they're not just another statistic, right? The numbers represent individuals, so you should approach the data in that way. You don't have to tell every individual's story. However, there's a subtle yet important difference between the unemployment rate increasing by 5 percentage points and several hundred thousand people left jobless. The former reads as a number without much context, whereas the latter is more relatable.

Journalism

A graphics internship at *The New York Times* drove the point home for me. It was only for 3 months during the summer after my second year of graduate school, but it's had a lasting impact on how I approach data. I didn't just learn how to create graphics for the news. I learned how to report data as the news, and with that came a lot of design, organization, fact checking, sleuthing, and research.

There was one day when my only goal was to verify three numbers in a dataset, because when *The New York Times* graphics desk creates a graphic, it makes sure what it reports is accurate. Only after we knew the data was reliable did we move on to the presentation. It's this attention to detail that makes its graphics so good.

Take a look at any *New York Times* graphic. It presents the data clearly, concisely, and ever so nicely. What does that mean though? When you look at a graphic, you get the chance to understand the data. Important points or areas are annotated; symbols and colors are carefully explained in a legend or with points; and the *Times* makes it easy for readers to see the story in the data. It's not just a graph. It's a graphic.

The graphic in Figure 1-1 is similar to what you will find in *The New York Times*. It shows the increasing probability that you will die within one year given your age.

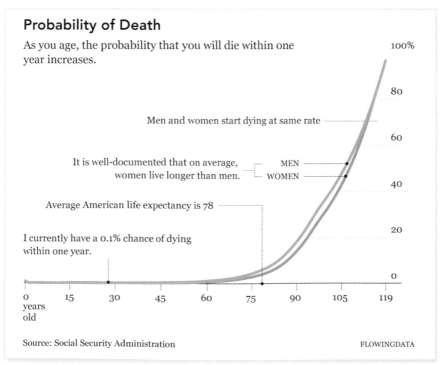

FIGURE 1-1 Probability of death given your age

▶ Check out some of the best *New York Times* graphics at `http://datafl.ws/nytimes`.

The base of the graphic is simply a line chart. However, design elements help tell the story better. Labeling and pointers provide context and help you see why the data is interesting; and line width and color direct your eyes to what's important.

Chart and graph design isn't just about making statistical visualization but also explaining what the visualization shows.

NOTE

See Geoff McGhee's video documentary "Journalism in the Age of Data" for more on how journalists use data to report current events. This includes great interviews with some of the best in the business.

Art

The New York Times is objective. It presents the data and gives you the facts. It does a great job at that. On the opposite side of the spectrum, visualization is less about analytics and more about tapping into your emotions. Jonathan Harris and Sep Kamvar did this quite literally in *We Feel Fine* (Figure 1-2).

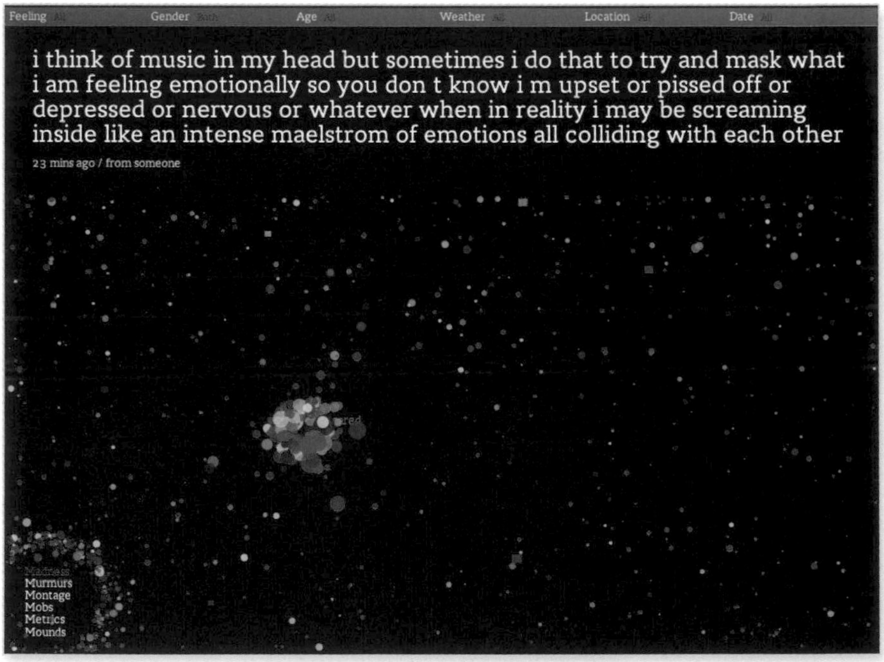
Feeling
Gender
Age
Weather
Location
Date
i think of music in my head but sometimes i do that to try and mask what i am feeling emotionally so you don t know i m upset or pissed off or depressed or nervous or whatever when in reality i may be screaming inside like an intense maelstrom of emotions all colliding with each other
23 mins ago / from someone
Murmurs
Montage
Mobs
Metrics
Mounds

FIGURE 1-2 We Feel Fine by Jonathan Harris and Sep Kamvar

The interactive piece scrapes sentences and phrases from personal public blogs and then visualizes them as a box of floating bubbles. Each bubble represents an emotion and is color-coded accordingly. As a whole, it is like individuals floating through space, but watch a little longer and you see bubbles start to cluster. Apply sorts and categorization through the interface to see how these seemingly random vignettes connect. Click an individual bubble to see a single story. It's poetic and revealing at the same time.

There are lots of other examples such as Golan Levin's *The Dumpster*, which explores blog entries that mention breaking up with a significant other; Kim Asendorf's *Sumedicina*, which tells a fictional story of a man running from a corrupt organization, with not words, but graphs and charts; or Andreas Nicolas Fischer's physical sculptures that show economic downturn in the United States.

The main point is that data and visualization don't always have to be just about the cold, hard facts. Sometimes you're not looking for analytical insight. Rather, sometimes you can tell the story from an emotional point of view that encourages viewers to reflect on the data. Think of it like this. Not all movies have to be documentaries, and not all visualization has to be traditional charts and graphs.

▶ Interact and explore people's emotions in Jonathan Harris and Sep Kamvar's live and online piece at http://wefeelfine.org.

▶ See Flowing-Data for many more examples of art and data at http://datafl.ws/art.

Entertainment

Somewhere in between journalism and art, visualization has also found its way into entertainment. If you think of data in the more abstract sense, outside of spreadsheets and comma-delimited text files, where photos and status updates also qualify, this is easy to see.

Facebook used status updates to gauge the happiest day of the year, and online dating site OkCupid used online information to estimate the lies people tell to make their digital selves look better, as shown in Figure 1-3. These analyses had little to do with improving a business, increasing revenues, or finding glitches in a system. They circulated the web like wildfire because of their entertainment value. The data revealed a little bit about ourselves and society.

Facebook found the happiest day to be Thanksgiving, and OkCupid found that people tend to exaggerate their height by about 2 inches.

▶ Check out the OkTrends blog for more revelations from online dating such as what white people really like and how not to be ugly by accident: http://blog.okcupid.com.

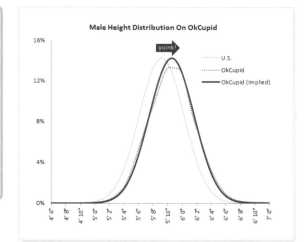

FIGURE 1-3 Male Height Distribution on OkCupid

Compelling

Of course, stories aren't always to keep people informed or entertained. Sometimes they're meant to provide urgency or compel people to action. Who can forget that point in *An Inconvenient Truth* when Al Gore stands on that scissor lift to show rising levels of carbon dioxide?

For my money though, no one has done this better than Hans Rosling, professor of International Health and director of the Gapminder Foundation. Using a tool called Trendalyzer, as shown in Figure 1-4, Rosling runs an animation that shows changes in poverty by country. He does this during a talk that first draws you in deep to the data and by the end, everyone is on their feet applauding. It's an amazing talk, so if you haven't seen it yet, I highly recommend it.

The visualization itself is fairly basic. It's a motion chart. Bubbles represent countries and move based on the corresponding country's poverty during a given year. Why is the talk so popular then? Because Rosling speaks with conviction and excitement. He tells a story. How often have you seen a presentation with charts and graphs that put everyone to sleep? Instead Rosling gets the meaning of the data and uses that to his advantage. Plus, the sword-swallowing at the end of his talk drives the point home. After I saw Rosling's talk, I wanted to get my hands on that data and take a look myself. It was a story I wanted to explore, too.

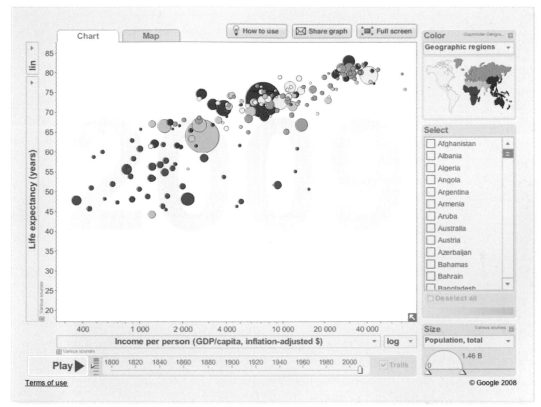

FIGURE 1-4 Trendalyzer by the Gapminder Foundation

I later saw a Gapminder talk on the same topic with the same visualizations but with a different speaker. It wasn't nearly as exciting. To be honest, it was kind of a snoozer. There wasn't any emotion. I didn't feel any conviction or excitement about the data. So it's not just about the data that makes for interesting chatter. It's how you present it and design it that can help people remember.

When it's all said and done, here's what you need to know. Approach visualization as if you were telling a story. What kind of story are you trying to tell? Is it a report, or is it a novel? Do you want to convince people that action is necessary?

Think character development. Every data point has a story behind it in the same way that every character in a book has a past, present, and future. There are interactions and relationships between those data points. It's up

▶ Watch Hans Rosling wow the audience with data and an amazing demonstration at http://datafl .ws/hans.

to you to find them. Of course, before expert storytellers write novels, they must first learn to construct sentences.

What to Look For

Okay, stories. Check. Now what kind of stories do you tell with data? Well, the specifics vary by dataset, but generally speaking, you should always be on the lookout for these two things whatever your graphic is for: patterns and relationships.

Patterns

Stuff changes as time goes by. You get older, your hair grays, and your sight starts to get kind of fuzzy (Figure 1-5). Prices change. Logos change. Businesses are born. Businesses die. Sometimes these changes are sudden and without warning. Other times the change happens so slowly you don't even notice.

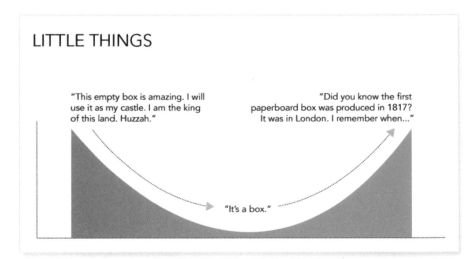

FIGURE 1-5 A comic look at aging

Whatever it is you're looking at, the change itself can be interesting as can the changing process. It is here you can explore patterns over time. For example, say you looked at stock prices over time. They of course increase and decrease, but by how much do they change per day? Per week? Per month? Are there periods when the stock went up more than usual? If so, why did it go up? Were there any specific events that triggered the change?

As you can see, when you start with a single question as a starting point, it can lead you to additional questions. This isn't just for time series data, but with all types of data. Try to approach your data in a more exploratory fashion, and you'll most likely end up with more interesting answers.

You can split your time series data in different ways. In some cases it makes sense to show hourly or daily values. Other times, it could be better to see that data on a monthly or annual basis. When you go with the former, your time series plot could show more noise, whereas the latter is more of an aggregate view.

Those with websites and some analytics software in place can identify with this quickly. When you look at traffic to your site on a daily basis, as shown in Figure 1-6, the graph is bumpier. There are a lot more fluctuations.

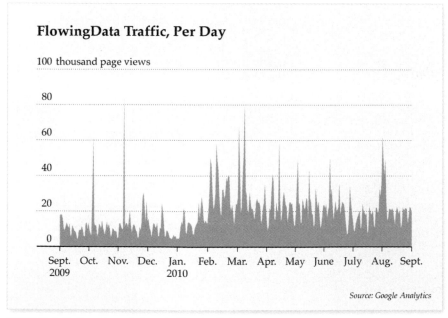

FIGURE 1-6 Daily unique visitors to FlowingData

When you look at it on a monthly basis, as shown in Figure 1-7, fewer data points are on the same graph, covering the same time span, so it looks much smoother.

I'm not saying one graph is better than the other. In fact, they can complement each other. How you split your data depends on how much detail you need (or don't need).

Of course, patterns over time are not the only ones to look for. You can also find patterns in aggregates that can help you compare groups, people, and things. What do you tend to eat or drink each week? What does the President usually talk about during the State of the Union address? What states usually vote Republican? Looking at patterns over geographic regions would be useful in this case. While the questions and data types are different, your approach is similar, as you'll see in the following chapters.

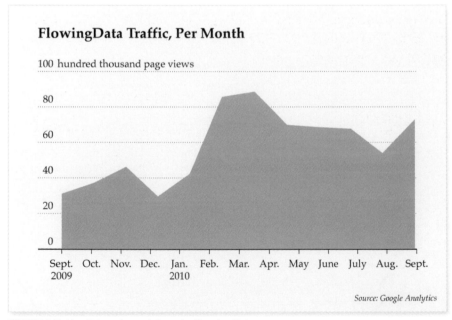

FIGURE 1-7 Monthly unique visitors to FlowingData

Relationships

Have you ever seen a graphic with a whole bunch of charts on it that seemed like they've been randomly placed? I'm talking about the graphics that seem to be missing that special something, as if the designer gave only a little bit of thought to the data itself and then belted out a graphic to meet a deadline. Often, that special something is relationships.

In statistics, this usually means correlation and causation. Multiple variables might be related in some way. Chapter 6, "Visualizing Relationships," covers these concepts and how to visualize them.

At a more abstract level though, where you're not thinking about equations and hypothesis tests, you can design your graphics to compare and contrast values and distributions visually. For a simple example, look at this excerpt on technology from the *World Progress Report* in Figure 1-8.

These are histograms that show the number of users of the Internet, Internet subscriptions, and broadband per 100 inhabitants. Notice that the range for Internet users (0 to 95 per 100 inhabitants) is much wider than that of the other two datasets.

▶ The World Progress Report was a graphical report that compared progress around the world using data from UNdata. See the full version at `http://datafl .ws/12i`.

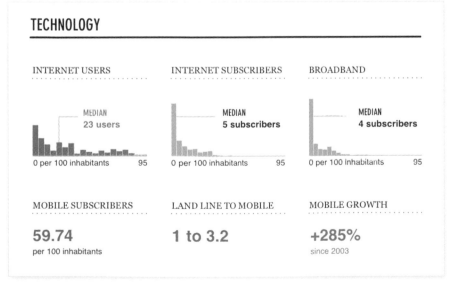

FIGURE 1-8 Technology adoption worldwide

The quick-and-easy thing to do would have been to let your software decide what range to use for each histogram. However, each histogram was made on the same range even though there were no countries who had 95 Internet subscribers or broadband users per 100 inhabitants. This enables you to easily compare the distributions between the groups.

So when you end up with a lot of different datasets, try to think of them as several groups instead of separate compartments that do not interact with each other. It can make for more interesting results.

Questionable Data

While you're looking for the stories in your data, you should always question what you see. Remember, just because it's numbers doesn't mean it's true.

I have to admit. Data checking is definitely my least favorite part of graph-making. I mean, when someone, a group, or a service provides you with a bunch of data, it should be up to them to make sure all their data is legit. But this is what good graph designers do. After all, reliable builders don't use shoddy cement for a house's foundation, so don't use shoddy data to build your data graphic.

Data-checking and verification is one of the most important—if not *the* most important—part of graph design.

Basically, what you're looking for is stuff that makes no sense. Maybe there was an error at data entry and someone added an extra zero or missed one. Maybe there were connectivity issues during a data scrape, and some bits got mucked up in random spots. Whatever it is, you need to verify with the source if anything looks funky.

The person who supplied the data usually has a sense of what to expect. If you were the one who collected the data, just ask yourself if it makes sense: That state is 90 percent of whatever and all other states are only in the 10 to 20 percent range. What's going on there?

Often, an anomaly is simply a typo, and other times it's actually an interesting point in your dataset that could form the whole drive for your story. Just make sure you know which one it is.

Design

When you have all your data in order, you're ready to visualize. Whatever you're making, whether it is for a report, an infographic online, or a piece of data art, you should follow a few basic rules. There's wiggle room with all of them, and you should think of what follows as more of a framework than a hard set of rules, but this is a good place to start if you are just getting into data graphics.

Explain Encodings

The design of every graph follows a familiar flow. You get the data; you encode the data with circles, bars, and colors; and then you let others read it. The readers have to decode your encodings at this point. What do these circles, bars, and colors represent?

William Cleveland and Robert McGill have written about encodings in detail. Some encodings work better than others. But it won't matter what you choose if readers don't know what the encodings represent in the first place. If they can't decode, the time you spend designing your graphic is a waste.

You sometimes see this lack of context with graphics that are somewhere in between data art and infographic. You definitely see it a lot with data art. A label or legend can completely mess up the vibe of a piece of work, but at the least, you can include some information in a short description paragraph. It helps others appreciate your efforts.

Other times you see this in actual data graphics, which can be frustrating for readers, which is the last thing you want. Sometimes you might forget because you're actually working with the data, so you know what everything means. Readers come to a graphic blind though without the context that you gain from analyses.

So how can you make sure readers can decode your encodings? Explain what they mean with labels, legends, and keys. Which one you choose can vary depending on the situation. For example, take a look at the world map in Figure 1-9 that shows usage of Firefox by country.

> **NOTE**
>
> See Cleveland and McGill's paper on *Graphical Perception and Graphical Methods for Analyzing Data* for more on how people encode shapes and colors.

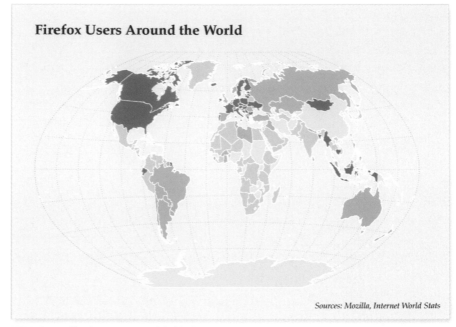

FIGURE 1-9 Firefox usage worldwide by country

You can see different shades of blue for different countries, but what do they mean? Does dark blue mean more or less usage? If dark blue means high usage, what qualifies as high usage? As-is, this map is pretty useless to us. But if you provide the legend in Figure 1-10, it clears things up. The color legend also serves double time as a histogram showing the distribution of usage by number of users.

You can also directly label shapes and objects in your graphic if you have enough space and not too many categories, as shown in Figure 1-11. This is a graph that shows the number of nominations an actor had before winning an Oscar for best actor.

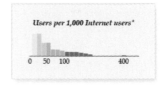

FIGURE 1-10 Legend for Firefox usage map

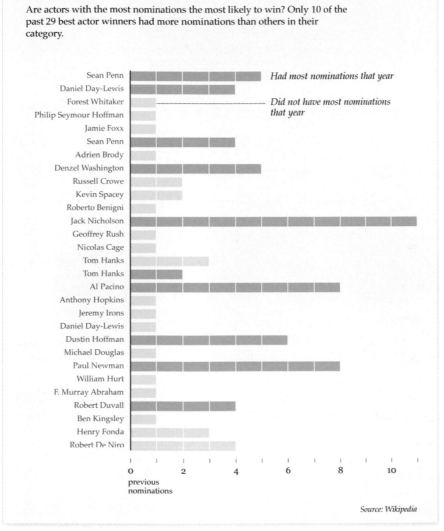

Best Actor Oscar Nominations Before Winning

Are actors with the most nominations the most likely to win? Only 10 of the past 29 best actor winners had more nominations than others in their category.

Sean Penn — *Had most nominations that year*
Forest Whitaker — *Did not have most nominations that year*

previous nominations

Source: Wikipedia

FIGURE 1-11 Directly labeled objects

A theory floated around the web that actors who had the most nominations among their cohorts in a given year generally won the statue. As labeled, dark orange shows actors who did have the most nominations, whereas light orange shows actors who did not.

As you can see, plenty of options are available to you. They're easy to use, but these small details can make a huge difference on how your graphic reads.

Label Axes

Along the same lines as explaining your encodings, you should always label your axes. Without labels or an explanation, your axes are just there for decoration. Label your axes so that readers know what scale points are plotted on. Is it logarithmic, incremental, exponential, or per 100 flushing toilets? Personally, I always assume it's that last one when I don't see labels.

To demonstrate my point, rewind to a contest I held on FlowingData a couple of years ago. I posted the image in Figure 1-12 and asked readers to label the axes for maximum amusement.

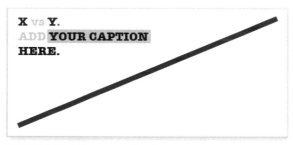

FIGURE 1-12 Add your caption here.

There were about 60 different captions for the same graph; Figure 1-13 shows a few.

As you can see, even though everyone looked at the same graph, a simple change in axis labels told a completely different story. Of course, this was just for play. Now just imagine if your graph were meant to be taken seriously. Without labels, your graph is meaningless.

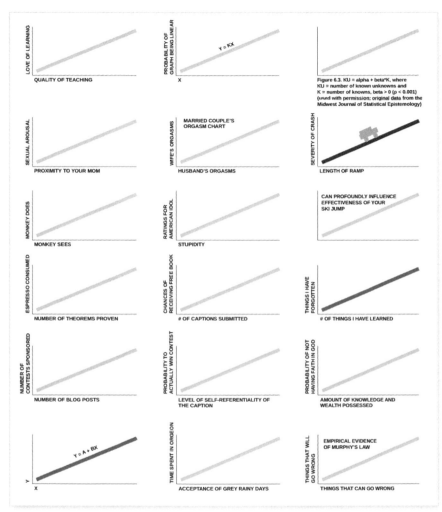

FIGURE 1-13 Some of the results from a caption contest on FlowingData

Keep Your Geometry in Check

When you design a graph, you use geometric shapes. A bar graph uses rectangles, and you use the length of the rectangles to represent values. In a dot plot, the position indicates value—same thing with a standard time series chart. Pie charts use angles to indicate value, and the sum of the values always equal 100 percent (see Figure 1-14). This is easy stuff, so be careful because it's also easy to mess up. You're going to make a mistake if you don't pay attention, and when you do mess up, people, especially on the web, won't be afraid to call you out on it.

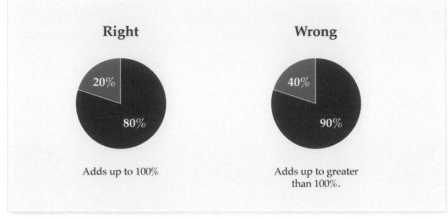

FIGURE 1-14 The right and wrong way to make a pie chart

Another common mistake is when designers start to use two-dimensional shapes to represent values, but size them as if they were using only a single dimension. The rectangles in a bar chart are two-dimensional, but you only use one length as an indicator. The width doesn't mean anything. However, when you create a bubble chart, you use an area to represent values. Beginners often use radius or diameter instead, and the scale is totally off.

Figure 1-15 shows a pair of circles that have been sized by area. This is the right way to do it.

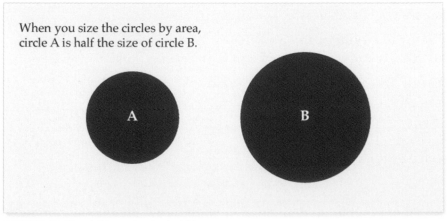

FIGURE 1-15 The right way to size bubbles

Figure 1-16 shows a pair of circles sized by diameter. The first circle has twice the diameter as that of the second but is four times the area.

It's the same deal with rectangles, like in a treemap. You use the area of the rectangles to indicate values instead of the length or width.

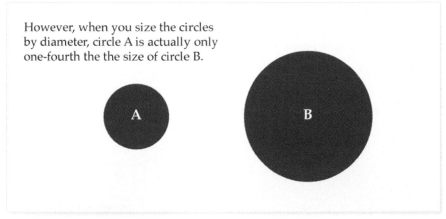

However, when you size the circles by diameter, circle A is actually only one-fourth the the size of circle B.

FIGURE 1-16 The wrong way to size bubbles

Include Your Sources

This should go without saying, but so many people miss this one. Where did the data come from? If you look at the graphics printed in the newspaper, you always see the source somewhere, usually in small print along the bottom. You should do the same. Otherwise readers have no idea how accurate your graphic is.

There's no way for them to know that the data wasn't just made up. Of course, you would never do that, but not everyone will know that. Other than making your graphics more reputable, including your source also lets others fact check or analyze the data.

Inclusion of your data source also provides more context to the numbers. Obviously a poll taken at a state fair is going to have a different interpretation than one conducted door-to-door by the U.S. Census.

Consider Your Audience

Finally, always consider your audience and the purpose of your graphics. For example, a chart designed for a slide presentation should be simple. You can include a bunch of details, but only the people sitting up front will see them. On the other hand, if you design a poster that's meant to be studied and examined, you can include a lot more details.

Are you working on a business report? Then don't try to create the most beautiful piece of data art the world has ever seen. Instead, create a clear and straight-to-the-point graphic. Are you using graphics in analyses? Then the graphic is just for you, and you probably don't need to spend a lot of time on aesthetics and annotation. Is your graphic meant for publication to a mass audience? Don't get too complicated, and explain any challenging concepts.

Wrapping Up

In short, start with a question, investigate your data with a critical eye, and figure out the purpose of your graphics and who they're for. This will help you design a clear graphic that's worth people's time—no matter what kind of graphic it is.

You learn how to do this in the following chapters. You learn how to handle and visualize data. You learn how to design graphics from start to finish. You then apply what you learn to your own data. Figure out what story you want to tell and design accordingly.

Handling Data

Before you start working on the visual part of any visualization, you actually need data. The data is what makes a visualization interesting. If you don't have interesting data, you just end up with a forgettable graph or a pretty but useless picture. Where can you find good data? How can you access it?

When you have your data, it needs to be formatted so that you can load it into your software. Maybe you got the data as a comma-delimited text file or an Excel spreadsheet, and you need to convert it to something such as XML, or vice versa. Maybe the data you want is accessible point-by-point from a web application, but you want an entire spreadsheet.

Learn to access and process data, and your visualization skills will follow.

Gather Data

Data is the core of any visualization. Fortunately, there are a lot of places to find it. You can get it from experts in the area you're interested in, a variety of online applications, or you can gather it yourself.

Provided by Others

This route is common, especially if you're a freelance designer or work in a graphics department of a larger organization. This is a good thing a lot of the time because someone else did all the data gathering work for you, but you still need to be careful. A lot of mistakes can happen along the way before that nicely formatted spreadsheet gets into your hands.

When you share data with spreadsheets, the most common mistake to look for is typos. Are there any missing zeros? Did your client or data supplier mean six instead of five? At some point, data was read from one source and then input into Excel or a different spreadsheet program (unless a delimited text file was imported), so it's easy for an innocent typo to make its way through the vetting stage and into your hands.

You also need to check for context. You don't need to become an expert in the data's subject matter, but you should know where the original data came from, how it was collected, and what it's about. This can help you build a better graphic and tell a more complete story when you design your graphic. For example, say you're looking at poll results. When did the poll take place? Who conducted the poll? Who answered? Obviously, poll results from 1970 are going to take on a different meaning from poll results from the present day.

Finding Sources

If the data isn't directly sent to you, it's your job to go out and find it. The bad news is that, well, that's more work on your shoulders, but the good news is that's it's getting easier and easier to find data that's relevant and machine-readable (as in, you can easily load it into software). Here's where you can start your search.

SEARCH ENGINES

How do you find anything online nowadays? You Google it. This is a no-brainer, but you'd be surprised how many times people email me asking if I know where to find a particular dataset and a quick search provided relevant results. Personally, I turn to Google and occasionally look to Wolfram|Alpha, the computational search engine.

DIRECT FROM THE SOURCE

If a direct query for "data" doesn't provide anything of use, try searching for academics who specialize in the area you're interested in finding data for. Sometimes they post data on their personal sites. If not, scan their papers and studies for possible leads. You can also try emailing them, but make sure they've actually done related studies. Otherwise, you'll just be wasting everyone's time.

You can also spot sources in graphics published by news outlets such as *The New York Times*. Usually data sources are included in small print somewhere on the graphic. If it's not in the graphic, it should be mentioned in the related article. This is particularly useful when you see a graphic in the paper or online that uses data you're interested in exploring. Search for a site for the source, and the data might be available.

This won't always work because finding contacts seems to be a little easier when you email saying that you're a reporter for the so-and-so paper, but it's worth a shot.

UNIVERSITIES

As a graduate student, I frequently make use of the academic resources available to me, namely the library. Many libraries have amped up their technology resources and actually have some expansive data archives. A number of statistics departments also keep a list of data files, many of which are publicly accessible. Albeit, many of the datasets made available by these departments are intended for use with course labs and homework. I suggest visiting the following resources:

- Data and Story Library (DASL) (http://lib.stat.cmu.edu/DASL/)—An online library of data files and stories that illustrate the use of basic statistics methods, from Carnegie Mellon

> ▶ See Wolfram| Alpha at http://wolframalpha.com. The search engine can be especially useful if you're looking for some basic statistics on a topic.

- Berkeley Data Lab (http://sunsite3.berkeley.edu/wikis/datalab/)—
  Part of the University of California, Berkeley library system
- UCLA Statistics Data Sets (www.stat.ucla.edu/data/)—Some of the
  data that the UCLA Department of Statistics uses in their labs and
  assignments

GENERAL DATA APPLICATIONS

A growing number of general data-supplying applications are available.
Some applications provide large data files that you can download for free
or for a fee. Others are built with developers in mind with data accessible
via Application Programming Interface (API). This lets you use data from a
service, such as Twitter, and integrate the data with your own application.
Following are a few suggested resources:

- Freebase (www.freebase.com)—A community effort that mostly provides data on people, places, and things. It's like Wikipedia for data
  but more structured. Download data dumps or use it as a backend
  for your application.
- Infochimps (http://infochimps.org)—A data marketplace with free
  and for-sale datasets. You can also access some datasets via
  their API.
- Numbrary (http://numbrary.com)—Serves as a catalog for (mostly
  government) data on the web.
- AggData (http://aggdata.com)—Another repository of for-sale datasets, mostly focused on comprehensive lists of retail locations.
- Amazon Public Data Sets (http://aws.amazon.com/publicdatasets)—
  There's not a lot of growth here, but it does host some large scientific datasets.
- Wikipedia (http://wikipedia.org)—A lot of smaller datasets in the
  form of HTML tables on this community-run encyclopedia.

TOPICAL DATA

Outside more general data suppliers, there's no shortage of subject-
specific sites offering loads of free data.

Following is a small taste of what's available for the topic of your choice.

Geography

Do you have mapping software, but no geographic data? You're in luck. Plenty of shapefiles and other geographic file types are at your disposal.

- TIGER (www.census.gov/geo/www/tiger/)—From the Census Bureau, probably the most extensive detailed data about roads, railroads, rivers, and ZIP codes you can find
- OpenStreetMap (www.openstreetmap.org/)—One of the best examples of data and community effort
- Geocommons (www.geocommons.com/)—Both data and a mapmaker
- Flickr Shapefiles (www.flickr.com/services/api/)—Geographic boundaries as defined by Flickr users

Sports

People love sports statistics, and you can find decades' worth of sports data. You can find it on *Sports Illustrated* or team organizations' sites, but you can also find more on sites dedicated to the data specifically.

- Basketball Reference (www.basketball-reference.com/)—Provides data as specific as play-by-play for NBA games.
- Baseball DataBank (http://baseball-databank.org/)—Super basic site where you can download full datasets.
- databaseFootball (www.databasefootball.com/)—Browse data for NFL games by team, player, and season.

World

Several noteworthy international organizations keep data about the world, mainly health and development indicators. It does take some sifting though, because a lot of the datasets are quite sparse. It's not easy to get standardized data across countries with varied methods.

- Global Health Facts (www.globalhealthfacts.org/)—Health-related data about countries in the world.

- UNdata (http://data.un.org/)—Aggregator of world data from a variety of sources

- World Health Organization (www.who.int/research/en/)—Again, a variety of health-related datasets such as mortality and life expectancy

- OECD Statistics (http://stats.oecd.org/)—Major source for economic indicators

- World Bank (http://data.worldbank.org/)—Data for hundreds of indicators and developer-friendly

Government and Politics

There has been a fresh emphasis on data and transparency in recent years, so many government organizations supply data, and groups such as the Sunlight Foundation encourage developers and designers to make use of it. Government organizations have been doing this for awhile, but with the launch of data.gov, much of the data is available in one place. You can also find plenty of nongovernmental sites that aim to make politicians more accountable.

- Census Bureau (www.census.gov/)—Find extensive demographics here.

- Data.gov (http://data.gov/)—Catalog for data supplied by government organizations. Still relatively new, but has a lot of sources.

- Data.gov.uk (http://data.gov.uk/)—The Data.gov equivalent for the United Kingdom.

- DataSF (http://datasf.org/)—Data specific to San Francisco.

- NYC DataMine (http://nyc.gov/data/)—Just like the above, but for New York.

- Follow the Money (www.followthemoney.org/)—Big set of tools and datasets to investigate money in state politics.

- OpenSecrets (www.opensecrets.org/)—Also provides details on government spending and lobbying.

Data Scraping

Often you can find the exact data that you need, except there's one problem. It's not all in one place or in one file. Instead it's in a bunch of HTML pages or on multiple websites. What should you do?

The straightforward, but most time-consuming method would be to visit every page and manually enter your data point of interest in a spreadsheet. If you have only a few pages, sure, no problem.

What if you have a thousand pages? That would take too long—even a hundred pages would be tedious. It would be much easier if you could automate the process, which is what *data scraping* is for. You write some code to visit a bunch of pages automatically, grab some content from that page, and store it in a database or a text file.

EXAMPLE: SCRAPE A WEBSITE

The best way to learn how to scrape data is to jump right into an example. Say you wanted to download temperature data for the past year, but you can't find a source that provides all the numbers for the right time frame or the correct city. Go to almost any weather website, and at the most, you'll usually see only temperatures for an extended 10-day forecast. That's not even close to what you want. You want actual temperatures from the past, not predictions about future weather.

Fortunately, the Weather Underground site does provide historic temperatures; however, you can see only one day at a time.

To make things more concrete, look up temperature in Buffalo. Go to the Weather Underground site and search for **BUF** in the search box. This should take you to the weather page for Buffalo Niagara International, which is the airport in Buffalo (see Figure 2-1).

> **NOTE**
>
> Although coding is the most flexible way to scrape the data you need, you can also try tools such as Needlebase and Able2Extract PDF converter. Use is straightforward, and they can save you time.

> ► Visit Weather Underground at http://wunderground.com.

FIGURE 2-1 Temperature in Buffalo, New York, according to Weather Underground

The top of the page provides the current temperature, a 5-day forecast, and other details about the current day. Scroll down toward the middle of the page to the History & Almanac panel, as shown in Figure 2-2. Notice the drop-down menu where you can select a specific date.

History & Almanac		
	Max Temperature:	Min Temperature:
Normal	52 °F	38 °F
Record	73 °F (1944)	24 °F (1965)
Yesterday	42 °F	29 °F
Yesterday's Heating Degree Days: 29		
Detailed History and Climate		
October ▾ 1 ▾ 2010 ▾ View		

FIGURE 2-2 Drop-down menu to see historical data for a selected date

Adjust the menu to show October 1, 2010, and click the View button. This takes you to a different view that shows you details for your selected date (see Figure 2-3).

Daily Summary

	Actual:	Average :	Record :
Temperature:			
Mean Temperature	56 °F	56 °F	
Max Temperature	62 °F	65 °F	83 °F (1898)
Min Temperature	49 °F	48 °F	34 °F (1993)
Degree Days:			
Heating Degree Days	10	9	
Month to date heating degree days	9	9	
Since 1 July heating degree days	149	187	
Cooling Degree Days	0	1	
Month to date cooling degree days	0	1	
Year to date cooling degree days	744	545	
Growing Degree Days	6 (Base 50)		
Moisture:			
Dew Point	46 °F		
Average Humidity	73		
Maximum Humidity	93		
Minimum Humidity	49		
Precipitation:			
Precipitation	0.00 in	0.11 in	3.00 in (1945)
Month to date precipitation	0.00	0.11	
Year to date precipitation	27.39	29.74	

FIGURE 2-3 Temperature data for a single day

There's temperature, degree days, moisture, precipitation, and plenty of other data points, but for now, all you're interested in is maximum temperature per day, which you can find in the second column, second row down. On October 1, 2010, the maximum temperature in Buffalo was 62 degrees Fahrenheit.

Getting that single value was easy enough. Now how can you get that maximum temperature value every day, during the year 2009? The easy-and-straightforward way would be to keep changing the date in the drop-down. Do that 365 times and you're done.

Wouldn't that be fun? No. You can speed up the process with a little bit of code and some know-how, and for that, turn to the Python programming language and Leonard Richardson's Python library called Beautiful Soup.

You're about to get your first taste of code in the next few paragraphs. If you have programming experience, you can go through the following relatively quickly. Don't worry if you don't have any programming experience though—I'll take you through it step-by-step. A lot of people like to keep everything within a safe click interface, but trust me. Pick up just a little bit of programming skills, and you can open up a whole bag of possibilities for what you can do with data. Ready? Here you go.

First, you need to make sure your computer has all the right software installed. If you work on Mac OS X, you should have Python installed already. Open the Terminal application and type **python** to start (see Figure 2-4).

▶ Visit http://
python.org to
download and in-
stall Python. Don't
worry; it's not too
hard.

FIGURE 2-4 Starting Python in OS X

▶ Visit
www.crummy
.com/software/
BeautifulSoup/ to
download Beauti-
ful Soup. Down-
load the version
that matches the
version of Python
that you use.

If you're on a Windows machine, you can visit the Python site and follow the directions on how to download and install.

Next, you need to download Beautiful Soup, which can help you read web pages quickly and easily. Save the Beautiful Soup Python (.py) file in the directory that you plan to save your code in. If you know your way around Python, you can also put Beautiful Soup in your library path, but it'll work the same either way.

After you install Python and download Beautiful Soup, start a file in your favorite text or code editor, and save it as get-weather-data.py. Now you can code.

The first thing you need to do is load the page that shows historical weather information. The URL for historical weather in Buffalo on October 1, 2010, follows:

```
www.wunderground.com/history/airport/KBUF/2010/10/1/DailyHistory
.html?req_city=NA&req_state=NA&req_statename=NA
```

If you remove everything after .html in the preceding URL, the same page still loads, so get rid of those. You don't care about those right now.

```
www.wunderground.com/history/airport/KBUF/2010/10/1/DailyHistory.html
```

The date is indicated in the URL with /2010/10/1. Using the drop-down menu, change the date to January 1, 2009, because you're going to scrape temperature for all of 2009. The URL is now this:

```
www.wunderground.com/history/airport/KBUF/2009/1/1/DailyHistory.html
```

Everything is the same as the URL for October 1, except the portion that indicates the date. It's /2009/1/1 now. Interesting. Without using the drop-down menu, how can you load the page for January 2, 2009? Simply change the date parameter so that the URL looks like this:

```
www.wunderground.com/history/airport/KBUF/2009/1/2/DailyHistory.html
```

Load the preceding URL in your browser and you get the historical summary for January 2, 2009. So all you have to do to get the weather for a specific date is to modify the Weather Underground URL. Keep this in mind for later.

Now load a single page with Python, using the urllib2 library by importing it with the following line of code:

```
import urllib2
```

To load the January 1 page with Python, use the urlopen function.

```
page = urllib2.urlopen("www.wunderground.com/history/airport/
KBUF/2009/1/1/DailyHistory.html")
```

This loads all the HTML that the URL points to in the page variable. The next step is to extract the maximum temperature value you're interested in from that HTML, and for that, Beautiful Soup makes your task much easier. After `urllib2`, import Beautiful Soup like so:

```
from BeautifulSoup import BeautifulSoup
```

At the end of your file, use Beautiful Soup to read (that is, parse) the page.

```
soup = BeautifulSoup(page)
```

Without getting into nitty-gritty details, this line of code reads the HTML, which is essentially one long string, and then stores elements of the page, such as the header or images, in a way that is easier to work with.

For example, if you want to find all the images in the page, you can use this:

```
images = soup.findAll('img')
```

This gives you a list of all the images on the Weather Underground page displayed with the `<img />` HTML tag. Want the first image on the page? Do this:

```
first_image = images[0]
```

Want the second image? Change the zero to a one. If you want the `src` value in the first `<img />` tag, you would use this:

```
src = first_image['src']
```

Okay, you don't want images. You just want that one value: maximum temperature on January 1, 2009, in Buffalo, New York. It was 26 degrees Fahrenheit. It's a little trickier finding that value in your soup than it was finding images, but you still use the same method. You just need to figure out what to put in `findAll()`, so look at the HTML source.

You can easily do this in all the major browsers. In Firefox, go to the View menu, and select Page Source. A window with the HTML for your current page appears, as shown in Figure 2-5.

Scroll down to where it shows Mean Temperature, or just search for it, which is faster. Spot the 26. That's what you want to extract.

The row is enclosed by a `<span>` tag with a `nobr` class. That's your key. You can find all the elements in the page with the `nobr` class.

```
nobrs = soup.findAll(attrs={"class":"nobr"})
```

FIGURE 2-5 HTML source for a page on Weather Underground

As before, this gives you a list of all the occurrences of nobr. The one that you're interested in is the sixth occurrence, which you can find with the following:

```
print nobrs[5]
```

This gives you the whole element, but you just want the 26. Inside the <span> tag with the nobr class is another <span> tag and *then* the 26. So here's what you need to use:

```
dayTemp = nobrs[5].span.string
print dayTemp
```

Ta Da! You scraped your first value from an HTML web page. Next step: scrape all the pages for 2009. For that, return to the original URL.

www.wunderground.com/history/airport/KBUF/2009/1/1/DailyHistory.html

Remember that you changed the URL manually to get the weather data for the date you want. The preceding code is for January 1, 2009. If you want the page for January 2, 2009, simply change the date portion of the URL to match that. To get the data for every day of 2009, load every month (1 through 12) and then load every day of each month. Here's the script in full with comments. Save it to your get-weather-data.py file.

```python
import urllib2
from BeautifulSoup import BeautifulSoup

# Create/open a file called wunder.txt (which will be a comma-delimited
file)
f = open('wunder-data.txt', 'w')

# Iterate through months and day
for m in range(1, 13):
    for d in range(1, 32):

        # Check if already gone through month
        if (m == 2 and d > 28):
          break
        elif (m in [4, 6, 9, 11] and d > 30):
          break

        # Open wunderground.com url
        timestamp = '2009' + str(m) + str(d)
        print "Getting data for " + timestamp
        url = "http://www.wunderground.com/history/airport/KBUF/2009/" +
str(m) + "/" + str(d) + "/DailyHistory.html"
        page = urllib2.urlopen(url)

        # Get temperature from page
        soup = BeautifulSoup(page)
        # dayTemp = soup.body.nobr.b.string
        dayTemp = soup.findAll(attrs={"class":"nobr"})[5].span.string

        # Format month for timestamp
        if len(str(m)) < 2:
          mStamp = '0' + str(m)
        else:
          mStamp = str(m)

        # Format day for timestamp
```

```
    if len(str(d)) < 2:
      dStamp = '0' + str(d)
    else:
      dStamp = str(d)

    # Build timestamp
    timestamp = '2009' + mStamp + dStamp

    # Write timestamp and temperature to file
    f.write(timestamp + ',' + dayTemp + '\n')

# Done getting data! Close file.
f.close()
```

You should recognize the first two lines of code to import the necessary libraries, urllib2 and BeautifulSoup.

```
import urllib2
from BeautifulSoup import BeautifulSoup
```

Next, start a text file called wunder-data-txt with write permissions, using the open() method. All the data that you scrape will be stored in this text file, in the same directory that you saved this script in.

```
# Create/open a file called wunder.txt (which will be a comma-delimited
file)
f = open('wunder-data.txt', 'w')
```

With the next line of code, use a for loop, which tells the computer to visit each month. The month number is stored in the m variable. The loop that follows then tells the computer to visit each day of each month. The day number is stored in the d variable.

> ► See Python documentation for more on how loops and iteration work: http:// docs.python .org/reference/ compound_stmts .html

```
# Iterate through months and day
for m in range(1, 13):
    for d in range(1, 32):
```

Notice that you used range (1, 32) to iterate through the days. This means you can iterate through the numbers 1 to 31. However, not every month of the year has 31 days. February has 28 days; April, June, September, and November have 30 days. There's no temperature value for April 31 because it doesn't exist. So check what month it is and act accordingly. If the current month is February and the day is greater than 28, break and move on to the next month. If you want to scrape multiple years, you need to use an additional if statement to handle leap years.

Similarly, if it's not February, but instead April, June, September, or November, move on to the next month if the current day is greater than 30.

```
# Check if already gone through month
if (m == 2 and d > 28):
    break
elif (m in [4, 6, 9, 11] and d > 30):
    break
```

Again, the next few lines of code should look familiar. You used them to scrape a single page from Weather Underground. The difference is in the month and day variable in the URL. Change that for each day instead of leaving it static; the rest is the same. Load the page with the urllib2 library, parse the contents with Beautiful Soup, and then extract the maximum temperature, but look for the sixth appearance of the nobr class.

```
# Open wunderground.com url
url = "http://www.wunderground.com/history/airport/KBUF/2009/" +
str(m) + "/" + str(d) + "/DailyHistory.html"
page = urllib2.urlopen(url)

# Get temperature from page
soup = BeautifulSoup(page)
# dayTemp = soup.body.nobr.b.string
dayTemp = soup.findAll(attrs={"class":"nobr"})[5].span.string
```

The next to last chunk of code puts together a timestamp based on the year, month, and day. Timestamps are put into this format: yyyymmdd. You can construct any format here, but keep it simple for now.

```
# Format day for timestamp
if len(str(d)) < 2:
    dStamp = '0' + str(d)
else:
    dStamp = str(d)

# Build timestamp
timestamp = '2009' + mStamp + dStamp
```

Finally, the temperature and timestamp are written to 'wunder-data.txt' using the write() method.

```
    # Write timestamp and temperature to file
    f.write(timestamp + ',' + dayTemp + '\n')
```

Then use close()when you finish with all the months and days.

```
# Done getting data! Close file.
f.close()
```

The only thing left to do is run the code, which you do in your terminal with the following:

```
$ python get-weather-data.py
```

It takes a little while to run, so be patient. In the process of running, your computer is essentially loading 365 pages, one for each day of 2009. You should have a file named wunder-data.txt in your working directory when the script is done running. Open it up, and there's your data, as a comma-separated file. The first column is for the timestamps, and the second column is temperatures. It should look similar to Figure 2-6.

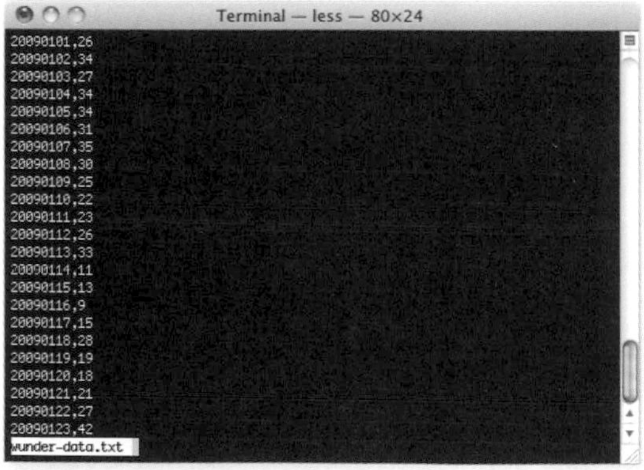

FIGURE 2-6 One year's worth of scraped temperature data

GENERALIZING THE EXAMPLE

Although you just scraped weather data from Weather Underground, you can generalize the process for use with other data sources. Data scraping typically involves three steps:

1. Identify the patterns.

2. Iterate.

3. Store the data.

In this example, you had to find two patterns. The first was in the URL, and the second was in the loaded web page to get the actual temperature value. To load the page for a different day in 2009, you changed the month and day portions of the URL. The temperature value was enclosed in the sixth occurrence of the nobr class in the HTML page. If there is no obvious pattern to the URL, try to figure out how you can get the URLs of all the pages you want to scrape. Maybe the site has a site map, or maybe you can go through the index via a search engine. In the end, you need to know all the URLs of the pages of data.

After you find the patterns, you iterate. That is, you visit all the pages programmatically, load them, and parse them. Here you did it with Beautiful Soup, which makes parsing XML and HTML easy in Python. There's probably a similar library if you choose a different programming language.

Lastly, you need to store it somewhere. The easiest solution is to store the data as a plain text file with comma-delimited values, but if you have a database set up, you can also store the values in there.

Things can get trickier as you run into web pages that use JavaScript to load all their data into view, but the process is still the same.

Formatting Data

Different visualization tools use different data formats, and the structure you use varies by the story you want to tell. So the more flexible you are with the structure of your data, the more possibilities you can gain. Make use of data formatting applications, and couple that with a little bit of programming know-how, and you can get your data in any format you want to fit your specific needs.

The easy way of course is to find a programmer who can format and parse all of your data, but you'll always be waiting on someone. This is especially evident during the early stages of any project where iteration and data exploration are key in designing a useful visualization. Honestly, if I were in a hiring position, I'd likely just get the person who knows how to work with data, over the one who needs help at the beginning of every project.

WHAT I LEARNED ABOUT FORMATTING

When I first learned statistics in high school, the data was always provided in a nice, rectangular format. All I had to do was plug some numbers into an Excel spreadsheet or my awesome graphing calculator (which was the best way to look like you were working in class, but actually playing Tetris). That's how it was all the way through my undergraduate education. Because I was learning about techniques and theorems for analyses, my teachers didn't spend any time on working with raw, preprocessed data. The data always seemed to be in just the right format.

This is perfectly understandable, given time constraints and such, but in graduate school, I realized that data in the real world never seems to be in the format that you need. There are missing values, inconsistent labels, typos, and values without any context. Often the data is spread across several tables, but you need everything in one, joined across a value, like a name or a unique id number.

This was also true when I started to work with visualization. It became increasingly important because I wanted to do more with the data I had. Nowadays, it's not out of the ordinary that I spend just as much time getting data in the format that I need as I do putting the visual part of a data graphic together. Sometimes I spend more time getting all my data in place. This might seem strange at first, but you'll find that the design of your data graphics comes much easier when you have your data neatly organized, just like it was back in that introductory statistics course in high school.

Various data formats, the tools available to deal with these formats, and finally, some programming, using the same logic you used to scrape data in the previous example are described next.

Data Formats

Most people are used to working with data in Excel. This is fine if you're going to do everything from analyses to visualization in the program, but if you want to step beyond that, you need to familiarize yourself with other data formats. The point of these formats is to make your data machine-readable, or in other words, to structure your data in a way that a computer can understand. Which data format you use can change by visualization tool and purpose, but the three following formats can cover most of your bases: delimited text, JavaScript Object Notation, and Extensible Markup Language.

DELIMITED TEXT

Most people are familiar with delimited text. You did after all just make a comma-delimited text file in your data scraping example. If you think of a dataset in the context of rows and columns, a delimited text file splits columns by a delimiter. The delimiter is a comma in a comma-delimited file. The delimiter might also be a tab. It can be spaces, semicolons, colons, slashes, or whatever you want; although a comma and tab are the most common.

Delimited text is widely used and can be read into most spreadsheet programs such as Excel or Google Documents. You can also export spreadsheets as delimited text. If multiple sheets are in your workbook, you usually have multiple delimited files, unless you specify otherwise.

This format is also good for sharing data with others because it doesn't depend on any particular program.

JAVASCRIPT OBJECT NOTATION (JSON)

This is a common format offered by web APIs. It's designed to be both machine- and human-readable; although, if you have a lot of it in front of you, it'll probably make you cross-eyed if you stare at it too long. It's based on JavaScript notation, but it's not dependent on the language. There are a lot of specifications for JSON, but you can get by for the most part with just the basics.

JSON works with keywords and values, and treats items like objects. If you were to convert JSON data to comma-separated values (CSV), each object might be a row.

As you can see later in this book, a number of applications, languages, and libraries accept JSON as input. If you plan to design data graphics for the web, you're likely to run into this format.

▶ Visit http://json.org for the full specification of JSON. You don't need to know every detail of the format, but it can be handy at times when you don't understand a JSON data source.

EXTENSIBLE MARKUP LANGUAGE (XML)

XML is another popular format on the web, often used to transfer data via APIs. There are lots of different types and specifications for XML, but at the most basic level, it is a text document with values enclosed by tags. For example, the Really Simple Syndication (RSS) feed that people use to subscribe to blogs, such as FlowingData, is actually an XML file, as shown in Figure 2-7.

The RSS lists recently published items enclosed in the <item></item> tag, and each item has a title, description, author, and publish date, along with some other attributes.

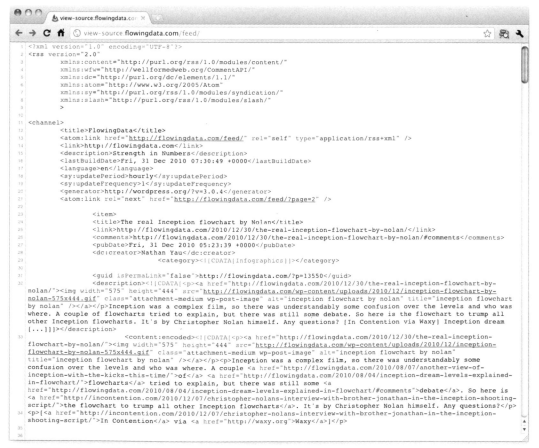

FIGURE 2-7 Snippet of FlowingData's RSS feed

XML is relatively easy to parse with libraries such as Beautiful Soup in Python. You can get a better feel for XML, along with CSV and JSON, in the sections that follow.

Formatting Tools

Just a couple of years ago, quick scripts were always written to handle and format data. After you've written a few scripts, you start to notice patterns in the logic, so it's not super hard to write new scripts for specific datasets, but it does take time. Luckily, with growing volumes of data, some tools have been developed to handle the boiler plate routines.

GOOGLE REFINE

Google Refine is the evolution of Freebase Gridworks. Gridworks was first developed as an in-house tool for an open data platform, Freebase; however, Freebase was acquired by Google, therefore the new name. Google Refine is essentially Gridworks 2.0 with an easier-to-use interface (Figure 2-8) with more features.

It runs on your desktop (but still through your browser), which is great, because you don't need to worry about uploading private data to Google's servers. All the processing happens on your computer. Refine is also open source, so if you feel ambitious, you can cater the tool to your own needs with extensions.

When you open Refine, you see a familiar spreadsheet interface with your rows and columns. You can easily sort by field and search for values. You can also find inconsistencies in your data and consolidate in a relatively easy way.

For example, say for some reason you have an inventory list for your kitchen. You can load the data in Refine and quickly find inconsistencies such as typos or differing classifications. Maybe a fork was misspelled as "frk," or you want to reclassify all the forks, spoons, and knives as utensils. You can easily find these things with Refine and make changes. If you don't like the changes you made or make a mistake, you can revert to the old dataset with a simple undo.

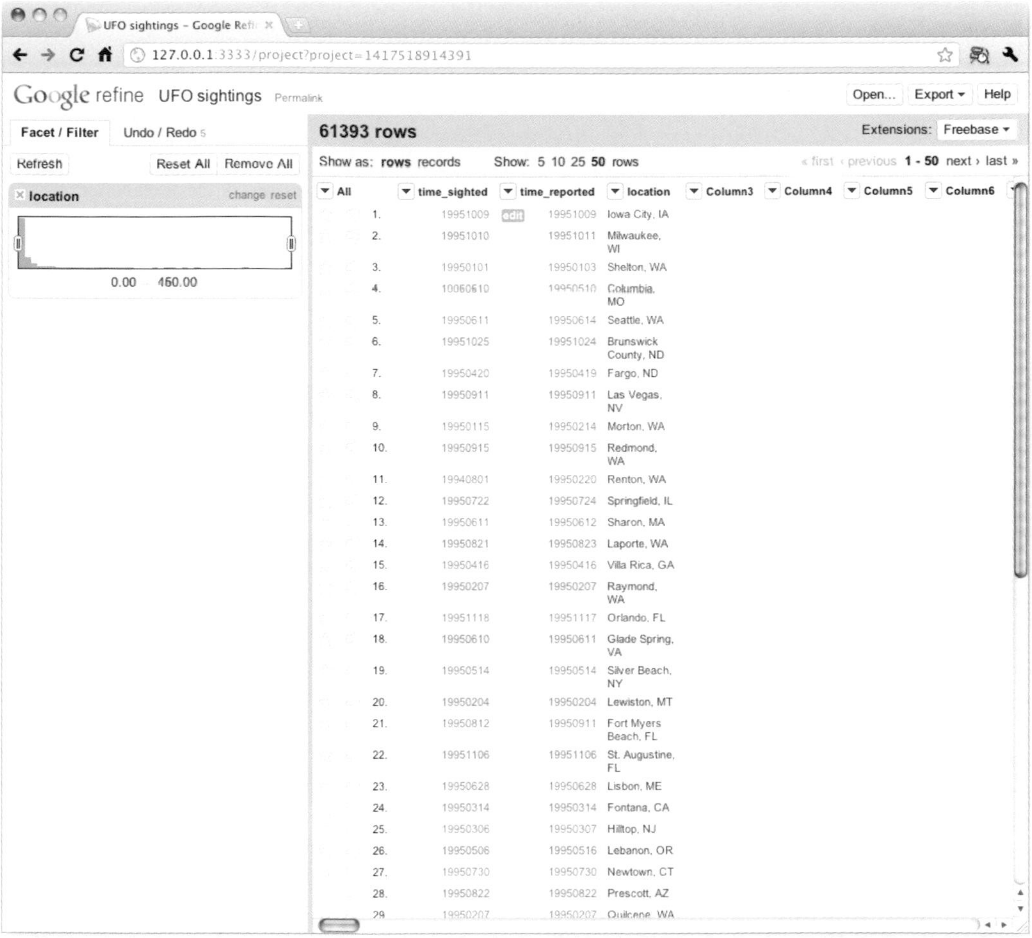

FIGURE 2-8 Google Refine user interface

Getting into the more advanced stuff, you can also incorporate data sources like your own with a dataset from Freebase to create a richer dataset.

If anything, Google Refine is a good tool to keep in your back pocket. It's powerful, and it's a free download, so I highly recommend you at least fiddle around with the tool.

MR. DATA CONVERTER

Often, you might get all your data in Excel but then need to convert it to another format to fit your needs. This is almost always the case when you

▶ Download the open-source Google Refine and view tutorials on how to make the most out of the tool at http://code.google.com/p/google-refine/.

create graphics for the web. You can already export Excel spreadsheets as CSV, but what if you need something other than that? Mr. Data Converter can help you.

Mr. Data Converter is a simple and free tool created by Shan Carter, who is a graphics editor for *The New York Times*. Carter spends most of his work time creating interactive graphics for the online version of the paper. He has to convert data often to fit the software that he uses, so it's not surprising he made a tool that streamlines the process.

It's easy to use, and Figure 2-9 shows that the interface is equally as simple. All you need to do is copy and paste data from Excel in the input section on the top and then select what output format you want in the bottom half of the screen. Choose from variants of XML, JSON, and a number of others.

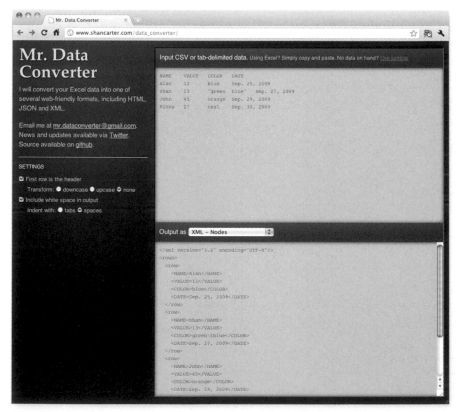

FIGURE 2-9 Mr. Data Converter makes switching between data formats easy.

The source code to Mr. Data Converter is also available if you want to make your own or extend.

MR. PEOPLE

Inspired by Carter's Mr. Data Converter, *The New York Times* graphics deputy director Matthew Ericson created Mr. People. Like Mr. Data Converter, Mr. People enables you to copy and paste data into a text field, and the tool parses and extracts for you. Mr. People, however, as you might guess, is specifically for parsing names.

Maybe you have a long list of names without a specific format, and you want to identify the first and last names, along with middle initial, prefix, and suffix. Maybe multiple people are listed on a single row. That's where Mr. People comes in. Copy and paste names, as shown in Figure 2-10, and you get a nice clean table that you can copy into your favorite spreadsheet software, as shown in Figure 2-11.

Like Mr. Data Converter, Mr. People is also available as open-source software on github.

SPREADSHEET SOFTWARE

Of course, if all you need is simple sorting, or you just need to make some small changes to individual data points, your favorite spreadsheet software is always available. Take this route if you're okay with manually editing data. Otherwise, try the preceding first (especially if you have a giganto dataset), or go with a custom coding solution.

> ▶ Try out Mr. Data Converter at www .shancarter.com/ data_converter/ or download the source on github at https://github .com/shancarter/ Mr-Data-Converter to convert your Excel spreadsheets to a web-friendly format.

> ▶ Use Mr. People at http://people .ericson.net/ or download the Ruby source on github to use the name parser in your own scripts: http://github .com/mericson/ people.

FIGURE 2-10 Input page for names on Mr. People

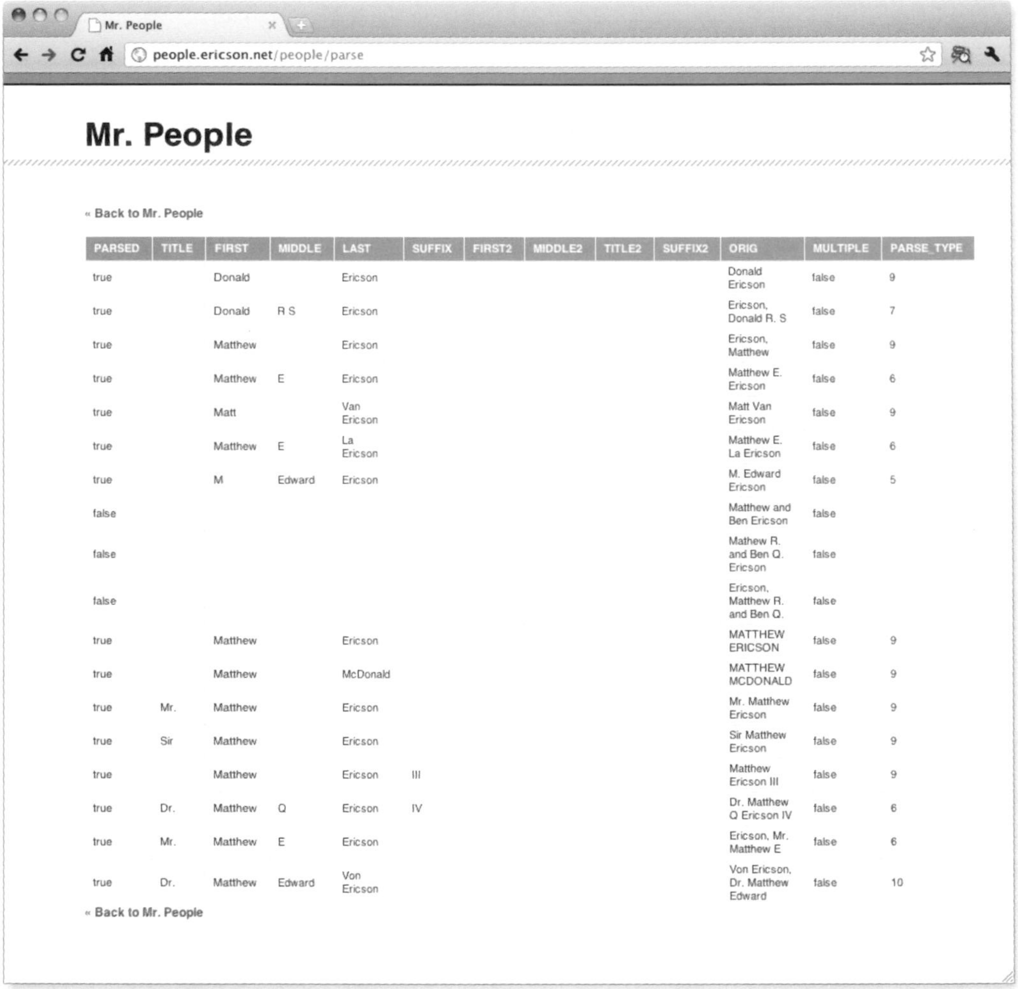

PARSED	TITLE	FIRST	MIDDLE	LAST	SUFFIX	FIRST2	MIDDLE2	TITLE2	SUFFIX2	ORIG	MULTIPLE	PARSE_TYPE
true		Donald		Ericson						Donald Ericson	false	9
true		Donald	R S	Ericson						Ericson, Donald R. S	false	7
true		Matthew		Ericson						Ericson, Matthew	false	9
true		Matthew	E	Ericson						Matthew E. Ericson	false	6
true		Matt		Van Ericson						Matt Van Ericson	false	9
true		Matthew	E	La Ericson						Matthew E. La Ericson	false	6
true		M	Edward	Ericson						M. Edward Ericson	false	5
false										Matthew and Ben Ericson	false	
false										Mathew R. and Ben Q. Ericson	false	
false										Ericson, Matthew R. and Ben Q.	false	
true		Matthew		Ericson						MATTHEW ERICSON	false	9
true		Matthew		McDonald						MATTHEW MCDONALD	false	9
true	Mr.	Matthew		Ericson						Mr. Matthew Ericson	false	9
true	Sir	Matthew		Ericson						Sir Matthew Ericson	false	9
true		Matthew		Ericson	III					Matthew Ericson III	false	9
true	Dr.	Matthew	Q	Ericson	IV					Dr. Matthew Q Ericson IV	false	6
true	Mr.	Matthew	E	Ericson						Ericson, Mr. Matthew E	false	6
true	Dr.	Matthew	Edward	Von Ericson						Von Ericson, Dr. Matthew Edward	false	10

FIGURE 2-11 Parsed names in table format with Mr. People

Formatting with Code

Although point-and-click software can be useful, sometimes the applications don't quite do what you want if you work with data long enough. Some software doesn't handle large data files well; they get slow or they crash.

What do you do at this point? You can throw your hands in the air and give up; although, that wouldn't be productive. Instead, you can write some code to get the job done. With code you become much more flexible, and you can tailor your scripts specifically for your data.

Now jump right into an example on how to easily switch between data formats with just a few lines of code.

EXAMPLE: SWITCH BETWEEN DATA FORMATS

This example uses Python, but you can of course use any language you want. The logic is the same, but the syntax will be different. (I like to develop applications in Python, so managing raw data with Python fits into my workflow.)

Going back to the previous example on scraping data, use the resulting wunder-data.txt file, which has dates and temperatures in Buffalo, New York, for 2009. The first rows look like this:

```
20090101,26
20090102,34
20090103,27
20090104,34
20090105,34
20090106,31
20090107,35
20090108,30
20090109,25
...
```

This is a CSV file, but say you want the data as XML in the following format:

```
<weather_data>
    <observation>
        <date>20090101</date>
        <max_temperature>26</max_temperature>
    </observation>
    <observation>
        <date>20090102</date>
        <max_temperature>34</max_temperature>
    </observation>
    <observation>
        <date>20090103</date>
        <max_temperature>27</max_temperature>
    </observation>
    <observation>
```

```
        <date>20090104</date>
        <max_temperature>34</max_temperature>
    </observation>
      ...
</weather_data>
```

Each day's temperature is enclosed in <observation> tags with a <date> and the <max_temperature>.

To convert the CSV into the preceding XML format, you can use the following code snippet:

```
import csv
reader = csv.reader(open('wunder-data.txt', 'r'), delimiter=",")
print '<weather_data>'

for row in reader:
    print '<observation>'
    print '<date>' + row[0] + '</date>'
    print '<max_temperature>' + row[1] + '</max_temperature>'
    print '</observation>'

print '</weather_data>'
```

As before, you import the necessary modules. You need only the csv module in this case to read in wunder-data.txt.

```
import csv
```

The second line of code opens wunder-data.txt to read using open() and then reads it with the csv.reader() method.

```
reader = csv.reader(open('wunder-data.txt', 'r'), delimiter=",")
```

Notice the delimiter is specified as a comma. If the file were a tab-delimited file, you could specify the delimiter as '\t'.

Then you can print the opening line of the XML file in line 3.

```
print '<weather_data>'
```

In the main chunk of the code, you can loop through each row of data and print in the format that you need the XML to be in. In this example, each row in the CSV header is equivalent to each observation in the XML.

```
for row in reader:
    print '<observation>'
```

```
print '<date>' + row[0] + '</date>'
print '<max_temperature>' + row[1] + '</max_temperature>'
print '</observation>'
```

Each row has two values: the date and the maximum temperature.

End the XML conversion with its closing tag.

```
print '</weather_data>'
```

Two main things are at play here. First, you read the data in, and then you iterate over the data, changing each row in some way. It's the same logic if you were to convert the resulting XML back to CSV. As shown in the following snippet, the difference is that you use a different module to parse the XML file.

```
from BeautifulSoup import BeautifulStoneSoup

f = open('wunder-data.xml', 'r')
xml = f.read()

soup = BeautifulStoneSoup(xml)
observations = soup.findAll('observation')
for o in observations:
    print o.date.string + "," + o.max_temperature.string
```

The code looks different, but you're basically doing the same thing. Instead of importing the csv module, you import BeautifulStoneSoup from BeautifulSoup. Remember you used BeautifulSoup to parse the HTML from Weather Underground. BeautifulStoneSoup parses the more general XML.

You can open the XML file for reading with open() and then load the contents in the xml variable. At this point, the contents are stored as a string. To parse, pass the xml string to BeautifulStoneSoup to iterate through each <observation> in the XML file. Use findAll() to fetch all the observations, and finally, like you did with the CSV to XML conversion, loop through each observation, printing the values in your desired format.

This takes you back to where you began:

```
20090101,26
20090102,34
20090103,27
20090104,34
...
```

To drive the point home, here's the code to convert your CSV to JSON format.

```
import csv
reader = csv.reader(open('wunder-data.txt', 'r'), delimiter=",")

print "{ observations: ["
rows_so_far = 0
for row in reader:

    rows_so_far += 1

    print '{'
    print '"date": ' + '"' + row[0] + '", '
    print '"temperature": ' + row[1]

    if rows_so_far < 365:
        print " },"
    else:
        print " }"

print "] }"
```

Go through the lines to figure out what's going on, but again, it's the same logic with different output. Here's what the JSON looks like if you run the preceding code.

```
{
    "observations": [
        {
            "date": "20090101",
            "temperature": 26
        },
        {
            "date": "20090102",
            "temperature": 34
        },
        ...
    ]
}
```

This is still the same data, with date and temperature but in a different format. Computers just love variety.

Put Logic in the Loop

If you look at the code to convert your CSV file to JSON, you should notice the *if-else* statement in the *for* loop, after the three print lines. This checks if the current iteration is the last row of data. If it isn't, don't put a comma at the end of the observation. Otherwise, you do. This is part of the JSON specification. You can do more here.

You can check if the max temperature is more than a certain amount and create a new field that is 1 if a day is more than the threshold, or 0 if it is not. You can create categories or flag days with missing values.

Actually, it doesn't have to be just a check for a threshold. You can calculate a moving average or the difference between the current day and the previous. There are lots of things you can do within the loop to augment the raw data. Everything isn't covered here because you can do anything from trivial changes to advanced analyses, but now look at a simple example.

Going back to your original CSV file, wunder-data.txt, create a third column that indicates whether a day's maximum temperature was at or below freezing. A 0 indicates above freezing, and 1 indicates at or below freezing.

```
import csv
reader = csv.reader(open('wunder-data.txt', 'r'), delimiter=",")
for row in reader:
    if int(row[1]) <= 32:
        is_freezing = '1'
    else:
        is_freezing = '0'

    print row[0] + "," + row[1] + "," + is_freezing
```

Like before, read the data from the CSV file into Python, and then iterate over each row. Check each day and flag accordingly.

This is of course a simple example, but it should be easy to see how you can expand on this logic to format or augment your data to your liking. Remember the three steps of load, loop, and process, and expand from there.

Wrapping Up

This chapter covered where you can find the data you need and how to manage it after you have it. This is an important step, if not the most important, in the visualization process. A data graphic is only as interesting as its underlying data. You can dress up a graphic all you want, but the data (or the results from your analysis of the data) is still the substance; and now that you know where and how to get your data, you're already a step ahead of the pack.

You also got your first taste of programming. You scraped data from a website and then formatted and rearranged that data, which will be a useful trick in later chapters. The main takeaway, however, is the logic in the code. You used Python, but you easily could have used Ruby, Perl, or PHP. The logic is the same across languages. When you learn one programming language (and if you're a programmer already, you can attest to this), it's much easier to learn other languages later.

You don't always have to turn to code. Sometimes there are click-and-drag applications that make your job a lot easier, and you should take advantage of that when you can. In the end, the more tools you have in your toolbox, the less likely you're going to get stuck somewhere in the process.

Okay, you have your data. Now it's time to get visual.

Choosing Tools to Visualize Data

3

In the last chapter, you learned where to find your data and how to get it in the format you need, so you're ready to start visualizing. One of the most common questions people ask me at this point is "What software should I use to visualize my data?"

Luckily, you have a lot of options. Some are out-of-the-box and click-and-drag. Others require a little bit of programming, whereas some tools weren't designed specifically for data graphics but are useful nevertheless. This chapter covers these options.

The more visualization tools you know how to use and take advantage of, the less likely you'll get stuck not knowing what to do with a dataset and the more likely you can make a graphic that matches your vision.

Out-of-the-Box Visualization

The out-of-the-box solutions are by far the easiest for beginners to pick up. Copy and paste some data or load a CSV file and you're set. Just click the graph type you want—maybe change some options here and there.

Options

The out-of-the-box tools available vary quite a bit, depending on the application they've been designed for. Some, such as Microsoft Excel or Google Documents, are meant for basic data management and graphs, whereas others were built for more thorough analyses and visual exploration.

MICROSOFT EXCEL

You know this one. You have the all-familiar spreadsheet where you put your data, such as in Figure 3-1.

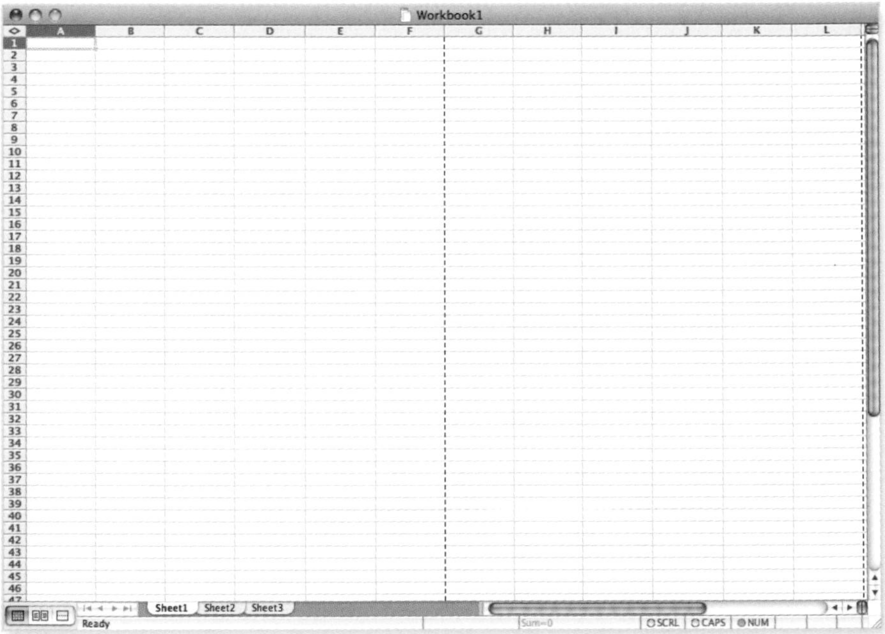

FIGURE 3-1 Microsoft Excel spreadsheet

Then you can click the button with the little bar graph on it to make the chart you want. You get all your standard chart types (Figure 3-2) such as the bar chart, line, pie, and scatterplot.

Some people scoff at Excel, but it's not all that bad for the right tasks. For example, I don't use Excel for any sort of deep analyses or graphics for a publication, but if I get a small dataset in an Excel file, as is often the case, and I want a quick feel for what is in front of me, then sure, I'll whip up a graph with a few clicks in everyone's favorite spreadsheet program.

GRAPHS REALLY *CAN* BE FUN

The first graph I made on a computer was in Microsoft Excel for my fifth grade science fair project. My project partner and I tried to find out which surface snails moved on the fastest. It was ground-breaking research, I assure you.

Even back then I remember enjoying the graph-making. It took me forever to learn (the computer was still new to me), but when I finally did, it was a nice treat. I entered numbers in a spreadsheet and then got a graph instantly that I could change to any color I wanted—blinding, bright yellow it is.

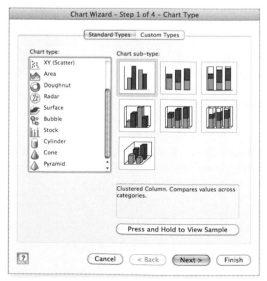

FIGURE 3-2 Microsoft Excel chart options

This ease of use is what makes Excel so appealing to the masses, and that's fine. If you want higher quality data graphics, don't stop here. Other tools are a better fit for that.

GOOGLE SPREADSHEETS

Google Spreadsheets is essentially the cloud version of Microsoft Excel with the familiar spreadsheet interface, obviously (Figure 3-3).

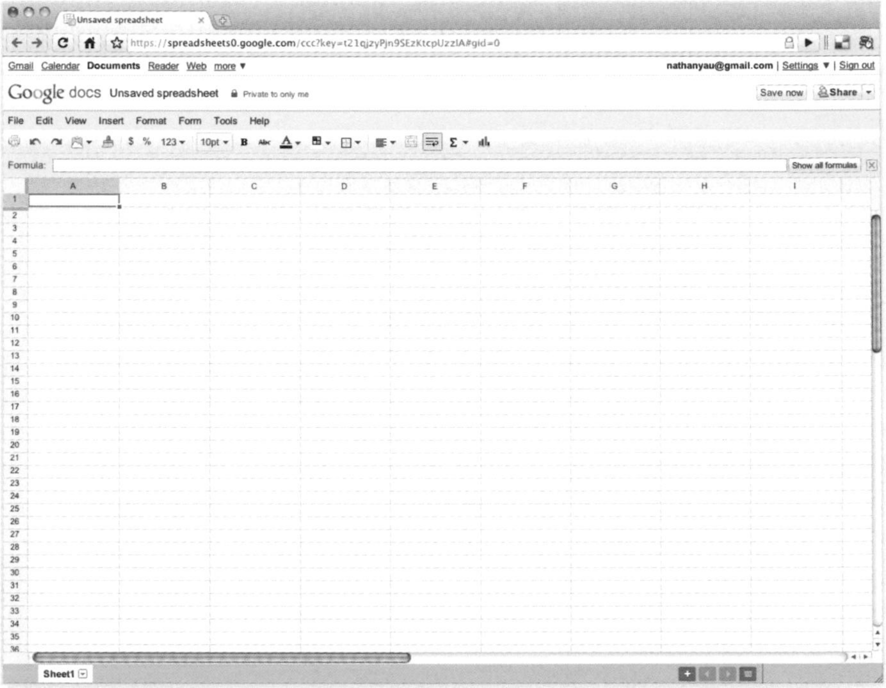

FIGURE 3-3 Google Spreadsheets

FIGURE 3-4 Google Spreadsheets charting options

It also offers your standard chart types, as shown in Figure 3-4.

Google Spreadsheets offers some advantages over Excel, however. First, because your data is stored on the Google servers, you can see your data on any computer as long as it has a web browser installed. Log in to your Google account and go. You can also easily share your spreadsheet with others and collaborate in real-time. Google Spreadsheets also offers some additional charting options via the Gadget option, as shown in Figure 3-5.

A lot of the gadgets are useless, but a few good ones are available. You can, for example, easily make a motion chart with your time series data (just like Hans Rosling). There's also an interactive time series chart that you might be familiar with if you've visited Google Finance, as shown in Figure 3-6.

▶ Visit Google Docs at http://docs.google.com to try spreadsheets.

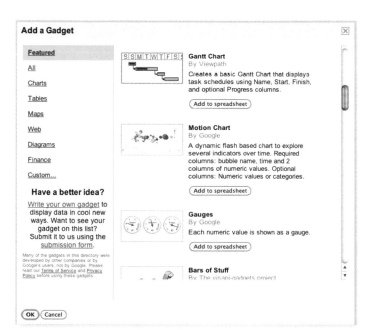

FIGURE 3-5 Google gadgets

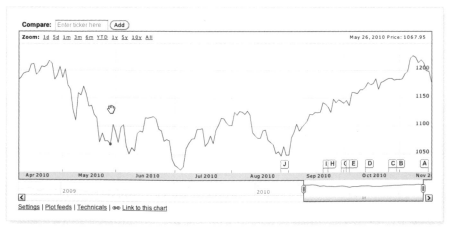

FIGURE 3-6 Google Finance

MANY EYES

Many Eyes is an ongoing research project by the IBM Visual Communication Lab. It's an online application that enables you to upload your data as a text-delimited file and explore through a set of interactive visualization tools. The original premise of Many Eyes was to see if people could explore large datasets as groups—therefore the name. If you have a lot of eyes on a large dataset, can a group find interesting points in the data quicker or more efficiently or find things in the data that you would not have found on your own?

Although social data analyses never caught on with Many Eyes, the tools can still be useful to the individual. Most traditional visualization types are available, such as the line graph (Figure 3-7) and the scatterplot (Figure 3-8).

One of the great things about all the visualizations on Many Eyes is that they are interactive and provide a number of customization options. The scatterplot, for example, enables you to scale dots by a third metric, and you can view individual values by rolling over a point of interest.

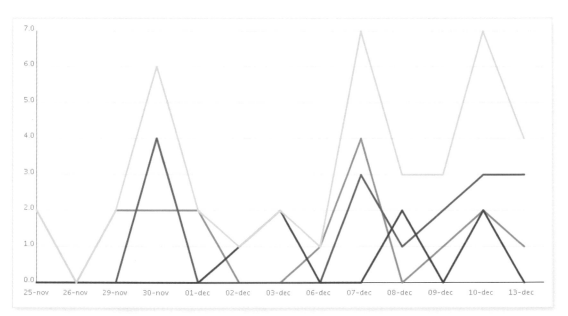

FIGURE 3-7 Line graph on Many Eyes

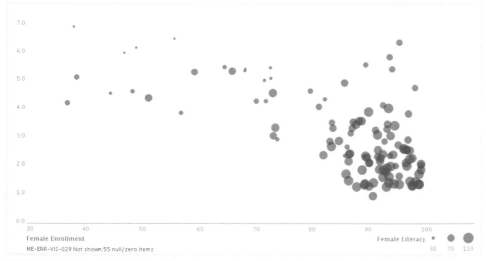

FIGURE 3-8 Scatterplot on Many Eyes

Many Eyes also provides a variety of more advanced and experimental visualizations, along with some basic mapping tools. A word tree helps you explore a full body of text, such as in a book or news article. You choose a word or a phrase, and you can see how your selection is used throughout the text by looking at what follows. Figure 3-9, for example, shows the results of a search for **right** in the United States Constitution.

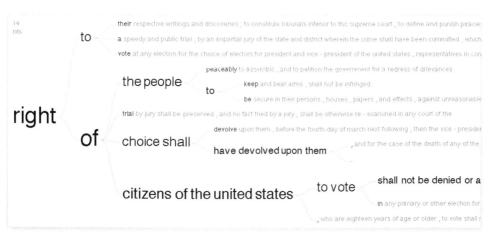

FIGURE 3-9 Word tree on Many Eyes showing parts of the United States Constitution

Alternatively, you can easily switch between tools, using the same data. Figure 3-10 shows the Constitution visualized with a stylized word cloud, known as a Wordle. Words used more often are sized larger.

FIGURE 3-10 Wordle of the United States Constitution

As you can see, Many Eyes has a lot of options to help you play with your data and is by far the most-extensive (and in my eyes, the best) free tool for data exploration; however, a couple of caveats exist. The first is that most of the tools are Java applets, so you can't do much if you don't have Java installed. (This isn't a big deal for most, but I know some people, for whatever reason, who are particular about what they put on their computer.)

The other caveat, which can be a deal breaker, is that all the data you upload to the site is in the public domain. So you can't use Many Eyes, for example, to dig into customer information or sales made by your business.

▶ Try uploading and visualizing your own data http://many-eyes.com.

TABLEAU SOFTWARE

Tableau Software, which is Windows-only software, is relatively new but has been growing in popularity for the past couple of years. It's designed mainly to explore and analyze data visually. It's clear that careful thought has been given to aesthetics and design, which is why so many people like it.

Tableau Software offers lots of interactive visualization tools and does a good job with data management, too. You can import data from Excel, text files, and database servers. Standard time series charts, bar graphs, pie charts, basic mapping, and so on are available. You can mix and match these displays, hook in a dynamic data source for a custom view, or a dashboard, for a snapshot of what's going on in your data.

Most recently, Tableau released Tableau Public, which is free and offers a subset of the functionality in the desktop editions. You can upload your data to Tableau's servers, build an interactive display, and easily publish it to your website or blog. Any data you upload to the servers though, like with Many Eyes, does become publicly available, so keep that in mind.

▶ Visit Tableau Software at `http://tableausoftware.com`. It has a full-functioning free trial.

If you want to use Tableau and keep your data private, you need to go with the desktop editions. At the time of this writing, the desktop software is on the pricier side at $999 and $1,999 for the Personal and Professional editions, respectively.

YOUR.FLOWINGDATA

My interest in personal data collection inspired my own application, your. flowingdata (YFD). It's an online application that enables you to collect data via Twitter and then explore patterns and relationships with a set of interactive visualization tools. Some people track their eating habits or when they go to sleep and wake up. Others have logged the habits of their newborn as sort of a baby scrapbook, with a data twist.

▶ Try personal data collection via Twitter at `http://your.flowingdata.com`.

YFD was originally designed with personal data in mind, but many have found the application useful for more general types of data collection, such as web activity or train arrivals and departures.

Trade-Offs

Although these tools are easy to use, there are some drawbacks. In exchange for click-and-drag, you give up some flexibility in what you can do. You can usually change colors, fonts, and titles, but you're restricted to what the software offers. If there is no button for the chart you want, you're out of luck.

On the flip side, some software might have a lot of functions, but in turn have a ton of buttons that you need to learn. For example, there was one program (not listed here) that I took a weekend crash course for, and it was obvious that it could do a lot if I put in the time. The processes to get things done though were so counterintuitive that it made me not want to learn anymore. It was also hard to repeat my work for different datasets, because I had to remember everything I clicked. In contrast, when you write code to handle your data, it's often easy to reuse code and plug in a different dataset.

Don't get me wrong. I'm not saying to avoid out-of-the-box software completely. They can help you explore your data quickly and easily. But as you work with more datasets, there will be times when the software doesn't fit, and when that time comes you can turn to programming.

Programming

This can't be stressed enough: Gain just a little bit of programming skills, and you can do so much more with data than if you were to stick only with out-of-the-box software. Programming skills give you the ability to be more flexible and more able to adapt to different types of data.

If you've ever been impressed by a data graphic that looked custom-made, most likely it was coded or designed in illustrative software. A lot of the time it's both. The latter is covered a little later.

Code can look cryptic to beginners—I've been there. But think of it as a new language because that's what it is. Each line of code tells the computer to do something. Your computer doesn't understand the way you talk to your friends, so you have to talk to the computer in its own language or syntax.

Like any language, you can't immediately start a conversation. Start with the basics first and then work your way up. Before you know it, you'll be coding. The cool thing about programming is that after you learn one language, it's much easier to learn others because the logic is similar.

Options

So you decide to get your hands dirty with code—good for you. A lot of options are freely available. Some languages are better at performing certain tasks better than others. Some solutions can handle large amounts of data, whereas others are not as robust in that department but can produce much better visuals or provide interaction. Which language you use largely depends on what your goals are for a specific data graphic and what you're most comfortable with.

Some people stick with one language and get to know it well. This is fine, and if you're new to programming, I highly recommend this strategy. Familiarize yourself with the basics and important concepts of code.

Use the language that best suits your needs. However, it's fun to learn new languages and new ways to play with data; so you should develop a good bit of programming experience before you decide on your favorite solution.

PYTHON

The previous chapter discussed how Python can handle data. Python is good at that and can handle large amounts of data without crashing. This makes the language especially useful for analyses and heavy computation.

Python also has a clean and easy-to-read syntax that programmers like, and you can work off of a lot of modules to create data graphics, such as the graph in Figure 3-11.

From an aesthetic point of view, it's not great. You probably don't want to take a graphic from Python direct to publication. The output usually looks kind of rough around the edges. Nevertheless, it can be a good starting point in the data exploration stages. You might also export images and then touch them up or add information using graphic editing software.

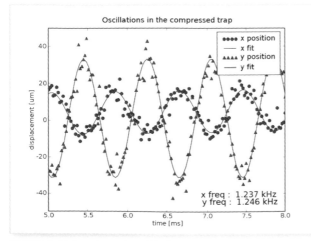

FIGURE 3-11 Graph produced in Python

USEFUL PYTHON RESOURCES

- Official Python website (http://python.org)
- NumPy and SciPy (http://numpy.scipy.org/)—Scientific computing

PHP

PHP was the first language I learned when I started programming for the web. Some people say it's messy, which it can be, but you can just as easily keep it organized. It's usually an easy setup because most web servers already have it installed, so it's easy to jump right in.

	5-Year	Close	High	Low
Cisco		19.55	80.06	8.60
EMC		13.05	101.05	3.83
Sun		5.09	64.32	2.42
Oracle		13.01	43.31	7.32

FIGURE 3-12 Sparklines using a PHP graphing library

There's a flexible PHP graphics library called GD that's also usually included in standard installs. The library enables you to create images from scratch or manipulate existing ones. Also a number of PHP graphing libraries exist that enable you to create basic charts and graphs. The most popular is the Sparklines Graphing Library, which enables you to embed small word-size graphs in text or add a visual component to a numeric table, as shown in Figure 3-12.

Most of the time PHP is coupled with a database such as MySQL, instead of working with a lot of CSV files, to maximize usage and to work with hefty datasets.

USEFUL PHP RESOURCES

- Official PHP website (http://php.net)
- Sparkline PHP Graphing Library (http://sparkline.org)

PROCESSING

Processing is an open-source programming language geared toward designers and data artists. It started as a coding sketchbook in which you could produce graphics quickly; however, it developed a lot since its early days, and many high-quality projects have been created in Processing. For example, *We Feel Fine*, mentioned in Chapter 1, "Telling Stories with Data," was created in Processing.

The great thing about Processing is that you can quickly get up and running. The programming environment is lightweight, and with just a few lines of code, you can create an animated and interactive graphic. It would of course be basic, but because it was designed with the creation of visuals in mind, you can easily learn how to create more advanced pieces.

Although the audience was originally for designers and artists, the community around Processing has grown to be a diverse group. Many libraries can help you do more with the language.

One of the drawbacks is that you do end up with a Java applet, which can be slow to load on some people's computers, and not everyone has Java installed. (Although most people do.) There's a solution for that, though. There's a JavaScript version of Processing recently out of development and ready to use.

Nevertheless, this is a great place to start for beginners. Even those who don't have any programming experience can make something useful.

USEFUL PROCESSING RESOURCE

■ Processing (**http://processing.org**)—Official site for Processing

FLASH AND ACTIONSCRIPT

Most interactive and animated data graphics on the web, especially on major news sites such as *The New York Times*, are built in Flash and ActionScript. You can design graphics in just Flash, which is a click-and-drag interface, but with ActionScript you have more control over interactions. Many applications are written completely in ActionScript, without the use of the Flash environment. However, the code compiles as a Flash application.

For example, an interactive map that animates the growth of Walmart, as shown in Figure 3-13, was written in ActionScript. The Modest Maps library was used, which is a display and interaction library for tile-based maps. It's BSD-licensed, meaning it's free, and you can use it for whatever you want.

NOTE

Although there are many free and open-source ActionScript libraries, Flash and Flash builders can be pricey, which you should consider in your choice of software.

FIGURE 3-13 Map animating the growth of Walmart, written in ActionScript

The interactive stacked area chart in Figure 3-14 was also written in ActionScript. It enables you to search for spending categories over the years. The Flare ActionScript library by the UC Berkeley Visualization Lab was used to do most of the heavy lifting.

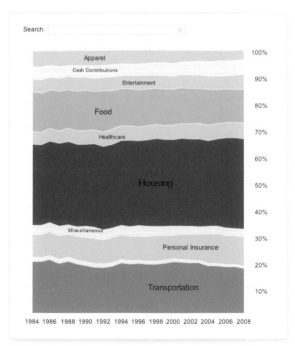

FIGURE 3-14 Interactive stacked area chart showing consumer spending breakdowns, written in ActionScript

If you want to get into interactive graphics for the web, Flash and Action-Script is an excellent option. Flash applications are relatively quick to load, and most people already have Flash installed on their computers.

It's not the easiest language to pick up; the syntax isn't that complicated, but the setup and code organization can overwhelm beginners. You're not going to have an application running with just a few lines of code like you would with Processing. Later chapters take you through the basic steps, and you can find a number of useful tutorials online because Flash is so widely used.

Also, as web browsers improve in speed and efficiency, you have a growing number of alternatives.

USEFUL FLASH AND ACTIONSCRIPT RESOURCES

- Adobe Support www.adobe.com/products/flash/whatisflash/)—Official documentation for Flash and ActionScript (and other Adobe products)
- Flare Visualization Toolkit (http://flare.prefuse.org)
- Modest Maps (http://modestmaps.com)

HTML, JAVASCRIPT, AND CSS

Web browsers continue to get faster and improve in functionality. A lot of people spend more time using their browsers than any other application on their computers. More recently, there has been a shift toward visualization that runs native in your browser via HTML, JavaScript, and CSS. Data graphics used to be primarily built in Flash and ActionScript if there were an interactive component or saved as a static image. This is still often the case, but it used to be that these were the only options.

Now there are several robust packages and libraries that can help you quickly build interactive and static visualizations. They also provide a lot of options so that you can customize the tools for your data needs.

For example, Protovis, maintained by the Stanford Visualization Group, is a free and open-source visualization library that enables you to create web-native visualizations. Protovis provides a number of out-of-the-box visualizations, but you're not at all limited by what you can make, geometrically speaking. Figure 3-15 shows a stacked area chart, which can be interactive.

This chart type is built into the Protovis, but you can also go with a less traditional streamgraph, as shown in Figure 3-16.

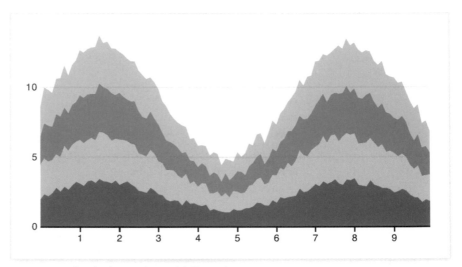

FIGURE 3-15 Stacked area chart with Protovis

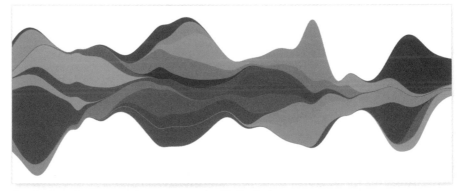

FIGURE 3-16 Custom-made streamgraph with Protovis

You can also easily use multiple libraries for increased functionality. This is possible in Flash, but JavaScript can be a lot less heavy code-wise. JavaScript is also a lot easier to read and use with libraries such as jQuery and MooTools. These are not visualization-specific but are useful. They provide a lot of basic functionality with only a few lines of code. Without the libraries, you'd have to write a lot more, and your code can get messy in a hurry.

Plugins for the libraries can also help you with some of your basic graphics. For example, you can use a Sparkline plugin for jQuery to make small charts (see Figure 3-17).

FIGURE 3-17 Sparklines with jQuery Sparklines plugin

You can also do this with PHP, but this method has a couple of advantages. First, the graphic is generated in a user's browser instead of the server. This relieves stress off your own machines, which can be an issue if you have a website with a lot of traffic.

The other advantage is that you don't need to set up your server with the PHP graphics library. A lot of servers are set up with graphics installed, but sometimes they are not. Installation can be tedious if you're unfamiliar with the system.

You might not want to use a plugin at all. You can also design a custom visualization with standard web programming. Figure 3-18, for example, is an interactive calendar that doubles as a heatmap in your.flowingdata.

There are, however, a couple of caveats. Because the software and technology are relatively new, your designs might look different in different browsers. Some of the previously mentioned tools won't work correctly in an old browser such as Internet Explorer 6. This is becoming less of a problem though, because most people use modern browsers such as Firefox or Google Chrome. In the end it depends on your audience. Less than 5 percent of visitors to FlowingData use old versions of Internet Explorer, so compatibility isn't much of an issue.

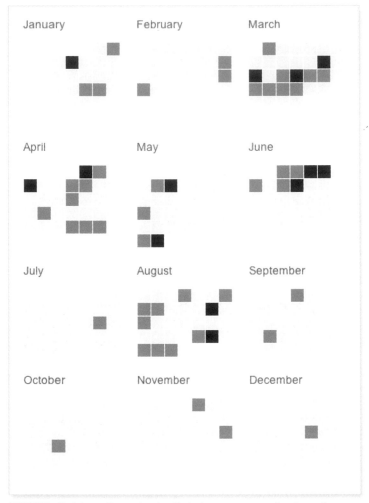

FIGURE 3-18 Interactive calendar that also serves as a heatmap in your.flowingdata

Also related to the age of the technology, there aren't as many libraries available for visualization in JavaScript as there are in Flash and Action-Script. This is why many major news organizations still use a lot of Flash, but this will change as development continues.

> ### USEFUL HTML, JAVASCRIPT, AND CSS RESOURCES
>
> - jQuery (http://jquery.com/)—A JavaScript library that makes coding in the language much more efficient and makes your finished product easier to read.
> - jQuery Sparklines (http://omnipotent.net/jquery.sparkline/)—Make static and animated sparklines in JavaScript.
> - Protovis (http://vis.stanford.edu/protovis/)—A visualization-specific JavaScript library designed to learn by example.
> - JavaScript InfoVis Toolkit (http://datafl.ws/15f)—Another visualization library, although not quite as developed as Protovis.
> - Google Charts API (http://code.google.com/apis/chart/)—Build traditional charts on-the-fly, simply by modifying a URL.

R

If you read FlowingData, you probably know that my favorite software for data graphics is R. It's free and open-source statistical computing software, which also has good statistical graphics functionality. It is also most statisticians' analysis software of choice. There are paid alternatives such as S-plus and SAS, but it's hard to beat the price of free and an active development community.

One of the advantages that R has over the previously mentioned software is that it was specifically designed to analyze data. HTML was designed to make web pages, and Flash is used for tons of other things, such as video and animated advertisements. R, on the other hand, was built and is maintained by statisticians for statisticians, which can be good and bad depending on what angle you're looking from.

There are lots of R packages that enable you to make data graphics with just a few lines of code. Load your data into R, and you can have a graphic with even just one line of code. For example, you can quickly make a treemap using the Portfolio package, as shown in Figure 3-19.

Just as easily, you can build a heatmap, as shown in Figure 3-20.

And of course, you can also make more traditional statistical graphics, such as scatterplots and time series charts, which are discussed in Chapter 4, "Visualizing Patterns over Time."

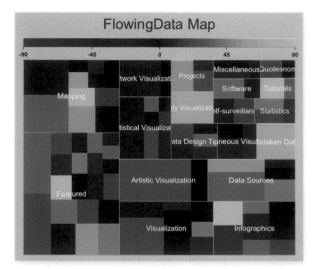

FIGURE 3-19 Treemap generated in R with the Portfolio package

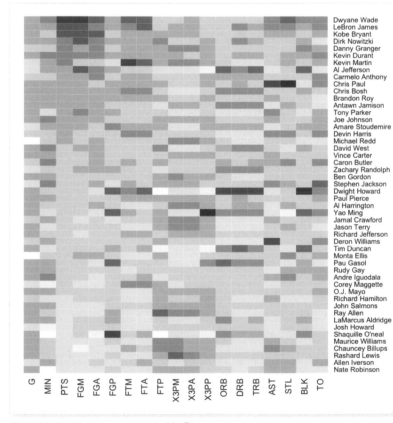

FIGURE 3-20 Heatmap generated in R

To be completely honest though, the R site looks horribly out-dated (Figure 3-21), and the software itself isn't very helpful in guiding new users. You need to remember though that R is a programming language, and you're going to get that with any language you use. The few bad things that I've read about R are usually written by people who are used to buttons and clicking and dragging. So when you come to R don't expect a clicky interface, or you will of course find the interface unfriendly.

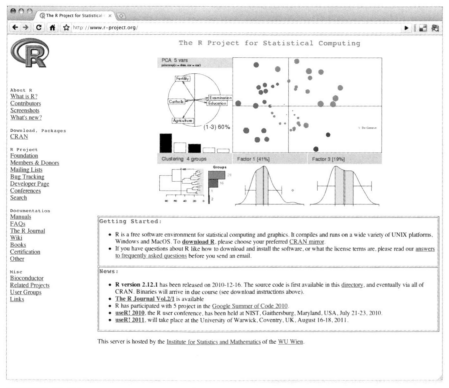

FIGURE 3-21 R homepage, www.r-project.org

But get past that, and there's a lot you can do. You can make publication-quality graphics (or at least the beginnings of them), and you can learn to embrace R's flexibility. If you like, you can write your own functions and packages to make graphics the way you want, or you can use the ones that others have made available in the R library.

TIP

When you search for something about R on the web via search engines, the basic name can sometimes throw off your results. Instead, try searching for **r-project** instead of just **R**, along with what you're looking for. You'll usually find more relevant search results.

R provides base drawing functions that basically enable you to draw what you want. You can draw lines, shapes, and axes within a plotting framework, so again, like the other programming solutions, you're limited only by your imagination. Then again, practically every chart type is available via some R package.

Why would you use anything besides R? Why not just do everything in R? Following are a few reasons. R works on your desktop, so it's not a good fit for the dynamic web. Saving graphics and images and putting them on a web page isn't a problem, but it's not going to happen automatically. You can generate graphics on-the-fly via the web, but so far, the solutions aren't particularly robust when you compare them to the web-native stuff such as JavaScript.

R is also not good with interactive graphics and animation. Again, you can do this in R, but there are better, more elegant ways to accomplish this using, for example, Flash or Processing.

Finally, you might have noticed that the graphics in Figures 3-19 and 3-20 lack a certain amount of polish. You probably won't see graphics like that in a newspaper any time soon. You can tighten up the design in R by messing with different options or writing additional code, but my strategy is usually to make the base graphic in R and then edit and refine in design software such as Adobe Illustrator, which is discussed soon. For analyses, the raw output from R does just fine, but for presentation and storytelling, it's best to adjust aesthetics.

USEFUL R RESOURCE

■ R Project for Statistical Computing (**www.r-project.org**)

Trade-Offs

Learning programming is learning a new language. It's your computer's language of bits and logic. When you work with Excel or Tableau for example, you essentially work with a translator. The buttons and menus are in your language, and when you click items, the software translates your interaction and then sends the translation to your computer. The computer then does something for you, such as makes a graph or processes some data.

So time is definitely a major hurdle. It takes time for you to learn a new language. For a lot of people, this hurdle is too high which I can relate to. You need to get work done now because you have a load of data sitting in front of you, and people waiting on results. If that's the case, in which you have only this single data-related task with nothing in the future, it might be better to go with the out of-the-box visualization tools.

However, if you want to tackle your data and will most likely have (or want) lots of data-related projects in the future, the time spent learning how to program now could end up as saved time on other projects, with more impressive results. You'll get better at programming on each project you go through, and it'll start to come much easier. Just like any foreign language, you don't start writing books in that language; you start with the essentials and then branch out.

Here's another way to look at it. Hypothetically speaking, say you're tossed into a foreign country, and you don't speak the language. Instead, you have a translator. (Stay with me on this one. I have a point.) To talk to a local, you speak, and then your translator forwards the message. What if the translator doesn't know the meaning or the right word for something you just said? He could leave the word out, or if he's resourceful, he can look it up in a translation dictionary.

For out-of-the-box visualization tools, the software is the translator. If it doesn't know how to do something, you're stuck or have to try an alternative method. Unlike the speaking translator, software usually doesn't instantly learn new words, or in this case, graph types or data handling features. New functions come in the form of software updates, which you have to wait for. So what if you learn the language yourself?

Again, I'm not saying to avoid out-of-the-box tools. I use them all the time. They make a lot of tedious tasks quick and easy, which is great. Just don't let the software restrict you.

As you see in later chapters, programming can help you get a lot done with much less effort than if you were to do it all by hand. That said, there are also things better done by hand, especially when you're telling stories with data. That brings you to the next section on illustration: the opposite end of the visualization spectrum.

Illustration

Now you're in graphic designers' comfort zone. If you're an analyst or in a more technical field, this is probably unfamiliar territory. You can do a lot with a combination of code and out-of-the-box visualization tools, but the resulting data graphics almost always have that look of something that was automatically generated. Maybe labels are out of place or a legend feels cluttered. For analyses, this is usually fine—you know what you're looking at.

However, when you make graphics for a presentation, a report, or a publication, more polished data graphics are usually appropriate so that people can clearly see the story you're telling.

For example, Figure 3-19 is the raw output from R. It shows views and comments on FlowingData for 100 popular posts. Posts are separated by category such as Mapping. The brighter the green, the more comments on that post, and the larger the rectangle, the more views. You wouldn't know that from the original, but when I was looking at the numbers, I knew what I was looking at, because I'm the one who wrote the code in R.

Figure 3-22 is a revised version. The labels have been adjusted so that they're all readable; lead-in copy has been added on the top so that readers know what they're looking at; and the red portion of the color legend was removed because there is no such thing as a post having a negative number of comments. I also changed the background to white from gray just because I think it looks better.

I could have edited the code to fit my specific needs, but it was a lot easier to click-and-drag in Adobe Illustrator. You can either make graphics completely with illustration software, or you can import graphics that you've made in, for example, R, and edit it to your liking. For the former, your visualization choices are limited because visualization is not the primary purpose of the software. For anything more complex than a bar chart, your best bet is to go with the latter. Otherwise, you will have to do a lot of things by hand, which is prone to mistakes.

The great thing about using illustration software is that you have more control over individual elements, and you can do everything by clicking and dragging. Change the color of bars or a single bar, modify axes width, or annotate important features with a few mouse clicks.

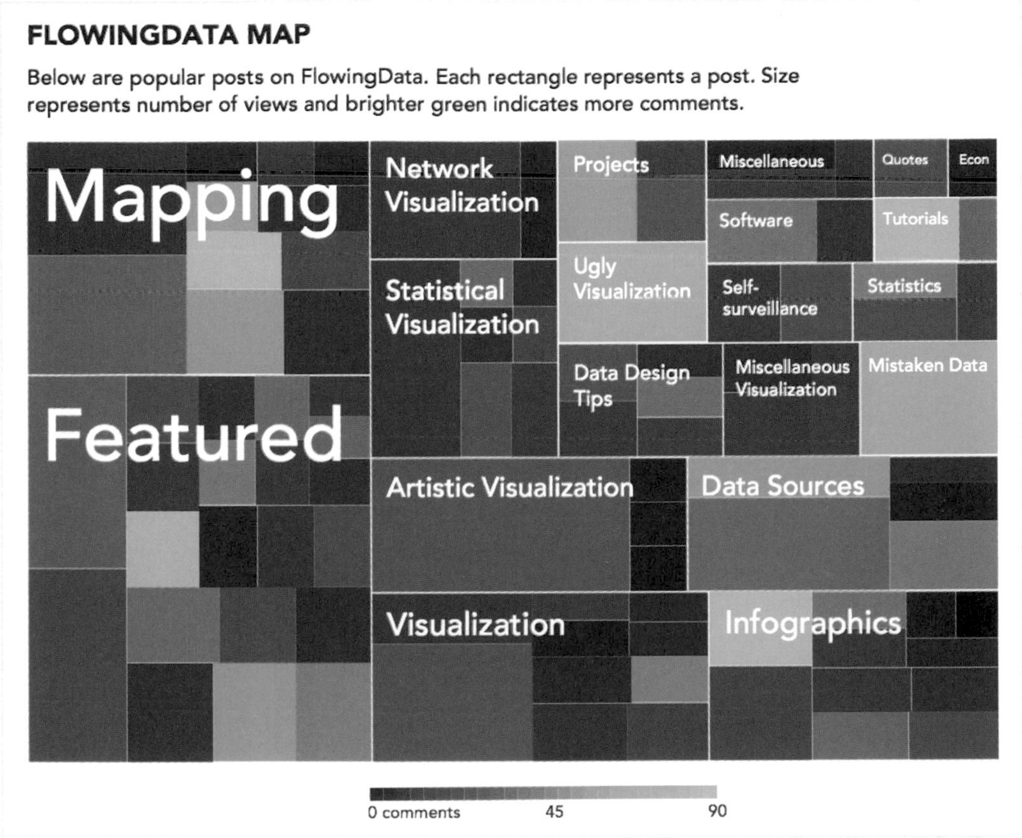

ILLUSTRATION 77

FLOWINGDATA MAP

Below are popular posts on FlowingData. Each rectangle represents a post. Size represents number of views and brighter green indicates more comments.

FIGURE 3-22 Treemap created in R, and edited in Adobe Illustrator

Options

A lot of illustration programs are available but only a few that most people use—and one that almost everyone uses. Cost will most likely be your deciding factor. Prices range from free (and open-source) to several hundred dollars.

ADOBE ILLUSTRATOR

Any static data graphic that looks custom-made or is in a major news publication most likely passed through Adobe Illustrator at some point. Adobe Illustrator is the industry standard. Every graphic that goes to print at *The New York Times* either was created or edited in Illustrator.

Illustrator is so popular for print because you work with vectors instead of pixels. This means you can make the graphics big without decreasing the quality of your image. In contrast, if you were to blow up a low-resolution photograph, which is a set number of pixels, you would end up with a pixelated image.

The software was originally designed for font development and later became popular among designers for illustrations such as logos and more art-focused graphics. And that's still what Illustrator is primarily used for.

However, Illustrator does offer some basic graphing functionality via its Graph tool. You can make the more basic graph types such as bar graphs, pie charts, and time series plots. You can paste your data into a small spreadsheet, but that's about the extent of the data management capabilities.

The best part about using Illustrator, in terms of data graphics, is the flexibility that it provides and its ease of use, with a lot of buttons and functions. It can be kind of confusing at first because there are so many, but it's easy to pick up, as you'll see in Chapter 4, "Visualizing Patterns over Time." It's this flexibility that enables the best data designers to create the most clear and concise graphics.

Illustrator is available for Windows and Mac. The downside though is that it's expensive when you compare it to doing everything with code, which is free, assuming you already have the machine to install things on. However, compared to some of the out-of-the-box solutions, Illustrator might not seem so pricey.

As of this writing, the most recent version of Illustrator is priced at $599 on the Adobe site, but you should find substantial discounts elsewhere (or go for an older version). Adobe also provides large discounts to students and those in academia, so be sure to check those out. (It's the most expensive software I've ever purchased, but I use it almost every day.)

USEFUL ADOBE ILLUSTRATOR RESOURCES

- Adobe Illustrator Product Page (www.adobe.com/products/illustrator/)
- VectorTuts (http://vectortuts.com)—Thorough and straightforward tutorials on how to use Illustrator

ILLUSTRATION   79

INKSCAPE

Inkscape is the free and open-source alternative to Adobe Illustrator. So if you want to avoid the hefty price tag, Inkscape is your best bet. I always use Illustrator because when I started to learn the finer points of data graphics on the job, Illustrator was what everyone used, so it just made sense. I have heard good things about Inkscape though, and because it's free, there's no harm in trying it. Just don't expect as many resources on how to use the software.

> **USEFUL INKSCAPE RESOURCES**
>
> - Inkscape (http://inkscape.org)
> - Inkscape Tutorials (http://inkscapetutorials.wordpress.com/)

TIP

Parts of this book use Adobe Illustrator to refine your data graphics; however, it shouldn't be too hard to figure out how to do the same thing in Inkscape. Many of the tools and functions are similarly named.

OTHERS

Illustrator and Inkscape are certainly not your only options to create and polish your data graphics. They just happen to be the programs that most people use. You might be comfortable with something else. Some people are fond of Corel Draw, which is Windows-only software and approximately the same price as Illustrator. It might be slightly cheaper, depending on where you look.

There are also programs such as Raven by Aviary and Lineform, that offer a smaller toolset. Remember that Illustrator and Inkscape are general tools for graphic designers, so they provide a lot of functionality. But if you just want to make a few edits to existing graphics, you might opt for the simpler (lower-priced) software.

Trade-Offs

Illustration software is for just that—illustration. It's not made specifically for data graphics. It's meant for graphic design, so many people do not use a lot of functions offered by Illustrator or Inkscape. The software is also not good for handling a lot of data, compared to when you program or use visualization-specific tools. Because of that, you can't explore your data in these programs.

That said, these programs are a must if you want to make publication-level data graphics. They don't just help with aesthetics, but also readability and clarity that's often hard to achieve with automatically generated output.

Mapping

Some overlap exists between the covered visualization tools and the ones that you use to map geographic data. However, the amount of geographic data has increased significantly in the past years as has the number of ways you can map. With mobile location services on the rise, there will be more data with latitude and longitude coordinates attached to it. Maps are also an incredibly intuitive way to visualize data, and this deserves a closer look.

Mapping in the early days of the web wasn't easy; it wasn't elegant either. Remember the days you would go to MapQuest, look up directions, and get this small static map? Yahoo had the same thing for a while.

It wasn't until a couple of years later until Google provided a *slippy map* implementation (Figure 3-23). The technology was around for a while, but it wasn't useful until most people's Internet speed was fast enough to handle the continuous updating. Slippy maps are what we're used to nowadays. We can pan and zoom maps with ease, and in some cases, maps aren't just for directions; they're the main interface to browse a dataset.

> **NOTE**
>
> *Slippy maps* are the map implementation that is now practically universal. Large maps, that would normally not fit on your screen, are split into smaller images, or tiles. Only the tiles that fit in your window display, and the rest are hidden from view. As you drag the map, other tiles display, making it seem as if you're moving around a single large map. You might have also seen this done with high-resolution photographs.

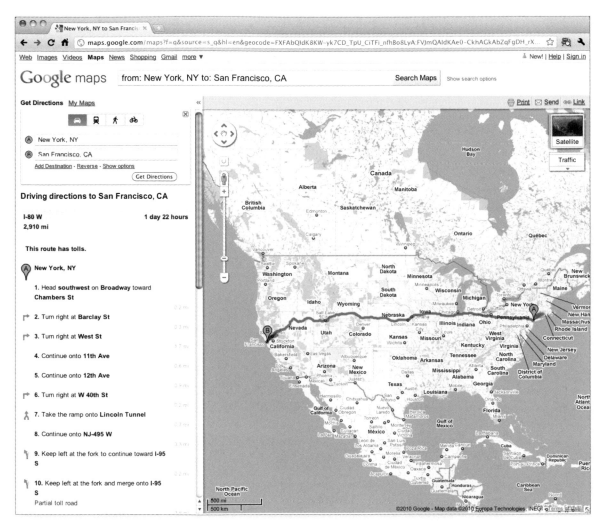

FIGURE 3-23 Google Maps to look up directions

Options

Along with all the geographic data making its way into the public domain, a variety of tools to map that data have also sprung up. Some require only a tiny bit of programming to get something up and running whereas others need a little more work. There are also a few other solutions that don't require programming.

GOOGLE, YAHOO, AND MICROSOFT MAPS

This is your easiest online solution; although, it does require a little bit of programming. The better you can code, the more you can do with the mapping APIs offered by Google, Yahoo, and Microsoft.

The base functionality of the three is fairly similar, but if you're just starting out, I recommend you go with Google. It seems to be the most reliable. They have a Maps API in both JavaScript and Flash, along with other geo-related services such as geocoding and directions. Go through the Getting Started tutorial and then branch out to other items such as placing markers (Figure 3-24), drawing paths, and adding overlays. The comprehensive set of code snippets and tutorials should quickly get you up and running .

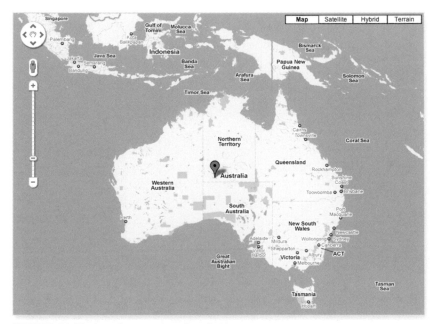

FIGURE 3-24 Marker placement on Google Maps

Yahoo also has JavaScript and Flash APIs for mapping, plus some geoservices, but I'm not sure how long it'll be around given the current state of the company. As of this writing, Yahoo has shifted focus from applications and development to content provider. Microsoft also provides a JavaScript API (under the Bing name) and one in Silverlight, which was its answer to Flash.

USEFUL MAPPING API RESOURCES

■ Google Maps API Family (http://code.google.com/apis/maps/)
■ Yahoo! Maps Web Services (http://code.google.com/apis/maps/index.html)
■ Bing Maps API (http://www.microsoft.com/maps/developers/web.aspx)

ARCGIS

The previously mentioned online mapping services are fairly basic in what they can do at the core. If you want more advanced mapping, you'll most likely need to implement the functionality yourself. ArcGIS, built for desktop mapping, is the opposite. It's a massive program that enables you to map lots of data and do lots of stuff with it, such as smoothing and processing. You can do all this through a user interface, so there's no code required.

Any graphics department with mapping specialists most likely uses ArcGIS. Professional cartographers use ArcGIS. Some people love it. So if you're interested in producing detailed maps, it's worth checking out ArcGIS.

I have used ArcGIS only for a few projects because I tend to take the programming route when I can, and I just didn't need all that functionality. The downside of such a rich feature set is that there are so many buttons and menus to go through. Online and server solutions are also available, but they feel kind of clunky compared to other implementations.

USEFUL ARCGIS RESOURCE

■ ArcGIS Product Page (www.esri.com/software/arcgis/)

MODEST MAPS

I mentioned Modest Maps earlier, with an example in Figure 3-13. It shows the growth of Walmart. Modest Maps is a Flash and ActionScript library for tile-based maps, and there is support for Python. It's maintained by a group of people who know their online mapping and do great work for both clients and for fun, which should tell you a little something about the quality of the library.

The fun thing about Modest Maps is that it's more of a framework than a mapping API like the one offered by Google. It provides the bare minimum of what it takes to create an online map and then gets out of the way to let you implement what you want. You can use tiles from different providers, and you can customize the maps to fit with your application. For example, Figure 3-13 has a black-and-blue theme, but you can just as easily change that to white and red, as shown in Figure 3-25.

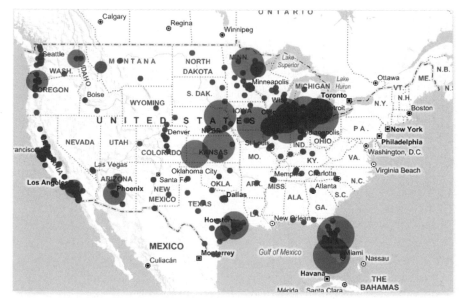

FIGURE 3-25 White-and-red themed map using Modest Maps

It's BSD-licensed, so you can do just about anything you want with it at no cost. You do have to know the ropes around Flash and ActionScript, but the basics are covered in Chapter 8, "Visualizing Spatial Relationships."

POLYMAPS

Polymaps is kind of like the JavaScript version of Modest Maps. It was developed and is maintained by some of the same people and provides the same functionality—and then some. Modest Maps provides only the basics of mapping, but Polymaps has some built-in features such as choropleths (Figure 3-26) and bubbles.

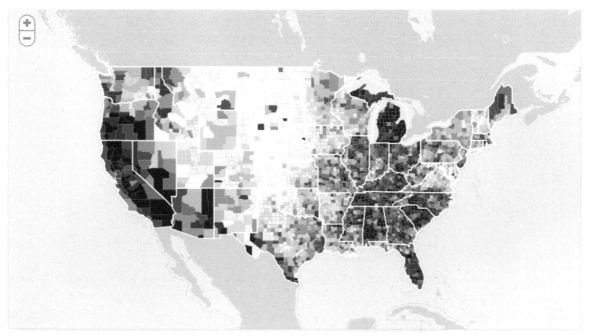

FIGURE 3-26 Choropleth map showing unemployment, implemented in Polymaps

Because it's JavaScript, it does feel more lightweight (because it requires less code), and it works in modern browsers. Polymaps uses Scalable Vector Graphics (SVG) to display data, so it doesn't work in the old versions of Internet Explorer, but most people are up-to-date. As a reference, only about 5 percent of FlowingData visitors use a browser that's too old, and I suspect that percentage will approach zero soon.

My favorite plus of a mapping library in JavaScript is that all the code runs native in the browser. You don't have to do any compiling or Flash exports, which makes it easier to get things running and to make updates later.

USEFUL POLYMAPS RESOURCE

- Polymaps (http://polymaps.org/)

R

R doesn't provide mapping functionality in the base distribution, but there are a few packages that let you do so. Figure 3-27 is a map that I made in R. The annotation was added after the fact in Adobe Illustrator.

Maps in R are limited in what they can do, and the documentation isn't great. So I use R for mapping if I have something simple and I happen to be using R. Otherwise, I tend to use the tools already mentioned.

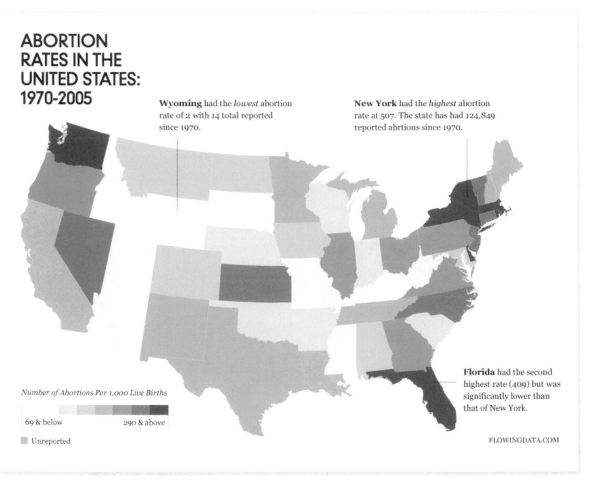

FIGURE 3-27 United States map created in R

USEFUL R MAPPING RESOURCES

- Analysis of Spatial Data (`http://cran.r-project.org/web/views/Spatial.html`)—Comprehensive list of packages in R for spatial analysis
- A Practical Guide to Geostatistical Mapping (`http://spatial-analyst.net/book/download`)—Free book download on how to use R and other tools for spatial data

ONLINE-BASED SOLUTIONS

A few online mapping solutions make it easy to visualize your geographic data. For the most part, they've taken the map types that people use the most and then stripped away the other stuff—kind of like a simplified ArcGIS. Many Eyes and GeoCommons are two free ones. The former, discussed previously, has only basic functionality for data by country or by state in the United States. GeoCommons, however, has more features and richer interaction. It also handles common geospatial file formats such as shapefiles and KML.

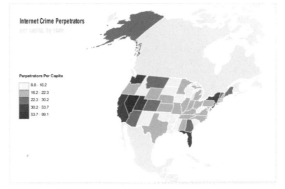

A number of paid solutions exist, but Indiemapper and SpatialKey are the most helpful. SpatialKey is geared more toward business and decision making whereas Indiemapper is geared toward cartographers and designers. Figure 3-28 shows an example I whipped up in just a few minutes in Indiemapper.

FIGURE 3-28 Choropleth map created in Indiemapper

Trade-Offs

Mapping software comes in all shapes and sizes suited to fit lots of different needs. It'd be great if you could learn one program and be able design every kind of map imaginable. Unfortunately, it doesn't work that way.

For example, ArcGIS has a lot of functions, but it might not be worth the time to learn or the money to purchase if you only want to create simple maps. On the other hand, R, which has basic mapping functionality and is free, could be too simple for what you want. If online and interactive maps are your goal, you can go open-source with Modest Maps or Polymaps, but that requires more programming skills. You'll learn more about how to use what's available in Chapter 8.

Survey Your Options

This isn't a comprehensive list of what you can use to visualize data, but it should be enough to get you started. There's a lot to consider and play with here. The tools you end up using largely depend on what you want to accomplish, and there are always multiple ways to accomplish a single task, even within the same software. Want to design static data graphics? Maybe try R or Illustrator. Do you want to build an interactive tool for a web application? Try JavaScript or Flash.

On FlowingData, I ran a poll that asked people what they mainly used to analyze and visualize data. A little more than 1,000 people responded. The results are shown in Figure 3-29.

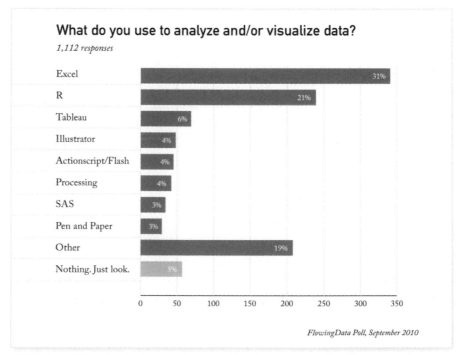

FIGURE 3-29 What FlowingData readers use to analyze and visualize data

There are some obvious leaders, given the topic of FlowingData. Excel was first, and R followed in second. But after that, there was a variety of software picks. More than 200 people chose the Other category. In the comments, many people stated that they use a combination of tools to fill different needs, which is usually the best route for the long term.

Combining Them

A lot of people like to stick to one program—it's comfortable and easy. They don't have to learn anything new. If that works, then by all means they should keep at it. But there comes a point after you've worked with data long enough when you hit the software's threshold. You know what you want to do with your data or how to visualize it, but the software doesn't let you do it or makes the process harder than it has to be.

You can either accept that, or you can use different software, which could take time to learn but helps you design what you envision—I say go with the latter. Learning a variety of tools ensures that you won't get stuck on a dataset, and you can be versatile enough to accomplish a variety of visualization tasks to get actual results.

Wrapping Up

Remember that none of these tools are a cure-all. In the end, the analyses and data design is still up to you. The tools are just that—they're tools. Just because you have a hammer doesn't mean you can build a house. Likewise, you can have great software and a super computer, but if you don't know how to use your tools, they might as well not exist. You decide what questions to ask, what data to use, and what facets to highlight, and this all becomes easier with practice.

But hey, you're in luck. That's what the rest of this book is for. The following chapters cover important data design concepts and teach you how to put the abstract into practice, using a combination of the tools that were just covered. You can learn what to look for in your data and how to visualize it.

Visualizing
Patterns over Time   4

Time series data is just about everywhere. Public opinion changes, populations shift, and businesses grow. You look to time series data to see how much these things have changed. This chapter looks at discrete and continuous data because the type of data graphics you use depends on the type of data you have. You also get your hands dirty with R and Adobe Illustrator—the two programs go great together.

What to Look for over Time

You look at time every day. It's on your computer, your watch, your phone, and just about anywhere else you look. Even without a clock, you feel time as you wake up and go to sleep and the sun rises and sets. So it's only natural to have data over time. It lets you see how things change.

The most common thing you look for in time series, or temporal, data is trends. Is something increasing or decreasing? Are there seasonal cycles? To find these patterns, you have to look beyond individual data points to get the whole picture. It's easy to pick out a single value from a point in time and call it a day, but when you look at what came before and after, you gain a better understanding of what that single value means, and the more you know about your data, the better the story that you can tell.

For example, there was a chart the Obama administration released a year into the new presidency, reproduced in Figure 4-1. It showed job loss during the tail end of the Bush administration through the first part of Obama's.

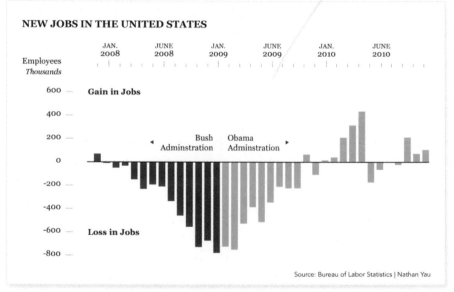

FIGURE 4-1 Change in job loss since Barack Obama took office

It looks like the new administration had a significant positive effect on job loss, but what if you zoom out and look at a larger time frame, as shown in Figure 4-2? Does it make a difference?

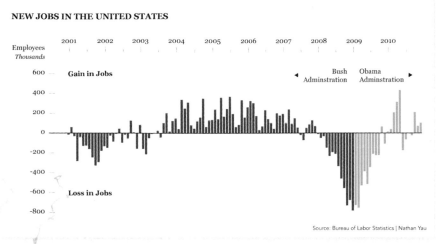

FIGURE 4-2 Change in job loss from 2001 through 2010

Although you always want to get the big picture, it's also useful to look at your data in more detail. Are there outliers? Are there any periods of time that look out of place? Are there spikes or dips? If so, what happened during that time? Often, these irregularities are where you want to focus. Other times the outliers can end up being a mistake in data entry. Looking at the big picture—the context—can help you determine what is what.

Discrete Points in Time

Temporal data can be categorized as discrete or continuous. Knowing which category your data belongs to can help you decide how to visualize it. In the discrete case, values are from specific points or blocks of time, and there is a finite number of possible values. For example, the percentage of people who pass a test each year is discrete. People take the test, and that's it. Their scores don't change afterward, and the test is taken on a specific date. Something like temperature, however, is continuous. It can be measured at any time of day during any interval, and it is constantly changing.

In this section you look at chart types that help you visualize discrete temporal data, and you see concrete examples on how to create these charts in R and Illustrator. The beginning will be the main introduction, and then you can apply the same design patterns throughout the chapter. This part is important. Although the examples are for specific charts, you can apply the same principles to all sorts of visualization. Remember it's all about the big picture.

Bars

The bar graph is one of the most common chart types. Most likely you've seen lots of them. You've probably made some. The bar graph can be used for various data types, but now take a look at how it can be used for temporal data.

Figure 4-3 shows a basic framework. The time axis (the horizontal one, that is, x-axis) provides a place for points in time that are ordered chronologically. In this case the points in time are months, from January to June 2011, but it could just as easily be by year, by day, or by some other time unit. Bar width and bar spacing typically do not represent values.

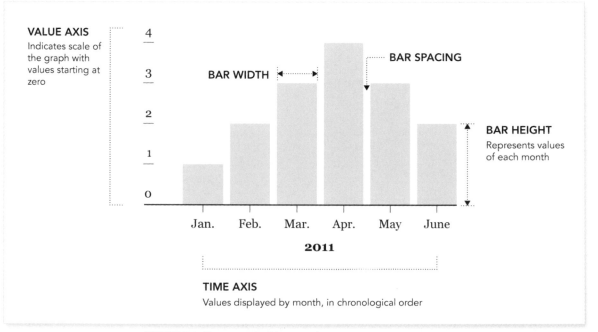

FIGURE 4-3 Framework of bar graphs

The value axis (the vertical one, that is, y-axis) indicates the scale of the graph. Figure 4-3 shows a linear scale where units are evenly spaced across the full axis. Bar height matches up with the value axis. The first bar, for example, goes up to one unit, whereas the highest bar goes up to four units.

This is important. The visual cue for value is bar height. The lower the value is, the shorter the bar will be. The greater a value is, the taller a bar will be. So you can see that the height of the four-unit bar in April is twice as tall as the two-unit bar in February.

Many programs, by default, set the lowest value of the value axis to the minimum of the dataset, as shown in Figure 4-4. In this case, the minimum is 1. However, if you were to start the value axis at 1, the height of the February bar wouldn't be half the height of the April bar anymore. It would look like February was one-third that of April. The bar for January would also be nonexistent. The point: Always start the value axis at zero. Otherwise, your bar graph could display incorrect relationships.

> **TIP**
>
> Always start the value axis of your bar graph at zero when you're dealing with all positive values. Anything else makes it harder to visually compare the height of the bars.

CREATE A BAR GRAPH

It's time to make your first graph, using real data, and it's an important part of history that is an absolute must for all people who call themselves a human. It's the results from the past three decades of Nathan's Hot Dog Eating Contest. Oh, yes.

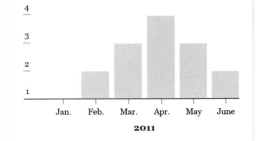

FIGURE 4-4 Bar graph with non-zero axis

Figure 4-5 is the final graph you're after. Do this in two steps. First, create a basic bar graph in R, and then you can refine that graph in Illustrator.

In case you're not in the know of the competitive eating circuit, Nathan's Hot Dog Eating Contest is an annual event that happens every July 4. That's Independence Day in the United States. The event has become so popular that it's even televised on ESPN.

Throughout the late 1990s, the winners ate 10 to 20 hot dogs and buns (HDBs) in about 15 minutes. However, in 2001, Takeru Kobayashi, a professional eater from Japan, obliterated the competition by eating 50 HDBs. That was more than twice the amount anyone in the world had eaten before him. And this is where the story begins.

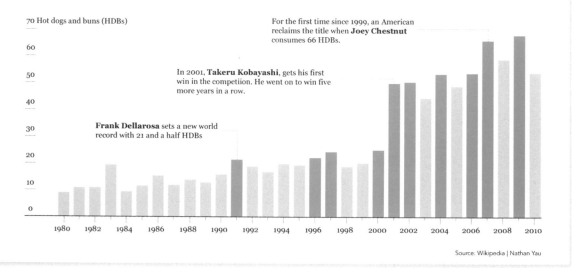

HOT DOG EATING

Nathan's hot dog eating contest every July 4th has been going on since the early 1900s, but it wasn't until 2001 when things got serious. Takeru Kobayashi from Japan raised the bar, more than doubling the previous world record. Highlighted bars indicate new records.

70 Hot dogs and buns (HDBs)

For the first time since 1999, an American reclaims the title when **Joey Chestnut** consumes 66 HDBs.

In 2001, **Takeru Kobayashi**, gets his first win in the competiion. He went on to win five more years in a row.

Frank Dellarosa sets a new world record with 21 and a half HDBs

Source: Wikipedia | Nathan Yau

FIGURE 4-5 Bar graph showing results from Nathan's Hot Dog Eating Contest

▶ Download the data in CSV format from `http://datasets .flowingdata.com/ hot-dog-contest- winners.csv`. See the page for "Nathan's Hot Dog Eating Contest" on Wikipedia for precompiled data and history of the contest.

Wikipedia has results from the contest dating back to 1916, but the hot dog eating didn't become a regular event until 1980, so we start here. The data is in an HTML table and includes the year, name, number of HDBs eaten, and country where the winner is from. I've compiled the data in a CSV file that you can download at `http://datasets.flowingdata.com/hot-dog-contest-winners .csv`. Here's what the first five rows of data look like:

```
"Year","Winner","Dogs eaten","Country","New record"
1980,"Paul Siederman & Joe Baldini",9.1,"United States",0
1981,"Thomas DeBerry ",11,"United States",0
1982,"Steven Abrams ",11,"United States",0
1983,"Luis Llamas ",19.5,"Mexico",1
1984,"Birgit Felden ",9.5,"Germany",0
```

To load the data in R, use the `read.csv()` command. You can either load the file locally from you own computer, or you can use a URL. Enter this line of code in R to do the latter:

```
hotdogs <-
    read.csv("http://datasets.flowingdata.com/hot-dog-contest-winners.csv",
    sep=",", header=TRUE)
```

Set your working directory in R to the same directory as your data file via the main menu if you want to load the data locally from your own computer, You can also use the setwd() function.

If you're new to programming, this probably looks cryptic, so now break it down so you can understand it. This is one line of R code. You load data with the read.csv() command, and it has three arguments. The first is the location of your data, which in this case is a URL.

The second argument, sep, specifies what character separates the columns in the data file. It's a comma-delimited file, so specify the comma. If it were a tab-delimited file, you would use \t instead of a comma to indicate the separator was a tab.

The last argument, header, tells R that the data file has a header, which contains the name of each column. The first column is year, the second is the winner's name, the third is number of HDBs eaten, and the fourth is the competitor's resident country. I've also added a new field that you might have noticed: new record. If the world record was broken on a year, the value is 1. Otherwise it is 0. You can put this to use soon.

The data is now loaded into R and is available via the hotdogs variable. Technically, the data is stored as a data frame, which isn't totally important but worth noting. Here's what the beginning of the data frame looks like if you type **hotdogs.**

```
  Year                          Winner Dogs.eaten       Country New.record
1 1980 Paul Siederman & Joe Baldini          9.10 United States          0
2 1981               Thomas DeBerry         11.00 United States          0
3 1982                Steven Abrams         11.00 United States          0
4 1983                 Luis Llamas         19.50         Mexico          1
5 1984                Birgit Felden          9.50        Germany          0
```

The spaces in the column names have been replaced with periods. Dogs eaten is now Dogs.eaten. It's the same thing with New record. To access a specific column of data, you use the name of the data frame followed by a dollar sign ($) and then the column name. For example, if you want to access Dogs.eaten you enter the following:

```
hotdogs$Dogs.eaten
```

Now that you have the data in R, you can go straight to graphing with the barplot() command.

```
barplot(hotdogs$Dogs.eaten)
```

This tells R to graph the `Dogs.eaten` column, and you should get Figure 4-6.

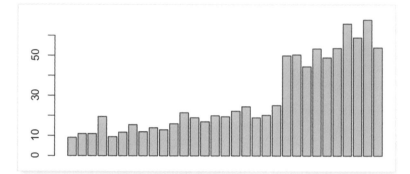

FIGURE 4-6 Default graph of number of hot dogs and buns eaten, using barplot() in R

Not bad, but you can do better. Use the `names.arg` argument in `barplot()` to specify the names of each bar. In this case, it is the year of each contest.

```
barplot(hotdogs$Dogs.eaten, names.arg=hotdogs$Year)
```

This gives you Figure 4-7. There are now labels on the bottom.

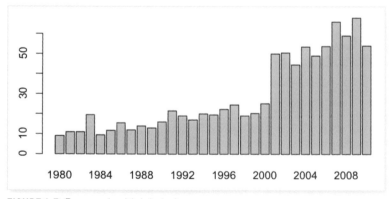

FIGURE 4-7 Bar graph with labels for years

You can apply a number of other arguments. You can add axis labels, change borders, and change colors, as shown in Figure 4-8.

```
barplot(hotdogs$Dogs.eaten, names.arg=hotdogs$Year, col="red",
    border=NA, xlab="Year", ylab="Hot dogs and buns (HDB) eaten")
```

The col argument can be your pick of colors (specified in R documentation) or a hexadecimal number such as #821122. Here you specified no border with *NA*, which is a logical constant meaning no value. You also labeled the x- and y-axes as "Year" and "Hot dogs and buns (HDB) eaten," respectively.

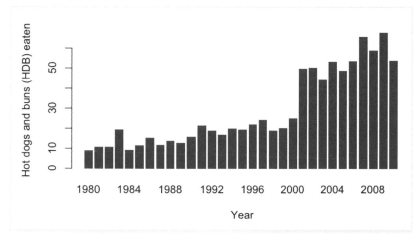

FIGURE 4-8 Bar graph with colored bars and labeled axes

You don't need to limit yourself to just one color. You can provide multiple colors to barplot() to shade each bar how you want. For example, say you want to highlight the years the United States won the contest. You can highlight those years in dark red (#821122) and the rest a light gray, as shown in Figure 4-9.

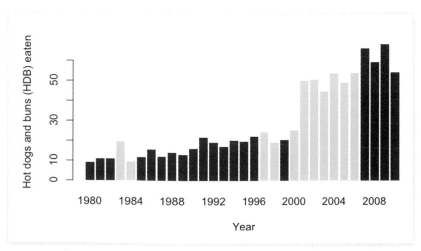

FIGURE 4-9 Bar graph with individually colored bars

To do this, you need to build a list, or vector in R, of colors. Visit each year and decide what color to make the corresponding bar. If it's a win for the United States, specify red. Otherwise, specify gray. Here's the code to do that:

```
fill_colors <- c()
for ( i in 1:length(hotdogs$Country) ) {
    if (hotdogs$Country[i] == "United States") {
        fill_colors <- c(fill_colors, "#821122")
    } else {
        fill_colors <- c(fill_colors, "#cccccc")
    }
}
```

The first line starts an empty vector named fill_colors. You use c() to create vectors in R.

The next line starts a for loop. You can tell R to loop through an index named i from 1 to the number of rows in your hotdogs data frame. More specifically, you can take a single column, Country, from the hotdogs data frame, and find the length. If you were to use length() with just hotdogs, you would get the number of columns, which is 5 in this case, but you want the number of rows, which is 31. There is one row for each year from 1980 to 2010, so the loop will execute the code inside the brackets 31 times, and for each loop, the *i* index will go up one.

So in the first iteration, where *i* equals 1, check if the country in the first row (that is, winner for 1980) is the United States. If it is, append the color #821122, which is a reddish color in hexadecimal form, to fill_colors. Otherwise, append #cccccc, which is a light gray.

In 1980, the winners were from the United States, so do the former. The loop checks 30 more times for the rest of the years. Enter **fill_colors** in the R console to see what you end up with. It's a vector of colors just like you want.

Pass the fill_colors vector in the col argument for barplot() like so.

```
barplot(hotdogs$Dogs.eaten, names.arg=hotdogs$Year, col=fill_colors,
    border=NA, xlab="Year", ylab="Hot dogs and buns (HDB) eaten")
```

The code is the same as before, except you use fill_colors instead of "red" in the col argument.

NOTE

Most languages use 0-based arrays or vectors where the first item is referenced with a 0-index. R, however, uses 1-based vectors.

The final bar graph in Figure 4-5 highlights years when a record was broken though—not when the United States won. The process and logic are the same. You just need to change some of the conditions. The New.record column in your data frame indicates new records, so if it's 1, you do dark red, and gray otherwise. Here's how to do it in R.

```
fill_colors <- c()
for ( i in 1:length(hotdogs$New.record) ) {
    if (hotdogs$New.record[i] == 1) {
        fill_colors <- c(fill_colors, "#821122")
    } else {
        fill_colors <- c(fill_colors, "#cccccc")
    }
}
barplot(hotdogs$Dogs.eaten, names.arg=hotdogs$Year, col=fill_colors,
    border=NA, xlab="Year", ylab="Hot dogs and buns (HDB) eaten")
```

It's the same as the United States example, just with different if statements. Your result should look like Figure 4-10.

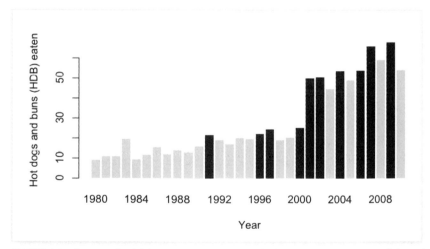

FIGURE 4-10 Bar graph with bars colored individually, but using different conditions than Figure 4-9

At this point you can play around with some of the other barplot() options such as spacing or adding a title.

```
barplot(hotdogs$Dogs.eaten, names.arg=hotdogs$Year, col=fill_colors,
    border=NA, space=0.3, xlab="Year", ylab="Hot dogs and buns (HDB)
eaten")
```

TIP

Be careful when you choose bar spacing. When the width of spacing is close to that of the width of the bars, there's a vibration effect visually. It's almost as if the roles of the bar and spacing have switched.

This gives you Figure 4-11. Notice the spacing is wider than before, and there is a title on the top.

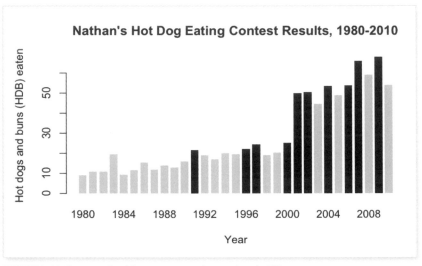

FIGURE 4-11 Bar graph with custom spacing and main title

Voilá! You've gotten your first taste of R.

In the File menu, there is an option to save your graph. Save it as a PDF. You're going to need it soon.

TIP

To see the documentation for any function in R, simply type a question mark followed by the function name. For example, to read more about `barplot()` in R, simply type **?barplot**. A description of the function is provided along with an explanation of available arguments. There are also usually working examples, which can be extremely helpful.

REFINE YOUR GRAPH IN ILLUSTRATOR

You now have a basic bar graph. It's not bad to look at, and if you use it only for analysis, it's not necessary to do much more with it. But if you want to make your graph into a standalone graphic, you can do some things to make it more readable.

Now look at this from a storytelling perspective. Pretend Figure 4-11 was by itself, and you're a reader who came across it somehow. What can you glean from the basic graph? You know the graph shows hot dogs and buns eaten by year. Is this one person's eating habits? That sure is a lot of hot dogs for one person. Is it food for animals? Are leftovers given to birds? Is it the average number of hot dogs eaten per person per year? Why are the bars colored?

As the one who made the graph, you know the context behind the numbers, but your readers don't, so you have to explain what's going on. Good data design can help your readers understand the story more clearly. Illustrator, which enables you to manipulate individual elements by hand, can help you do that. You can change fonts, add notes, modify axes, edit colors, and pretty much do whatever your imagination allows.

This book keeps the editing in Illustrator simple, but as you work through more examples, and start to design your own graphics, you'll see how these small changes can be a big help to make your graphic clear and concise.

First things first. Open the PDF file of your bar graph in Illustrator. You should see the graph you made in one window, and then there will most likely be several smaller windows with tools, colors, and fonts, among other things. The main window to make note of is the Tools window, as shown in Figure 4-12. You'll use this often. If you don't see the Tools window, go to the Window menu and click Tools to turn it on.

The black arrow is called the Selection tool. Select it, and your mouse pointer becomes a black arrow (if it wasn't already). Click-and-drag over the border. The borders appear highlighted, as shown in Figure 4-13. This is known as a clipping mask in Illustrator. It can be useful in various situations, but you don't care about it now, so press Delete on your keyboard to get rid of it. If this deletes the entire graphic, undo the edit, and use the Direct Selection tool, which is represented by a white arrow, to highlight the clipping mask instead.

TIP

Put yourself in a reader's shoes when you design data graphics. What parts of the data need explanation?

TIP

If you don't have Illustrator, you can try InkScape, the free and open-source alternative. Although the functions or buttons might not look exactly the same as Illustrator, you can still find many of the same things in InkScape.

FIGURE 4-12
Tools window in Illustrator

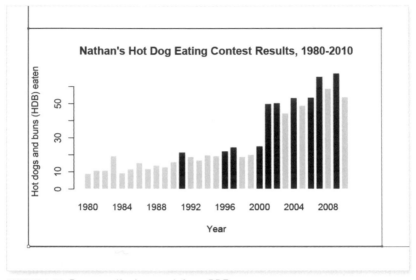

Nathan's Hot Dog Eating Contest Results, 1980-2010

FIGURE 4-13 Remove clipping mask from PDF

Now try to change the fonts, which is easy to do. Again, using the Selection tool, click the text to highlight what you want to change. Change the font to whatever you like through drop-down menus in the Font window, as shown in Figure 4-14. You can also change fonts through the Type menu. In Figure 4-15, the font is changed to Georgia Regular.

FIGURE 4-14 Font window in Illustrator

Next, something must be done about the number labels on the value axis. The numbers are turned on their side, but they should be turned right-side up to improve readability. Click those numbers. Notice that other stuff is highlighted, too. This is because the numbers are grouped with those elements of the graph. You need to ungroup them so that you can rotate each of the numbers, which you can do through the Object menu. Click Ungroup. Deselect the number labels and then select them again. Now only the numbers highlight. That's what you want. You might have to ungroup a few times before this happens. Alternatively, you can use the Direct Selection tool instead.

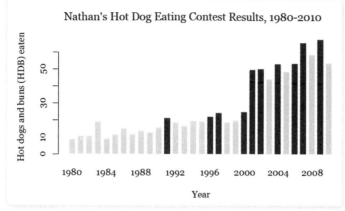

FIGURE 4-15 Graph with fonts changed to Georgia Regular

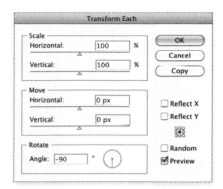

FIGURE 4-16 Transform menu

Go back to the Object menu, and select Transform ➪ Transform Each. As shown in Figure 4-16, change the rotation angle to –90 degrees. Click OK. The labels are now right-side up.

While you're at it, shift the labels (not the tick marks) up and to the right so that they're above the tick marks, instead of to the left. Shift items either with the arrow keys on your keyboard or drag with your mouse. You can also directly specify the units as hot dogs and buns (HDBs) instead of having them off to the side. Again, this improves readability as a reader's eyes move from left to right. You should now have something like Figure 4-17.

This is starting to look more like the final graph in Figure 4-5. It's still missing a few things, though. There aren't any tick marks on the horizontal axis, nothing is annotated, and it'd be nice if you incorporated green, one of the colors in Nathan's Hot Dogs' logo.

You can also simplify the graphic by removing the vertical line on the value axis. It doesn't help communicate the data more clearly. Notice how in the final graphic there are only tick marks. If you click the vertical line with the Selection Tool, the labels also highlight. That's because they're all part of a group. To select just the line, use the Direct Selection tool. After you highlight the line, press Delete and it'll be gone.

There are a bunch of ways to create tick marks, but here's one way to do it. Using the Pen tool, you can easily draw straight lines. Select it from the

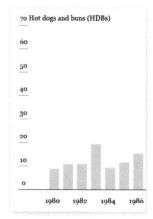

FIGURE 4-17 Bar graph with simplified value axis

TIP

Data graphics are meant to shine a light on your data. Try to remove any elements that don't help you do that.

Tools window, and then specify the style of your line via the Stroke window. Make the weight 0.3 pt, and make sure the Dashed Line check box is not selected.

To draw a line, click where you want to put the first point of the line (or tick mark in this case); then click where you want to put the second point. If you press the Shift key during the second click, the line will automatically be straight. You should now have a single tick mark. You need 30 more because you need a tick mark for each year.

You can draw them all by hand, but there's a better way. If you're on a Mac, hold down Option, or if you're on a PC, hold down Alt. Click the single tick with the Selection tool and drag to where you want the next tick, while still holding down Option or Alt. This creates a copy, so you should now have two tick marks. Now press Command+D for Mac or Control+D for PC. This duplicates the new tick mark spaced the same distance that the second was from the first. Press Command/Control+D until you have all the tick marks you need.

Finally, arrange all the marks correctly. Move the last tick mark so that it's centered with the last bar. The first tick should already be centered with the first bar. Now highlight all the ticks, and click Horizontal Distribute Center in the Align window (Figure 4-18).

This distributes the ticks so that they're evenly spaced between the outermost marks. Optionally, you can highlight every other tick with the Selection Tool and resize it vertically to make them smaller. This makes it obvious that the longer ticks are for the year labels.

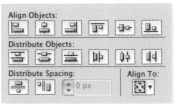

FIGURE 4-18 Align window in Illustrator

To change the fill color from red to green, you could go back to the Direct Selection tool and select every red box. Because there aren't that many, it would be quick, but what if you have a lot of elements to click? Instead, click a single red bar; then go to Select ⇨ Same ⇨ Fill Color. This does what you'd expect. It selects all the bars that have a red fill. Now simply change the color to your liking via the Color window. You can change both border and fill color here, but just change fill for now, as shown in Figure 4-19.

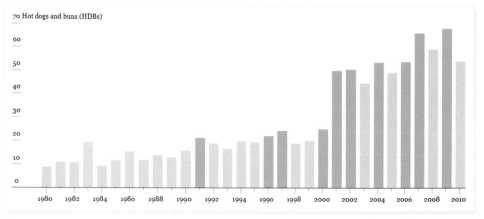

FIGURE 4-19 Changing color of graph elements

Using the Type tool, found in the Tools window, you can add text boxes to the graphic. This is your chance to explain what readers are looking at in your graphic and to clarify any spots that might seem unclear. Choose fonts that you think will work, using size and style to differentiate the label from graph elements like axis labels.

In the case of this ever important hot dog graphic, highlight the first record since 1980, Takeru Kobayashi's dominance, and Joey Chestnut's current reign. Also include a title and a lead-in that explains the gist of the graphic.

Last but not least: Remember to include the data source. There's no way to tell if your graphic is accurate otherwise.

Put all this together, and you have the final graphic, as shown in Figure 4-5.

I know this was a lot to take in, but it gets much easier as you work on more graphics. You'll see how coding in R, or any language for that matter, follows a certain pattern, and although Illustrator has a huge toolset, you'll just learn the ones that pertain to the task at hand.

The following examples look at other charting types for temporal data and spend more time with R and Illustrator. They'll go by quicker now that you covered some of the basics of the two tools.

TIP

Always include your data source in your graphics. It not only provides credibility but also context.

Stack the Bars

As shown in Figure 4-20, the geometry of stacked bar charts is similar to regular bar charts. The difference of course is that rectangles are stacked on top of each other. You use stacked bar charts when there are subcategories, and the sum of these subcategories is meaningful.

Like bar charts, stacked bar charts are not just for temporal data; they can be used for more categorical data. But in Figure 4-19, for example, the categories are months.

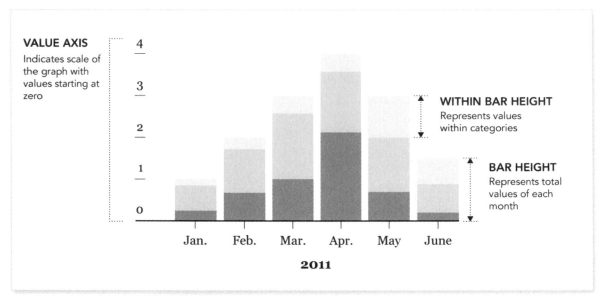

FIGURE 4-20 Framework for stacked bar charts

CREATE A STACKED BAR CHART

Because the stacked bar chart is a relatively common chart type, there are plenty of ways to make one (like its unstacked sibling), but here's how to do it in R. Follow a similar process to what you did to make a regular bar chart.

1. Load the data.

2. Make sure the data is properly formatted.

3. Use an R function to produce a plot.

This is generally what you'll do every time you use R to make data graphics. Sometimes you'll spend more time on one part than the other. It might take longer to get your data in the right format, or you might write your own functions in R to get exactly what you want. Whatever the case may be, you'll almost always follow the preceding three steps, and this will carry over to other languages, as you'll see in later chapters.

Back to your stacked bar chart. Go back to Nathan's Hot Dog Contest. This is the last time you look at hot dog eating data in this book, so savor the moment. Figure 4-21 is the graphic you want to make.

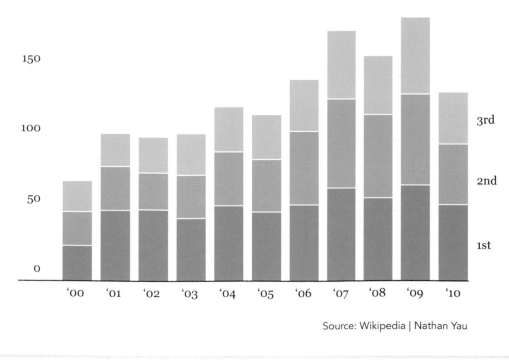

TOP THREE HOT DOG EATERS

The year before Takeru Kobayashi started to compete in Nathan's Hot Dog Eating Contest, the top three eaters were close in skills. However, from 2001 to 2005, Kobayashi always had a substantial lead. That changed in 2006 when Joey Chestnut started competing.

200 Hot dogs and buns (HDBs)

Source: Wikipedia | Nathan Yau

FIGURE 4-21 Stacked bar charts showing top three eaters from 2000 to 2010

Instead of looking at only the number of HDBs eaten by the winners, look at the top three for each year. Each stack represents a year, each with three bars, and one for each top-three eater. Wikipedia has this data consistently starting only in 2000, so start there.

First things first. Load the data in R. You can load it directly from the URL with the following.

```
hot_dog_places <-
    read.csv('http://datasets.flowingdata.com/hot-dog-places.csv',
    sep=",", header=TRUE)
```

Type **hot_dog_places** to view the data. Each column shows the results for a year, and each row is for places 1 through 3.

	X2000	X2001	X2002	X2003	X2004	X2005	X2006	X2007	X2008	X2009	X2010
1	25	50.0	50.5	44.5	53.5	49	54	66	59	68.0	54
2	24	31.0	26.0	30.5	38.0	37	52	63	59	64.5	43
3	22	23.5	25.5	29.5	32.0	32	37	49	42	55.0	37

See how an "X" precedes all the column names, which were added by default when you loaded the data because the header names are numbers? R doesn't like that, so it adds a letter to make it word-like, or more technically speaking, a *string*. You need to use the header names for labels in the stacked bar chart, so change those back.

```
names(hot_dog_places) <- c("2000", "2001", "2002", "2003", "2004",
    "2005", "2006", "2007", "2008", "2009", "2010")
```

Use quotes around each year to specify that it is a string. Type **hot_dog_places** again, and the headers are just the years now.

	2000	2001	2002	2003	2004	2005	2006	2007	2008	2009	2010
1	25	50.0	50.5	44.5	53.5	49	54	66	59	68.0	54
2	24	31.0	26.0	30.5	38.0	37	52	63	59	64.5	43
3	22	23.5	25.5	29.5	32.0	32	37	49	42	55.0	37

Like before, use the `barplot()` function, but use data that's in a different format. To pass all the preceding values to `barplot()`, you need to convert `hot_dog_places` to a matrix. Right now it's a data frame. These are different structures in R, but the differences between the two are not so important right now. What you need to know is how to convert a data frame to a matrix.

```
hot_dog_matrix <- as.matrix(hot_dog_places)
```

You stored our newly created matrix as *hot_dog_matrix*. You can pass this into barplot().

```
barplot(hot_dog_matrix, border=NA, space=0.25, ylim=c(0, 200),
    xlab="Year", ylab="Hot dogs and buns (HDBs) eaten",
    main="Hot Dog Eating Contest Results, 1980-2010")
```

You specified no borders around the bar, spacing to be 0.25 the width of bar width, and the limits of the value axis to go from 0 to 200, along with title and axis labels. Figure 4-22 is the result.

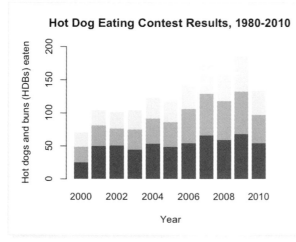

FIGURE 4-22 Stacked bar chart using R

Not bad for a few lines of code, but you're not quite done. Now you can refine. Save the image as a PDF and open it in Illustrator. Use the same tools that you did before. You can add text with the Type tool, change fonts, simplify the vertical axis, edit colors with the ability to select elements with the same fill, and of course include the data source (Figure 4-23).

Add some lead-in text and change the title to what you want, and Figure 4-21 shows the final result.

The next chapter covers the stacked bar chart's continuous cousin: the stacked area chart. The geometry is similar; just imagine if you connected all the stacks for a continuous flow.

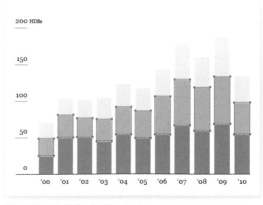

FIGURE 4-23 Edits in Illustrator

Points

Sometimes it makes more sense to use points instead of bars. They use less space and because there are no bins, points can provide a better feeling of flow from one point to the next. Figure 4-24 shows the common geometry when using points to graph temporal data.

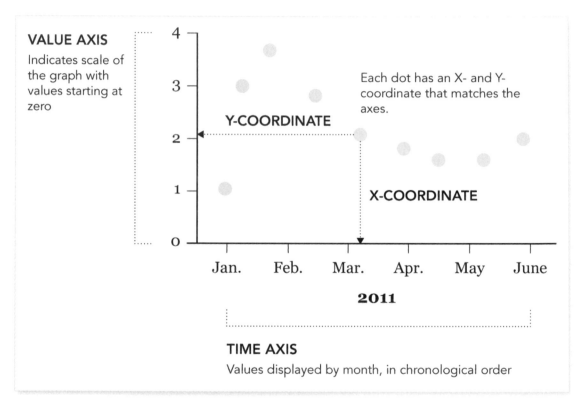

FIGURE 4-24 Framework for using points to chart

This type of chart is commonly known as a scatterplot and you can also use it to visualize nontemporal data. It's often used to show the relationship between two variables, which is covered in Chapter 6, "Visualizing Relationships." For temporal data, time is represented on the horizontal axis, and values or measurements are represented on the vertical axis.

Unlike the bar graph, which uses length as the visual cue, scatterplots use position. You can think of each point with an X- and Y-coordinate, and you can compare to other points in time based on where they are placed.

Because of this, the value axis of scatterplots doesn't always have to start at zero, but it's usually good practice.

CREATE A SCATTERPLOT

R makes it easy to create a scatterplot via the plot() function, but you can use variations, depending on what data you look at. Figure 4-25 shows the final graphic.

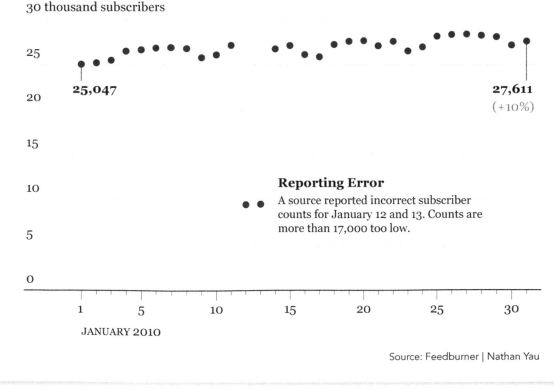

INCREASE IN SUBSCRIBERS

In January 2010, the number of subscribers via RSS and email increase to 27,611, making it the tenth month in a row with at least a ten percent increase.

30 thousand subscribers

25

20   **25,047**   **27,611**
                                                                       (+10%)

15

10   **Reporting Error**
                                A source reported incorrect subscriber
                                counts for January 12 and 13. Counts are
5   more than 17,000 too low.

0

     1   5   10   15   20   25   30

JANUARY 2010

Source: Feedburner | Nathan Yau

FIGURE 4-25 Scatterplot created in R and designed in Illustrator

This is the story of FlowingData subscriber counts in January 2010, as reported by Feedburner, the service that keeps track of how many people read FlowingData on a daily basis. On January 1, 2010, there were 25,047 subscribers, and by the end of the month, there were 27,611 subscribers. Probably the most interesting part though was what wasn't reported in the middle of the month. Did I actually say something to offend 17,000 readers that made them unsubscribe? Not likely.

Do you remember the first thing to do when you make a graph in R? You load your data. Use read.csv() to load the data directly from a URL.

```
subscribers <-
    read.csv("http://datasets.flowingdata.com/flowingdata_subscribers.csv",
    sep=",", header=TRUE)
```

To look at the first five rows of the data, enter the following:

```
subscribers[1:5,]
```

And here's what it looks like:

```
     Date Subscribers Reach Item.Views  Hits
1 01-01-2010       25047  4627       9682 27225
2 01-02-2010       25204  1676       5434 28042
3 01-03-2010       25491  1485       6318 29824
4 01-04-2010       26503  6290      17238 48911
5 01-04-2010       26654  6544      16224 45521
```

There are five columns on date, subscribers, reach, item views, and hits. You care only about subscribers.

You can also incorporate the date, but counts are already in chronological order, so you actually don't need the first column to plot subscribers. To plot the points, enter the following, and you'll get the result in Figure 4-26.

```
plot(subscribers$Subscribers)
```

Easy, right? The plot() function actually enables you to make several different types of graphs, but the point type is the default. You used only the subscriber counts. When you provide only one data array to the plot() function, it assumes that the array contains values, and it automatically generates an index for the x-coordinates.

Now explicitly specify that you want the point type, and set the range of the vertical axis from 0 to 30,000.

```
plot(subscribers$Subscribers, type="p", ylim=c(0, 30000))
```

Figure 4-27 is same thing as Figure 4-26, but with a wider vertical axis as you specified with the ylim argument. Notice you use the type argument to tell R to use points. If you changed type to h, R would make high-density vertical lines.

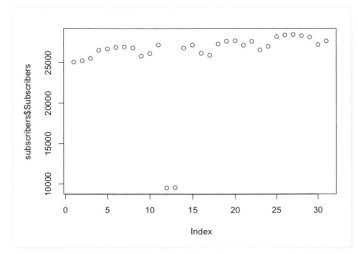

FIGURE 4-26 Default plot in R

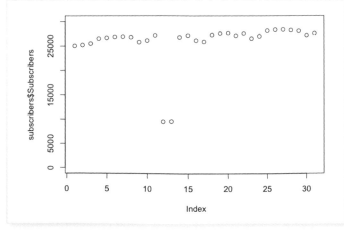

FIGURE 4-27 Point plot in R with y-limits specified

You could also combine the two, as shown in Figure 4-28. However, you'd also need to use the `points()` method. Whenever you use the `plot()` function, you create a new graphic, instead of adding new elements to an existing graph. Following is how you would combine vertical lines and points if you were so inclined.

```
plot(subscribers$Subscribers, type="h", ylim=c(0, 30000),
     xlab="Day", ylab="Subscribers")
points(subscribers$Subscribers, pch=19, col="black")
```

The plot with vertical lines is drawn first, this time with axis labels. Points are then added to the existing plot. The `pch` argument is for size, and the `col` argument, which you used with the bar chart, specifies fill color.

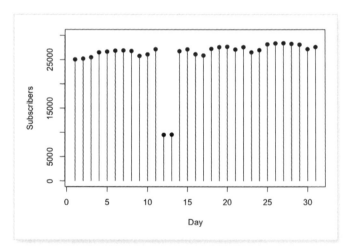

FIGURE 4-28 Plot with high-density vertical lines

Let's go back to Figure 4-27. Save it as a PDF and then open it in Illustrator so that we can do some designing.

Using the Selection tool, highlight labels, and change the font to your liking. Then ungroup the labels so that you can edit the vertical axis labels individually. Use Transform ⇨ Transform Each to turn the labels right-side up. Then use the Direct Selection tool to remove the vertical bar from the axis. You don't need that—it's just taking up space.

Finally, highlight the actual points, which are plain white circles, and use the options in the Color window to take your pick of fill and stroke color. You might need to change the color scheme to CMYK (that's Cyan, Magenta, Yellow, and key) from Grayscale to get more color choices via the options menu of the Color window (Figure 4-29).

This should bring you to Figure 4-30. It already looks more like the finished graphic.

FIGURE 4-29 Options menu for Color window

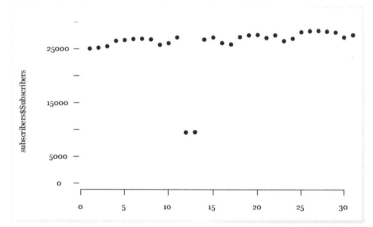

FIGURE 4-30 Point plot after editing vertical axis and color

Now try adding a grid so that it's easier to see what values the points on the far right represent and how they relate to previous points. Highlight the ticks on the value axis with the Selection tool, and then click-and-drag across to extend the ticks all the way across the graph. As-is, they're kind of blunt, so change the style for those. Like before, you can change the style of lines with the options available in the Stroke window. Use the options in Figure 4-31 if you want thin, dotted lines.

Figure 4-32 is what you have after those changes.

From here, use the same tools and techniques to get Figure 4-32 to your final graphic. Make tick marks on the horizontal axis with the Pen tool, and edit and add labels with the Type tool. Don't forget to add the source of your data on the bottom to complete the story.

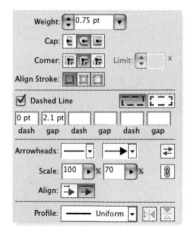

FIGURE 4-31 Options for dotted lines in Stroke window

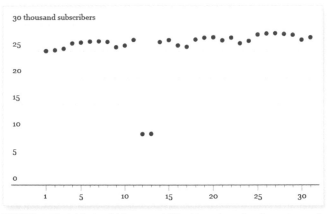

FIGURE 4-32 Added grid lines and filled in values for the value axis

Continuous Data

Visualizing continuous time series data is similar to visualizing discrete data. You do, after all, still have a discrete number of data points, even if the dataset is continuous. The structure of continuous and discrete is the same. The difference between the two is what they represent in the physical world. As previously covered, continuous data represents constantly changing phenomena, so to this end, you want to visualize the data in a way that shows that.

Connect the Dots

You're probably familiar with this one. The time series chart is similar to drawing points, except you also connect the points with lines. Often, you don't show the points. Figure 4-33 shows the geometry of the popular chart type.

You have the nodes, or points, that take on X- and Y-coordinates, and then the edges, or connecting lines that help you see trends in your data. It's usually a good idea to start the value axis at zero because starting anywhere else could affect the scale.

How far you stretch the horizontal axis can also affect the appearance of trends. Squish too much, and an increase from point to point might look more than it is. Stretch too far out, and you might not see patterns.

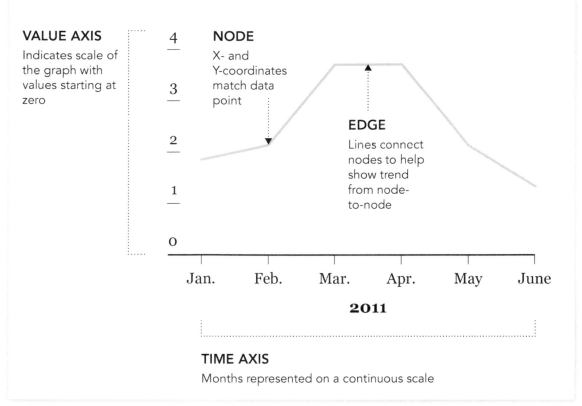

VALUE AXIS

Indicates scale of the graph with values starting at zero

NODE

X- and Y-coordinates match data point

EDGE

Lines connect nodes to help show trend from node-to-node

Jan.   Feb.   Mar.   Apr.   May   June

2011

TIME AXIS

Months represented on a continuous scale

FIGURE 4-33 Time series chart framework

CREATE A TIME SERIES CHART

If you know how to make a scatterplot in R, you know how to make a time series chart. Load your data and use the plot() function, but instead of using p in the type argument, you use 1 as the type, which stands for line.

To demonstrate, use world population data from the World Bank from 1960 to 2009. As usual load the data with the read.csv() function.

```
population <-
    read.csv("http://datasets.flowingdata.com/world-population.csv",
    sep=",", header=TRUE)
```

Here's what the first few rows of the data look like. It's just the year and population.

```
  Year Population
1 1960 3028654024
2 1961 3068356747
3 1962 3121963107
4 1963 3187471383
5 1964 3253112403
```

Use the plot() function and specify the X- and Y-coordinates, the type, the value axis limits, and axis labels.

```
plot(population$Year, population$Population, type="l",
    ylim=c(0, 7000000000), xlab="Year", ylab="Population")
```

Your chart will look like Figure 4-34.

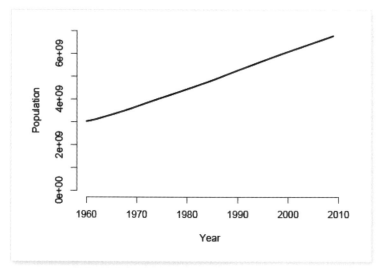

FIGURE 4-34 Default time series chart in R

At this point, you can save the image as a PDF and edit it in Illustrator like you've done a couple of times, but now try something else. Design the entire chart in Illustrator with the Line Graph tool. This is one of several graphing tools in Illustrator that enables you to create basic charts (Figure 4-35).

FIGURE 4-35 Graph tools in Illustrator

To start, select the Line Graph tool from the Tool window. You should see an icon of some kind of chart. Press and hold down the icon to choose the chart type.

Then download the population data at http://datasets.flowingdata.com/world-population.csv. You can't load data directly from a URL like you can in R, so you have to save the file on your computer. Open the CSV file in Excel or Google Documents, so that it's like Figure 4-36. Copy all the rows, except for the header row that names each column. You're going to paste the data into Illustrator.

Go back to Illustrator. Using the Line Graph tool, which you already selected from the Tool window, click-and-drag a rectangle that is approximately the size that you want your graph to be. A spreadsheet, as shown in Figure 4-37 will pop up.

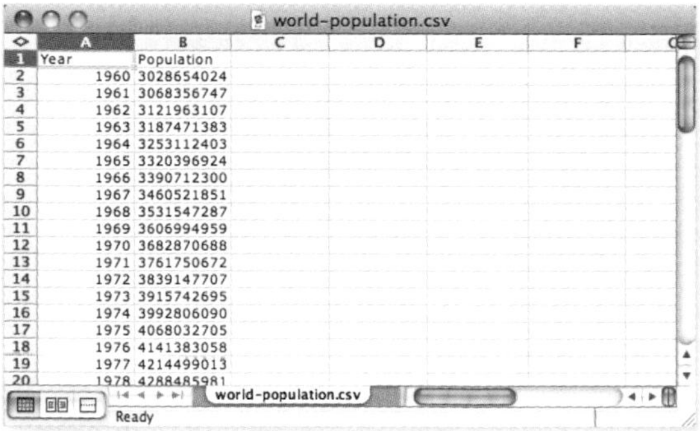

FIGURE 4-36 CSV file opened in Excel

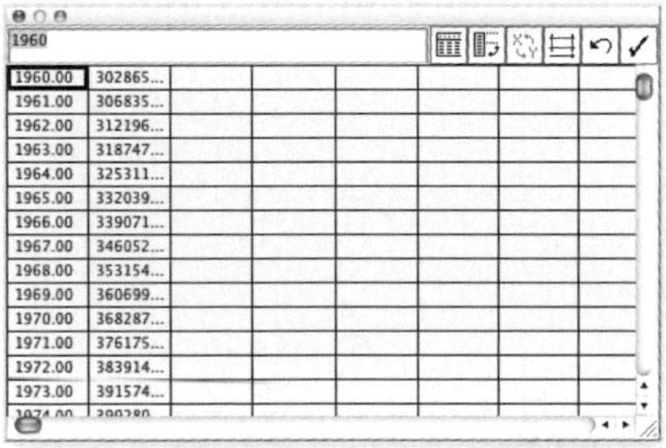

FIGURE 4-37 Spreadsheet to enter data in Illustrator

Paste the data that you copied from Excel, and then click the check mark on the top right. You should see an image that resembles Figure 4-38.

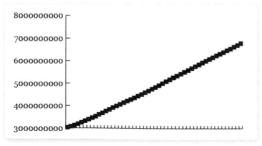

FIGURE 4-38 Default line graph in Illustrator

TIP

If you're going to edit in Illustrator and use a basic graph type, save some time and make the graph directly in Illustrator. You don't need to make everything in R first. That said, you don't have to make everything in Illustrator either.

Here's your base, but you need to change some options so that the graph doesn't look so rough. Right-click and select Type. Uncheck the box to Mark Data Points to match Figure 4-39.

Select Category Axis from the drop-down menu, and choose None for tick mark length. Press OK. This can give you a cleaner, less cluttered looking graph. From here, follow the same process that you followed when you edited graphs generated in R.

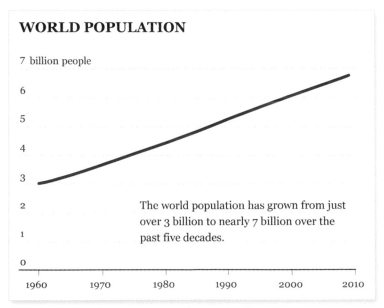

FIGURE 4-39 Graph options in Illustrator

You can clean up the vertical axis, simplify the value labels, add ticks and labels on the horizontal axis for years, and add a title and some copy. You can also change the stroke style for the actual line so that it stands out more. The default light gray makes it seem like the data is in the background when it should be front and center. Make these changes, and you should end up with Figure 4-40.

WORLD POPULATION

7 billion people

The world population has grown from just over 3 billion to nearly 7 billion over the past five decades.

FIGURE 4-40 World population over the past five decades

The main takeaway here is that you can make the same graph in both Illustrator and R—you still would have the same end result no matter. To that end, figure out what you're comfortable with tool-wise and go with it. The most important part is getting results.

Step It Up

One of the drawbacks of the standard line plot is that it implies steady change from point A to point B. That's about right with a measure like world population, but some things stay at a value for a long time and then all of a sudden see a boost or a decline. Interest rates, for example, can stay the same for months and then drop in a day. Use a step chart, as shown in Figure 4-41, for this type of data.

Instead of connecting point A to point B directly, the line stays at the same value until there is a change, at which point it jumps up (or down) to the next value. You end up with a bunch of steps.

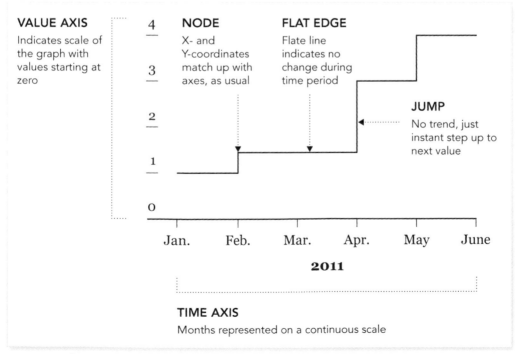

FIGURE 4-41 Step chart basic framework

CREATE A STEP CHART

Illustrator doesn't have a tool to easily create step charts. R does, however, so you can create a base chart in R and then edit in Illustrator. Are you starting to see a pattern here?

Figure 4-42 shows the final chart. It shows the change in postage rate for letters via the United States Postal Service. Notice the changes don't happen on a scheduled basis. From 1995 to 1999, postage stuck at 32 cents. That's 4 years without a change. However, more recently, there has been a change once a year from 2006 to 2009.

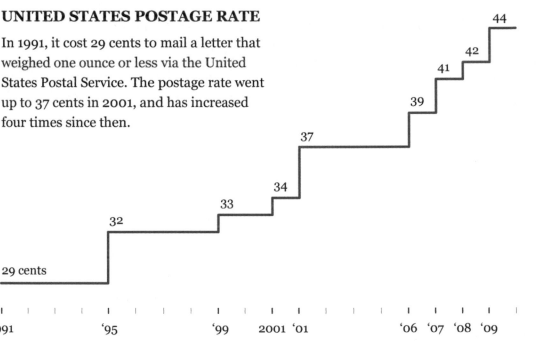

FIGURE 4-42 Step chart showing change in postage rate

To create the step chart in R, follow the same process you've been using throughout the chapter:

1. Load the data.

2. Make sure the data is properly formatted.

3. Use an R function to produce a plot.

You can find historical postage rates, along with many other datasets, from the United States Statistical Abstract. I've put it in a CSV file found at http://datasets.flowingdata.com/us-postage.csv. Plug that URL into read.csv() as the source to load the data file into R.

```
postage <- read.csv("http://datasets.flowingdata.com/us-postage.csv",
 sep=",", header=TRUE)
```

Following is the full dataset. It's only ten points, one for each postage rate change from 1991 to 2009, and a last point to indicate the current rate. The first column is year and the second column is rate in U.S. dollars.

```
   Year Price
1  1991  0.29
2  1995  0.32
3  1999  0.33
4  2001  0.34
5  2002  0.37
6  2006  0.39
7  2007  0.41
8  2008  0.42
9  2009  0.44
10 2010  0.44
```

The plot() function makes it easy to create a step chart. As you would expect, you plug in the year as the X-coordinate, price as the Y-coordinate, and use "s" as the *type*, which of course stands for step.

```
plot(postage$Year, postage$Price, type="s")
```

You can also specify main title and axis labels, if you like.

```
plot(postage$Year, postage$Price, type="s",
    main="US Postage Rates for Letters, First Ounce, 1991-2010",
    xlab="Year", ylab="Postage Rate (Dollars)")
```

This gives you the step chart for postage rate, as shown in Figure 4-43.

Just for fun, see what the graph would like if you used a line plot instead (Figure 4-44).

There's an increasing trend, but notice how it looks like it was a steady increase? At no point during 2001 and 2006 was the rate at 38 cents, but you wouldn't know that from the line plot unless you looked at the raw data.

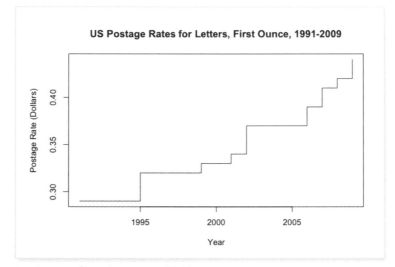

FIGURE 4-43 Step chart created in R

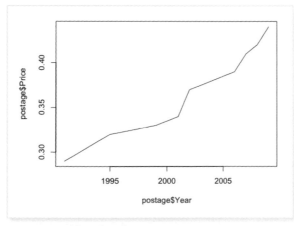

FIGURE 4-44 Line plot of postage rates

Save the image as a PDF and then open it in Illustrator. Follow the same process that you've used previously to edit the step chart to your liking. Design-wise, I got rid of the vertical axis altogether and directly labeled each jump (with the Type tool). I also made evenly spaced tick marks, but only labeled the years when there were changes.

Finally, I used a gray background. This was a personal preference, but the background helps highlight the graph, especially placed within text. It provides more surrounding space while not being annoyingly flashy. To make a background behind the graph and text, instead of on the top covering everything, you need to create a new layer in Illustrator. You can do this in, what else, the Layers window. Click the button to create a new layer. By default, the layer will be placed on top, but you want it on the bottom, so click-and-drag the new layer below Layer 1, as shown in Figure 4-45.

You can rename your layers, which can be especially useful when you start to design more complex graphics. I renamed the new layer "background." Then draw a rectangle using the Rectangle tool. Click and draw to make the size you want, and then change color via the Color window.

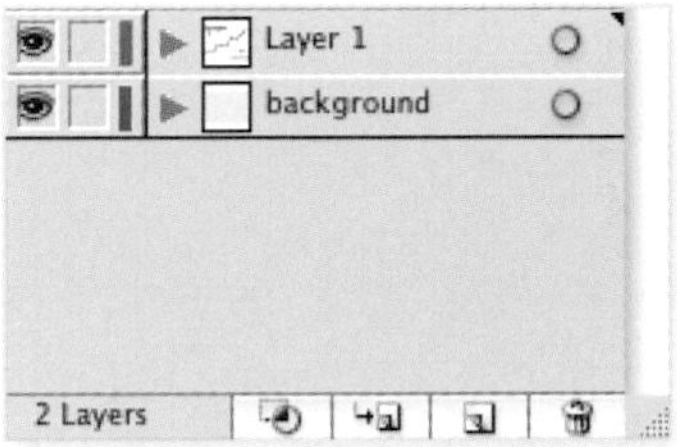

FIGURE 4-45 Layer window in Illustrator

> **TIP**
>
> When you have a small dataset, it can sometimes be useful to label points directly instead of using a value axis and grid. This places more emphasis on the data, and because there aren't that many points, the labels won't clutter and confuse.

Smoothing and Estimation

When you have a lot of data, or the data you have is noisy, it can be hard to spot trends and patterns. So to make it easier, you can estimate a trend line. Figure 4-46 shows the basic idea.

Draw a line that goes through the most points as possible, and minimize the summed distance from the points to the fitted line. The most straightforward route is to create a straight fitted line using the basic slope-intercept equation you probably learned in high school.

$$y = mx + b$$

Slope is m and the intercept is b. What happens when your trend is not linear? It doesn't make sense to fit a straight line to data that shows winds and curves. Instead use a statistical method created by William Cleveland and Susan Devlin called LOESS, or locally weighted scatterplot smoothing. It enables you to fit a curve to your data.

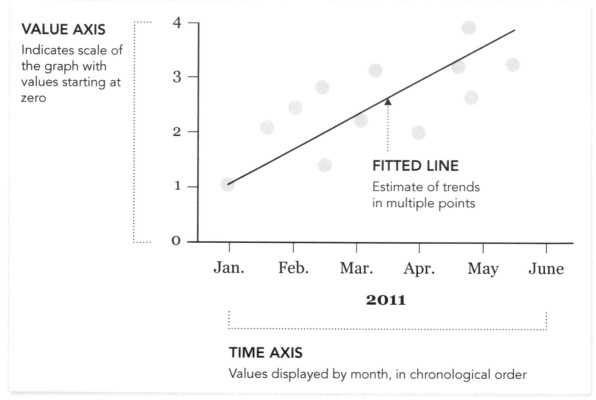

VALUE AXIS
Indicates scale of the graph with values starting at zero

FITTED LINE
Estimate of trends in multiple points

2011

TIME AXIS
Values displayed by month, in chronological order

FIGURE 4-46 Fitting a line to data points

▶ See "Robust Locally Weighted Regression and Smoothing Scatterplots" in the *Journal of the American Statistical Association* by William Cleveland for full details on LOESS.

LOESS starts at the beginning of the data and takes small slices. At each slice it estimates a low-degree polynomial for just the data in the slice. LOESS moves along the data, fitting a bunch of tiny curves, and together they form a single curve. You can Google it for more details. There are several papers on the topic. Now get into how to use LOESS with your data.

FIT A LOESS CURVE

The story you look at is unemployment in the United States over the past few decades. There have been ups and downs, along with seasonal fluctuations. What is the extent of the overall trends? As shown in Figure 4-47, the unemployment rate peaked in the 1980s, declined through the 1990s, and then shot up around 2008.

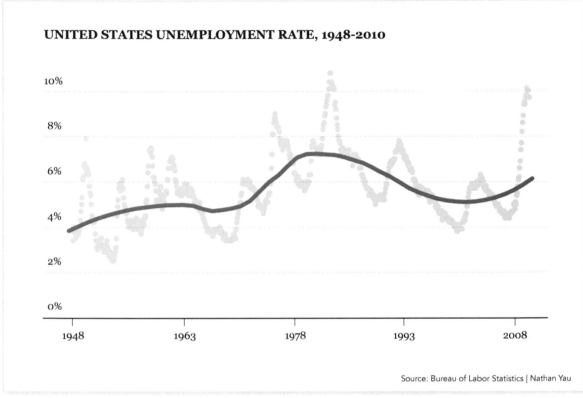

UNITED STATES UNEMPLOYMENT RATE, 1948-2010

FIGURE 4-47 Unemployment rates with fitted LOESS curve

Figure 4-48 shows what the unemployment graph looks like using only points with the R plot() function.

```
# Load data
unemployment <-
    read.csv(
        "http://datasets.flowingdata.com/unemployment-rate-1948-2010.csv",
        sep=",")
unemployment[1:10,]

# Plain scatter plot
plot(1:length(unemployment$Value), unemployment$Value)
```

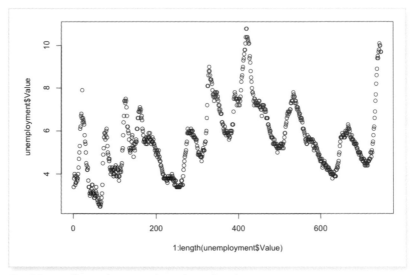

FIGURE 4-48 Unemployment plot using only points

Now here's what a straight fitted line would look like, as shown in Figure 4-49.

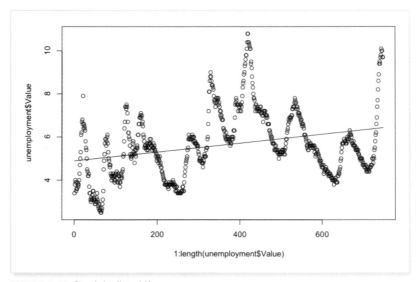

FIGURE 4-49 Straight fitted line

It's not helpful. It looks as if it ignores all the fluctuations in the unemployment rate. To fit a LOESS curve instead, you use the scatter.smooth() function.

```
scatter.smooth(x=1:length(unemployment$Value), y=unemployment$Value)
```

You can see the result in Figure 4-50. The line curves up now, accounting for the spike in the 1980s. That's a little better.

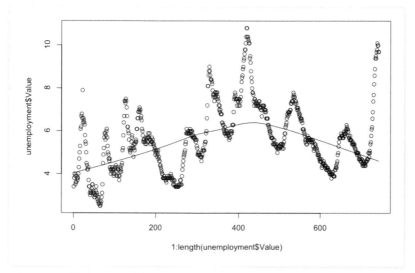

FIGURE 4-50 Fitting a LOESS curve

You can adjust how fitted the curve is via the degree and span arguments in the scatter.smooth() function. The former controls the degree of the polynomials that are fitted, and the latter controls how smooth the curve is. The closer the span is to zero, the closer the fit. Figure 4-51 is what you get if you change degree to 2 and span to 0.5. Now change the colors and adjust the axis limits.

```
scatter.smooth(x=1:length(unemployment$Value),
    y=unemployment$Value, ylim=c(0,11), degree=2, col="#CCCCCC", span=0.5)
```

The ups and downs of the curve are more prominent with these settings. Try messing around with span to get a better feel for how it changes smoothness.

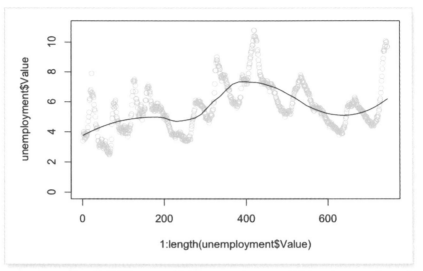

FIGURE 4-51 Fitted LOESS curve with less smoothness and higher degree polynomial

To get to the final graphic in Figure 4-47, save the image as a PDF and bring it into Illustrator. The same tools (for example, Selection, Type, Pen) are used to add titles, a background, and ticks for a horizontal axis. The fitted line was made more prominent to place more focus on the trends than on the individual data points.

Wrapping Up

It's fun to explore patterns over time. Time is so embedded in our day-to-day life that so many aspects of visualizing temporal data are fairly intuitive. You understand things changing and evolving—the hard part is figuring out by how much and learning what to look for in your graphs.

It's easy to glance over some lines on a plot and say something is increasing, and that's good. That's what visualization is for—to quickly get a general view of your data. But you can take it further. You can use visualization as an exploratory tool. Zoom in on sections of time and question why there was a small blip on some day but nowhere else or why there was a spike on a different day. That's when data is fun and interesting—the more you know about your data, the better story you can tell.

After you learn what your data is about, explain those details in your data graphic. Highlight the interesting parts so that your readers know where to look. A plain graph can be cool for you, but without context, the graph is boring for everyone else.

You used R with Illustrator to accomplish this. R built the base, and you used Illustrator to design graphics that pointed out what was important in the data. The covered chart types are of course only a subset of what you can do with temporal data. You open a whole new bag of tricks when you bring animation and interaction to the party, which you see in the next chapter. While you move on to a new data type—proportions—you can apply the same programming process and design principles that you used in this chapter, even if you code in a different language.

Visualizing Proportions

## 5

Time series data is naturally grouped by, well, time. A series of events happen during a specific time frame. Proportion data is also grouped, but by categories, subcategories, and population. By population, I don't mean just human population. Rather, population in this case represents all possible choices or outcomes. It's the sample space.

In a poll, people might be asked if they approve, disapprove, or have no opinion on some issue. Each category represents something, and the sum of the parts represent a whole.

This chapter discusses how to represent the individual categories, but still provides the bigger picture of how each choice relates to the other. You use some of what you learned in the previous chapter and get your first taste of interactive graphics using HTML, CSS, and JavaScript and then have a look at graphics with Flash.

What to Look for in Proportions

For proportions you usually look for three things: maximum, minimum, and the overall distribution. The first two are straightforward. Sort your data from least to greatest, and pick the ends for your maximum and minimum. If you were dealing with poll results, these could mean the most popular and least popular answers from participants; or if you were graphing calories from separate parts of a meal, you would see the biggest and smallest contributor to the overall calorie count.

You don't need a chart though to show you minimum and maximum. What you are most interested in is the distribution of proportions. How does the selection of one poll choice compare to the others? Are calories spread evenly across fat, protein, and carbohydrates, or does one group dominate? The following chart types can help you figure that out.

Parts of a Whole

This is proportions in their simplest form. You have a set of proportions that add up to 1 or a set of percentages that add up to 100 percent. You want to show the individual parts relative to the other parts but you also want to maintain the sense of a whole.

The Pie

Pie charts are the old standby. You see them everywhere these days, from business presentations to sites that use charts as a medium for jokes. The first known pie chart was published by William Playfair, who also invented the line graph and bar chart, in 1801. Smart guy.

You know how they work. As shown in Figure 5-1, you start with a circle, which represents a whole, and then cut wedges, like you would a pie. Each wedge represents a part of the whole. Remember that last part, because a lot of beginners make this mistake. The percentage of all the wedges should add up to 100 percent. If the sum is anything else, you have done something wrong.

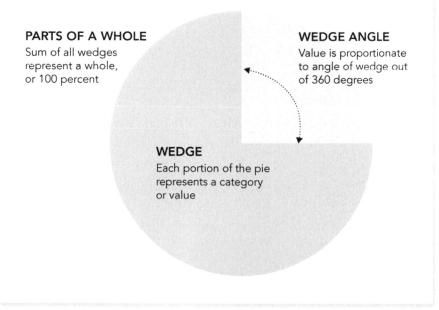

PARTS OF A WHOLE
Sum of all wedges
represent a whole,
or 100 percent

WEDGE ANGLE
Value is proportionate
to angle of wedge out
of 360 degrees

WEDGE
Each portion of the pie
represents a category
or value

FIGURE 5-1 Pie chart generalized

Pie charts have developed a stigma for not being as accurate as bar charts or position-based visuals, so some think you should avoid them completely. It's easier to judge length than it is to judge areas and angles. That doesn't mean you have to completely avoid them though.

You can use the pie chart without any problems just as long you know its limitations. It's simple. Keep your data organized, and don't put too many wedges in one pie.

CREATE A PIE CHART

Although just about every charting program enables you to make pie charts, you can make one in Illustrator just like you did in the previous chapter. The process of adding data, making a default chart, and then refining should feel familiar.

To build the base of your chart—the actual pie—is fairly straightforward. After you create a new document, select the Pie Graph tool from the Tool window, as shown in Figure 5-2. Click and drag a rectangle so that it is roughly the size of what you want your graph to be. You can resize it later.

FIGURE 5-2 Tool window in Illustrator

When you release the mouse button, a spreadsheet window pops up where you enter your data. For a single pie chart, enter each data point from left to right, and the values show up in your chart in the same order.

For this example, use the results from a poll on FlowingData. Readers were asked what data-related field they were most interested in. There were 831 responses.

AREA OF INTEREST	NUMBER OF VOTES
Statistics	172
Design	136
Business	135
Cartography	101
Information Science	80
Web Analytics	68
Programming	50
Engineering	29
Mathematics	19
Other	41

Enter the numbers in the spreadsheet in Illustrator, as shown in Figure 5-3. The order you enter the numbers will match the order the wedges appear in your pie chart, starting at the top and then rotating clockwise.

Notice that the poll results are organized from greatest to least and then end with the Other category. This kind of sorting can make your pie charts easier to read. Click the check mark in the top right of the pop-up when you finish.

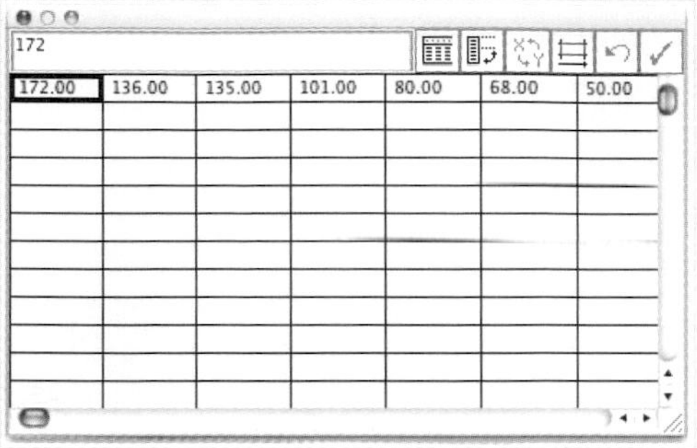

FIGURE 5-3 Spreadsheet in Illustrator

TIP

The spreadsheet in Illustrator is fairly bare bones, so you can't easily manipulate or rearrange your data. A way to get around this is to do all your data handling in Microsoft Excel, and then copy and paste into Illustrator.

The default pie chart appears with eight shades of gray, in a seemingly random sequence with a black border, as shown in Figure 5-4. It kind of looks like a grayscale lollipop, but you can easily do something about that. The important thing here is that you have the base of your pie chart.

Now make the pie chart more readable by changing some colors and adding text to explain to readers what they are looking at. As it is now, the colors don't make much sense. They just separate the wedges, but you can use colors as a way to tell readers what to look at and in what order. You did after all go through the trouble of sorting your data from greatest to least.

FIGURE 5-4 Default pie chart

If you start at 12 o'clock and rotate clockwise, you should see a descending order. However, because of the arbitrary color scheme, some of the smaller wedges are emphasized with darker shades. The dark shade acts as a highlighter, so instead, make larger wedges darker and smaller wedges lighter. If for some reason, you want to highlight answers that have fewer responses, you might want to color in reverse. In the case of this poll though, you want to know what data-related fields were the most popular.

TIP

Color can play an important role in how people read your graph. It's not just an aesthetic component— although sometimes it can be. Color can be a visual cue just like length or area, so choose wisely.

Choose the Direct Selection tool in the Tool window, and then click a wedge. Change fill and stroke color via the controls in the Color window. Figure 5-5 shows the same pie chart with a white stroke and wedges colored from darkest to lightest. Now it's easier to see that numbers go from greatest to least, with the exception of the last wedge for Other.

Of course, you don't have to be so frugal with your colors. You can use whatever colors you want, as shown Figure 5-6. Although it's usually a good idea to not use colors that are bright—you don't want to blind your readers. If a blinding color scheme fits with your topic though, go wild.

Because this is a FlowingData poll, I used the shade of red from the FlowingData logo and then made lighter color wedges by decreasing opacity. You can find the option in the Transparency window. At 0 percent opacity, the fill is completely see-through; at 100 percent opacity, the fill is not see-through.

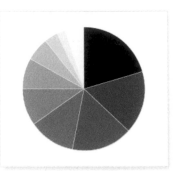

FIGURE 5-5 Pie chart with colors arranged darkest to lightest

Finally, add a title, a lead-in sentence, and labels for the graph with the Type tool. With practice, you can have a better idea what fonts you like to use for headers and copy, but whatever you use, Illustrator's alignment tools are your best friend when it comes to placing your text. Properly aligned and evenly spaced labels make your charts more readable. You can also make use of the Pen tool to create pointers, as shown in Figure 5-7, for the last three poll categories. These sections are too small to put the labels inside and are too close together to place the labels adjacent.

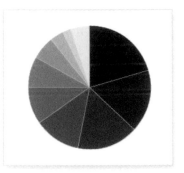

FIGURE 5-6 Colored pie chart

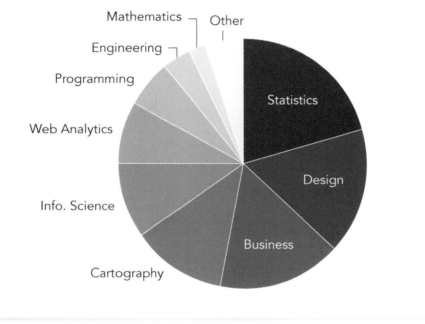

**WHAT DATA-RELATED AREA
ARE YOU MOST INTERESTED IN?**

Below are results of a poll on FlowingData in May 2009.
Readers come from a variety of fields, but Statistics, Design,
and Business led the way.

FIGURE 5-7 Final pie chart with labels and lead-in copy

The Donut

Your good friend the pie chart also has a lesser cousin: the donut chart.
It's like a pie chart, but with a hole cut out in the middle so that it looks like
a donut, as shown in Figure 5-8.

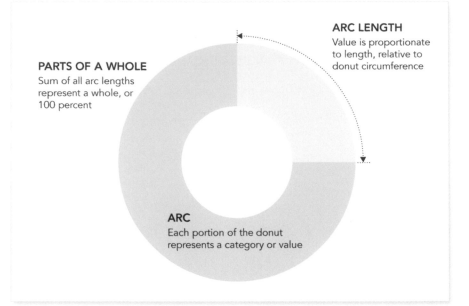

ARC LENGTH
Value is proportionate to length, relative to donut circumference

PARTS OF A WHOLE
Sum of all arc lengths represent a whole, or 100 percent

ARC
Each portion of the donut represents a category or value

FIGURE 5-8 Donut chart framework

Because there's a hole in the middle, you don't judge values by angle anymore. Instead you use arc length. This introduces many of the same problems when you use a single chart with too many categories, but in cases with fewer categories the donut chart can still come in handy.

CREATE A DONUT CHART

It's straightforward to make a donut chart in Illustrator. Create a pie chart like you just did; then put a filled circle in the middle, as shown in Figure 5-9. Again, use color to guide readers' eyes.

A lot of the time the middle of donut charts are used for a label or some other content like was done in the figure.

Now make the same chart using Protovis, the free and open-source visualization toolkit. It's a library implemented in JavaScript and makes use of modern browsers' Scalable Vector Graphics (SVG) capabilities. Graphics are generated dynamically and enable animation and interactivity, which makes Protovis great for online graphics.

WHAT DATA-RELATED AREA ARE YOU MOST INTERESTED IN?

Below are results of a poll on FlowingData in May 2009. Readers come from a variety of fields, but Statistics, Design, and Business led the way.

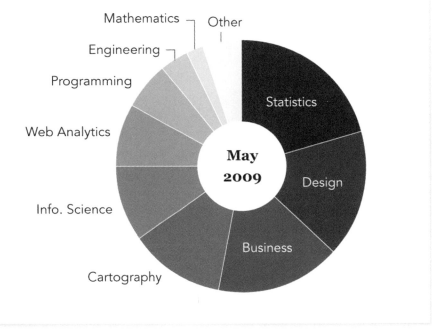

FIGURE 5-9 From pie to donut chart

Although you're about to get into a different programming language, you still follow the same process like you did in R and Illustrator. First, load the data, then build the base, and finally, customize the aesthetics.

Figure 5-10 shows what you want to make. It's similar to Figure 5-9, except the labels are set at an angle, and when you mouse over an arc, you can see how many votes there were for the corresponding category. Interaction can get much more advanced, but you have to learn the basics before you get fancy.

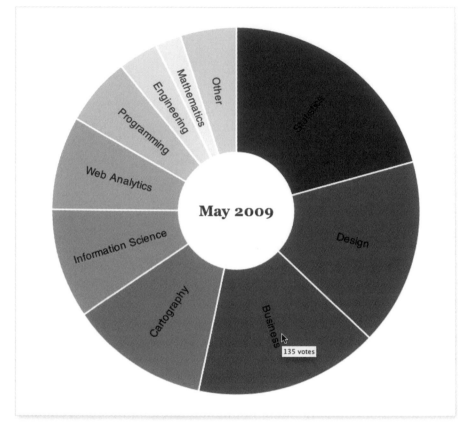

FIGURE 5-10 Donut chart using Protovis

The first thing you do is create an HTML page—call it **donut.html**.

```
<html>
<head>
    <title>Donut Chart</title>
    <script type="text/javascript" src="protovis-r3.2.js"></script>
    <style type="text/css">
        #figure {
            width: 400px;
            height: 400px;
        }
    </style>
</head>
<body>
```

```
    <div id="figure">

    </div><!-- @end figure -->
</body>
</html>
```

If you've ever created a web page, this should be straightforward, but in case you haven't, the preceding is basic HTML that you'll find almost everywhere online. Every page starts with an <html> tag and is followed by a <head> that contains information about the page but doesn't show in your browser window. Everything enclosed by the <body> tag is visible. Title the page **Donut Chart** and load the Protovis library, a JavaScript file, with the <script> tag. Then specify some CSS, which is used to style HTML pages. Keeping it simple, set the width and height of the <div> with the id "figure" at 400 pixels. This is where you draw our chart. The preceding HTML isn't actually part of the chart but necessary so that the JavaScript that follows loads properly in your browser. All you see is a blank page if you load the preceding donut.html file in your browser now.

Inside the figure <div>, specify that the code that you're going to write is JavaScript. Everything else goes in these <script> tags.

```
<script type="text/javascript+protovis">
</script>
```

Okay, first things first: the data. You're still looking at the results from the FlowingData poll, which you store in arrays. The vote counts are stored in one array, and the corresponding category names are stored in another.

```
var data = [172,136,135,101,80,68,50,29,19,41];
var cats = ["Statistics", "Design", "Business", "Cartography",
    "Information Science", "Web Analytics", "Programming",
    "Engineering", "Mathematics", "Other"];
```

Then specify the width and height of the donut chart and the radius length and scale for arc length.

```
var w = 350,
    h = 350,
    r = w / 2,
    a = pv.Scale.linear(0, pv.sum(data)).range(0, 2 * Math.PI);
```

The width and height of the donut chart are both 350 pixels, and the radius (that is, the center of the chart to the outer edge) is half the width, or 175 pixels. The fourth line specifies the arc scale. Here's how to read it. The actual data is on a linear scale from 0 to the sum of all votes, or total votes. This scale is then translated to the scale to that of the donut, which is from 0 to 2π radians, or 0 to 360 degrees if you want to think of it in that way.

Next create a color scale. The more votes a category receives, the darker the red it should be. In Illustrator, you did this by hand, but Protovis can pick the colors for you. You just pick the range of colors you want.

```
var depthColors = pv.Scale.linear(0, 172).range("white", "#821122");
```

Now you have a color scale from white to a dark red (that is #821122) on a linear range from 0 to 172, the highest vote count. In other words, a category with 0 votes will be white, and one with 172 votes will be dark red. Categories with vote counts in between will be somewhere in between white and red.

So far all you have are variables. You specified size and scale. To create the actual chart, first make a blank panel 350 (w) by 350 (h) pixels.

```
var vis = new pv.Panel()
    .width(w)
    .height(h);
```

Then add stuff to the panel, in this case wedges. It might be a little confusing, but now look over it line by line.

```
vis.add(pv.Wedge)
    .data(data)
    .bottom(w / 2)
    .left(w / 2)
    .innerRadius(r - 120)
    .outerRadius(r)
    .fillStyle(function(d) depthColors(d))
    .strokeStyle("#fff")
    .angle(a)
    .title(function(d) String(d) + " votes")
    .anchor("center").add(pv.Label)
        .text(function(d) cats[this.index]);
```

The first line says that you're adding wedges to the panel, one for each point in the data array. The bottom() and left() properties orient the wedges so that the points are situated in the center of the circle. The innerRadius() specifies the radius of the hole in the middle whereas the outerRadius is the radius of the full circle. That covers the structure of the donut chart.

Rather than setting the fill style to a static shade, fill colors are determined by the value of the data point and the color scale stored as depth-Colors, or in other words, color is determined by a function of each point. A white (#fff) border is used, which is specified by strokeStyle(). The circular scale you made can determine the angle of each wedge.

To get a tooltip that says how many votes there were when you mouse over a section, title() is used. Another option would be to create a *mouseover event* where you specify what happens when a user places a pointer over an object, but because browsers automatically show the value of the title attribute, it's easier to use title(). Make the title the value of each data point followed by "votes." Finally, add labels for each section. The only thing left to do is add May 2009 in the hole of the chart.

```
vis.anchor("center").add(pv.Label)
    .font("bold 14px Georgia")
    .text("May 2009");
```

This reads as, "Put a label in the center of the chart in bold 14-pixel Georgia font that says May 2009."

The full chart is now built, so now you can render it.

```
vis.render();
```

When you open donut.html in your browser, you should see Figure 5-10.

If you're new to programming, this section might have felt kind of daunting, but the good news is that Protovis was designed to be learned by example. The library's site has many working examples to learn from and that you can use with your own data. It has traditional statistical graphics to the more advanced interactive and animated graphics. So don't get discouraged if you were a little confused. The effort you put in now will pay off

▶ Visit http:// book.flowingdata .com/ch05/donut .html to see the live chart and view the source for the code in its entirety.

after you get the hang of things. Now have another look at Protovis in the next section.

Stack Them Up

In the previous chapter you used the stacked bar chart to show data over time, but it's not just temporal data. As shown in Figure 5-11, you can also use the stacked bar chart for categorical data.

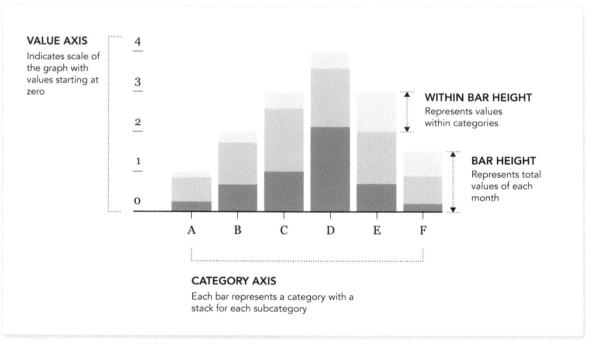

FIGURE 5-11 Stacked bar chart with categories

For example, look at approval ratings for Barack Obama as estimated from a Gallup and CBS poll taken in July and August 2010. Participants were asked whether they approved or disapproved of how Obama has dealt with 13 issues.

Here are the numbers in table form.

ISSUE	APPROVE	DISAPPROVE	NO OPINION
Race relations	52	38	10
Education	49	40	11
Terrorism	48	45	7
Energy policy	47	42	11
Foreign affairs	44	48	8
Environment	43	51	6
Situation in Iraq	41	53	6
Taxes	41	54	5
Healthcare policy	40	57	3
Economy	38	59	3
Situation in Afghanistan	36	57	7
Federal budget deficit	31	64	5
Immigration	29	62	9

One option would be to make a pie chart for every issue, as shown in Figure 5-12. To do this in Illustrator, all you have to do is enter multiple rows of data instead of just a single one. One pie chart is generated for each row.

However, a stacked bar chart enables you to compare approval ratings for the issues more easily because it's easier to judge bar length than wedge angles, so try that. In the previous chapter, you made a stacked bar chart in Illustrator using the Stacked Graph tool. This time you add some simple interactions.

CREATE AN INTERACTIVE STACKED BAR CHART

Like in the donut chart example, use Protovis to create an interactive stacked bar chart. Figure 5-13 shows the final graphic. There are two basic interactions to implement. The first shows the percentage value of any given stack when you place the mouse pointer over it. The second highlights bars in the approve, disapprove, and no opinion categories based on where you put your mouse.

APPROVAL RATINGS FOR BARACK OBAMA

Recent polls show a 52% approval rating for Barack Obama in race relations. It is the only issue out of the below thirteen where he has a majority approval. In eight of the thirteen, results show a majority disapproval.

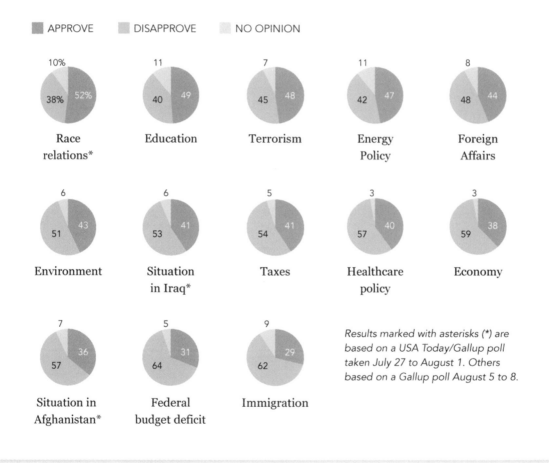

FIGURE 5-12 Series of pie charts

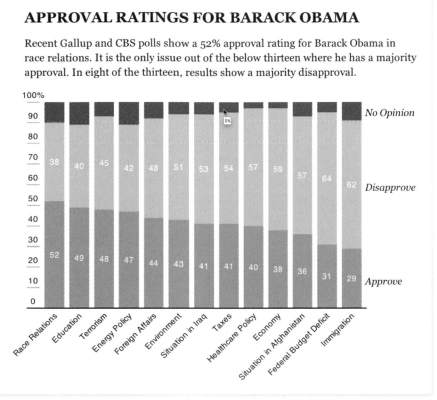

APPROVAL RATINGS FOR BARACK OBAMA

Recent Gallup and CBS polls show a 52% approval rating for Barack Obama in race relations. It is the only issue out of the below thirteen where he has a majority approval. In eight of the thirteen, results show a majority disapproval.

FIGURE 5-13 Interactive stacked bar chart in Protovis

To start, set up the HTML page and load the necessary Protovis JavaScript file.

```html
<html>
<head>
    <title>Stacked Bar Chart</title>
    <script type="text/javascript" src="protovis-r3.2.js"></script>
</head>
<body>
    <div id="figure-wrapper">
        <div id="figure">

    </div><!-- @end figure -->
    </div><!-- @end figure-wrapper -->
</body>
</html>
```

This should look familiar. You did the same thing to make a donut chart with Protovis. The only difference is that the title of the page is "Stacked Bar Chart" and there's an additional <div> with a "figure-wrapper" id. We also haven't added any CSS yet to style the page, because we're saving that for later.

Now on to JavaScript. Within the figure <div>, load and prepare the data (Obama ratings, in this case) in arrays.

```
<script type="text/javascript+protovis">
    var data = {
        "Issue":["Race Relations","Education","Terrorism","Energy Policy",
            "Foreign Affairs","Environment","Situation in Iraq",
            "Taxes","Healthcare Policy","Economy","Situation in Afghanistan",
            "Federal Budget Deficit","Immigration"],
        "Approve":[52,49,48,47,44,43,41,41,40,38,36,31,29],
        "Disapprove":[38,40,45,42,48,51,53,54,57,59,57,64,62],
        "None":[10,11,7,11,8,6,6,5,3,3,7,5,9]
    };
</script>
```

You can read this as 52 percent and 38 percent approval and disapproval ratings, respectively, for race relations. Similarly, there were 49 percent and 40 percent approval and disapproval ratings for education.

To make it easier to code the actual graph, you can split the data and store it in two variables.

```
var cat = data.Issue;
var data = [data.Approve, data.Disapprove, data.None];
```

The issues array is stored in cat and the data is now an array of arrays.

Set up the necessary variables for width, height, scale, and colors with the following:

```
var w = 400,
h = 250,
x = pv.Scale.ordinal(cat).splitBanded(0, w, 4/5),
y = pv.Scale.linear(0, 100).range(0, h),
fill = ["#809EAD", "#B1C0C9", "#D7D6CB"];
```

The graph will be 400 pixels wide and 250 pixels tall. The horizontal scale is ordinal, meaning you have set categories, as opposed to a continuous scale. The categories are the issues that the polls covered. Four-fifths of the graph width will be used for the bars, whereas the rest is for padding in between the bars.

The vertical axis, which represents percentages, is a linear scale from 0 to 100 percent. The height of the bars can be anywhere in between 0 pixels to the height of the graph, or 250 pixels.

Finally, fill is specified in an array with hexadecimal numbers. That's dark blue for approval, light blue for disapproval, and light gray for no opinion. You can change the colors to whatever you like.

Next step: Initialize the visualization with specified width and height. The rest provides padding around the actual graph, so you can fit axis labels. For example, bottom(90) moves the zero-axis up 90 pixels. Think of this part as setting up a blank canvas.

```
var vis = new pv.Panel()
    .width(w)
    .height(h)
    .bottom(90)
    .left(32)
    .right(10)
    .top(15);
```

► If you're not sure what colors to use, ColorBrewer at http:// colorbrewer2.org is a good place to start. The tool enables you to specify the number of colors you want to use and the type of colors, and it provides a color scale that you can copy in various formats. 0to255 at http://0to255.com is a more general color tool, but I use it often.

To add stacked bars to your canvas, Protovis provides a special layout for stacked charts appropriately named Stack. Although you use this for a stacked bar chart in this example, the layout can also be used with stacked area charts and streamgraphs. Store the new layout in the "bar" variable.

```
var bar - vis.add(pv.Layout.Stack)
    .layers(data)
    .x(function() x(this.index))
    .y(function(d) y(d))
    .layer.add(pv.Bar)
        .fillStyle(function() fill[this.parent.index])
    .width(x.range().band)
    .title(function(d) d + "%")
    .event("mouseover", function() this.fillStyle("#555"))
    .event("mouseout", function()
        this.fillStyle(fill[this.parent.index]));
```

Another way to think about this chart is as a set of three layers, one each for approval, disapproval, and no opinion. Remember how you structured those three as an array of three arrays? That goes in `layers()`, where x and y follow the scales that you already made.

For each layer, add bars using `pv.Bar`. Specify the fill style with `fillStyle()`. Notice that we used a function that goes by `this.parent.index`. This is so that the bar is colored by what layer it belongs to, of which there are three. If you were to use `this.index`, you would need color specifications for every bar, of which there are 39 (3 times 13). The width of each bar is the same across, and you can get that from the ordinal scale you already specified.

The final three lines of the preceding code are what make the graph interactive. Using `title()` in Protovis is the equivalent of setting the title attribute of an HTML element such as an image. When you roll over an image on a web page, a tooltip shows up if you set the title. Similarly, a tooltip appears as you place the mouse pointer over a bar for a second. Here simply make the tooltip show the percentage value that the bar represents followed with a percent sign (%).

TIP

Interaction in Protovis isn't just limited to mouse over and out. You can also set events for things such as click and double-click. See Protovis documentation for more details.

To make the layers highlight whenever you mouse over a bar, use `event()`. On "mouseover" the fill color is set to a dark gray (#555), and when the mouse pointer is moved off, the bar is set to its original color using the "mouseout" event.

To make the graph appear, you need to render it. Enter this at the end of our JavaScript.

```
vis.render();
```

This basically says, "Okay, we've put together all the pieces. Now draw the visualization." Open the page in your web browser (a modern one, such as Firefox or Safari), and you should see something like Figure 5-14.

Mouse over a bar, and the layer appears highlighted. A tooltip shows up, too. A few things are still missing, namely the axes and labels. Add those now.

In Figure 5-13, a number of labels are on the bars. It's only on the larger bars though, that is, not the gray ones. Here's how to do that. Keep in mind that this goes before `vis.render()`. Always save rendering for last.

```
bar.anchor("center").add(pv.Label)
    .visible(function(d) d > 11)
    .textStyle("white")
    .text(function(d) d.toFixed(0));
```

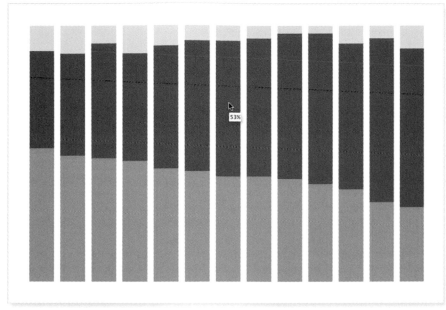

FIGURE 5-14 Stacked bar graph without any labels

For each bar, look to see if it is greater than 11 percent. If it is, a white label that reads the percentage rounded to the nearest integer is drawn in the middle of the bar.

Now add the labels for each issue on the x-axis. Ideally, you want to make all labels read horizontally, but there is obviously not enough space to do that. If the graph were a horizontal bar chart, you could fit horizontal labels, but for this you want to see them at 45-degree angles. You can make the labels completely vertical, but that'd make them harder to read.

```
bar.anchor("bottom").add(pv.Label)
    .visible(function() !this.parent.index)
    .textAlign("right")
    .top(260)
    .left(function() x(this.index)+20)
    .textAngle(-Math.PI / 4)
    .text(function() cat[this.index]);
```

This works in the same way you added number labels to the middle of each bar. However, this time around add labels only to the bars at the bottom, that is, the ones for approval. Then right-align the text and set their absolute vertical position with textAlign() and top(). Their x-position is based on what bar they label, each is rotated 45 degrees, and the text is the category.

That gives the categorical labels. The labels for values on the vertical axis are added in the same way, but you also need to add tick marks.

```
vis.add(pv.Rule)
    .data(y.ticks())
    .bottom(y)
    .left(-15)
    .width(15)
    .strokeStyle(function(d) d > 0 ? "rgba(0,0,0,0.3)" : "#000")
    .anchor("top").add(pv.Label)
    .bottom(function(d) y(d)+2)
    .text(function(d) d == 100 ? "100%" : d.toFixed(0));
```

This adds a Rule, or lines, according to y.ticks(). If the tick mark is for anything other than the zero line, its color is gray. Otherwise, the tick is black. The second section then adds labels on top of the tick marks.

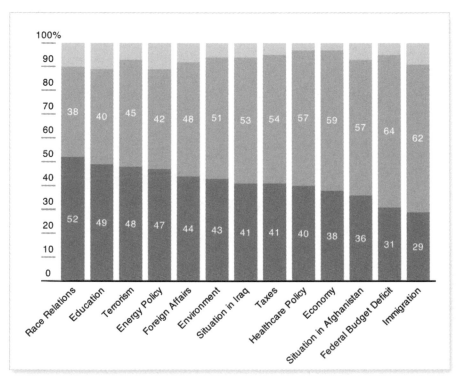

FIGURE 5-15 Adding the horizontal axis

You're still missing the horizontal axis, so add another Rule, separately to get what you see in Figure 5-15.

```
vis.add(pv.Rule)
    .bottom(y)
    .left(-15)
    .right(0)
    .strokeStyle("#000")
```

Lead-in copy and remaining labels are added with HTML and CSS. There are entire books for web design though, so I'll leave it at that. The cool thing here is that you can easily combine the HTML and CSS with Protovis, which is just JavaScript and still make it look seamless.

Hierarchy and Rectangles

In 1990, Ben Shneiderman, of the University of Maryland, wanted to visualize what was going on in his always-full hard drive. He wanted to know what was taking up so much space. Given the hierarchical structure of directories and files, he first tried a tree diagram. It got too big too fast to be useful though. Too many nodes. Too many branches.

The treemap was his solution. As shown in Figure 5-16, it's an area-based visualization where the size of each rectangle represents a metric. Outer rectangles represent parent categories, and rectangles within the parent are like subcategories. You can use a treemap to visualize straight-up proportions, but to fully put the technique to use, it's best served with hierarchical, or rather, tree-structured data.

▶ To see and interact with the stacked bar graph, visit http://book.flowingdata.com/ch05/stacked-bar.html. Check out the source code to see how HTML, CSS, and JavaScript fit together.

▶ See http://datafl.ws/11m for a full history of treemaps and additional examples described by the creator, Ben Shneiderman.

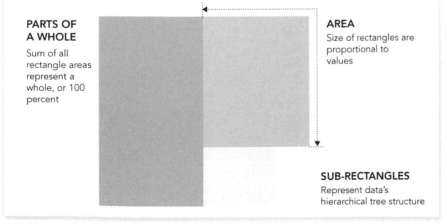

PARTS OF A WHOLE
Sum of all rectangle areas represent a whole, or 100 percent

AREA
Size of rectangles are proportional to values

SUB-RECTANGLES
Represent data's hierarchical tree structure

FIGURE 5-16 Treemap generalized

TIP

R is an open-source software environment for statistical computing. You can download it for free from www.r-project.org/. The great thing about R is that there is an active community around the software that is always developing packages to add functionality. If you're looking to make a static chart, and don't know where to start, the R archives are a great place to look.

CREATE A TREEMAP

Illustrator doesn't have a Treemap tool, but there is an R package by Jeff Enos and David Kane called Portfolio. It was originally intended to visualize stock market portfolios (hence the name), but you can easily apply it to your own data. Look at page views and comments of 100 popular posts on FlowingData and separate them by their post categories, such as visualization or data design tips.

As always, the first step is to load the data into R. You can load data directly from your computer or point to a URL. Do the latter in this example because the data is already available online. If, however, you want to do the former when you apply the following steps to your own data, just make sure you put your data file in your working directory in R. You can change your working directory through the Miscellaneous menu.

Loading a CSV file from a URL is easy. It's only one line of code with the read.csv()function in R (Figure 5-17).

```
posts <- read.csv("http://datasets.flowingdata.com/post-data.txt")
```

FIGURE 5-17 Loading CSV in R

Easy, right? We've loaded a text file (in CSV format) using read.csv() and stored the values for page views and comments in a variable called *posts*. As mentioned in the previous chapter, the read.csv() function assumes that your data file is comma-delimited. If your data were say, tab-delimited, you would use the sep argument and set the value to \t. If you want to load the data from a local directory, the preceding line might look something like this.

```
posts <- read.csv("post-data.txt")
```

This is assuming you've changed your working directory accordingly. For more options and instructions on how to load data using the read.csv() function, type the following in the R console:

```
?read.csv
```

Moving on, now that the data is stored in the *posts* variable, enter the following line to see the first five rows of the data.

```
posts[1:5,]
```

You should see four columns that correspond to the original CSV file, with *id*, *views*, *comments*, and *category*. Now that the data is loaded in R, make use of the Portfolio package. Try loading it with the following:

```
library(portfolio)
```

Get an error? You probably need to install the package before you begin:

```
install.packages("portfolio")
```

You should load the package now. Go ahead and do that. Loaded with no errors? Okay, good, now go to the next step.

The Portfolio package does the hard work with a function called map.market(). The function takes several arguments, but you use only five of them.

```
map.market(id=data$id, area=posts$views, group=posts$category,
    color=posts$comments, main="FlowingData Map")
```

The id is the column that indicates a unique point, and you tell R to use *views* to decide the areas of the rectangles in the treemap, the categories to form groups, and the number of comments in a post to decide color. Finally, enter **FlowingData Map** as the main title. Press Enter on your keyboard to get a treemap, as shown in Figure 5-18.

It's still kind of rough around the edges, but the base and hierarchy is set up, which is the hard part. Just like you specified, rectangles, each of which represent a post, are sized by the number of page views and sorted by category. Brighter shades of green indicate posts that received more comments; posts with a lot of views don't necessarily get the most comments.

You can save the image as a PDF in R and then open the file in Illustrator. All regular edit options apply. You can change stroke and fill colors, fonts, remove anything extraneous, and add comments if you like.

> **TIP**
>
> You can also install packages in R through the user interface. Go to Packages & Data ➪ Package Installer. Click Get List, and then find the package of interest. Double-click to install.

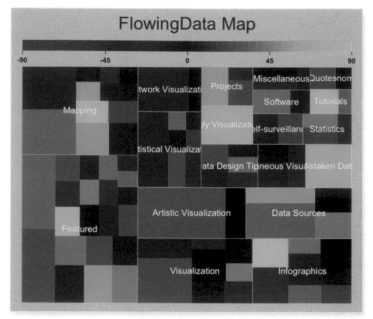

FIGURE 5-18 Default treemap in R

▶ *The New York Times* used an animated treemap to show changes in the stock market during the financial crisis in its piece titled "How the Giants of Finance Shrank, Then Grew, Under the Financial Crisis." See it in action at `http://nyti.ms/9JUkWL`.

For this particular graphic you need to change the scale of the legend that goes from –90 to 90. It doesn't make sense to have a negative scale because there's no such thing as a negative number of comments. You can also fix the labels. Some of them are obscured in the small rectangles. Size the labels by popularity instead of the uniform scale it now has using the Selection tool. Also thicken the category borders so that they're more prominent. That should give you something like Figure 5-19.

There you go. The graphic is much more readable now with unobscured labeling and a color scale that makes more sense. You also got rid of the dark gray background, which makes it cleaner. Oh, and of course, you included a title and lead-in to briefly explain what the graphic shows.

Because the Portfolio package does most of the heavy lifting, the only tough part in applying this to your own data is getting it into the right format. Remember, you need three things. You need a unique id for each row, a metric to size rectangles, and parent categories. Optionally, you can use a fourth metric to color your rectangles. Check out Chapter 2, "Handling Data," for instructions on how to get your data into the format you need.

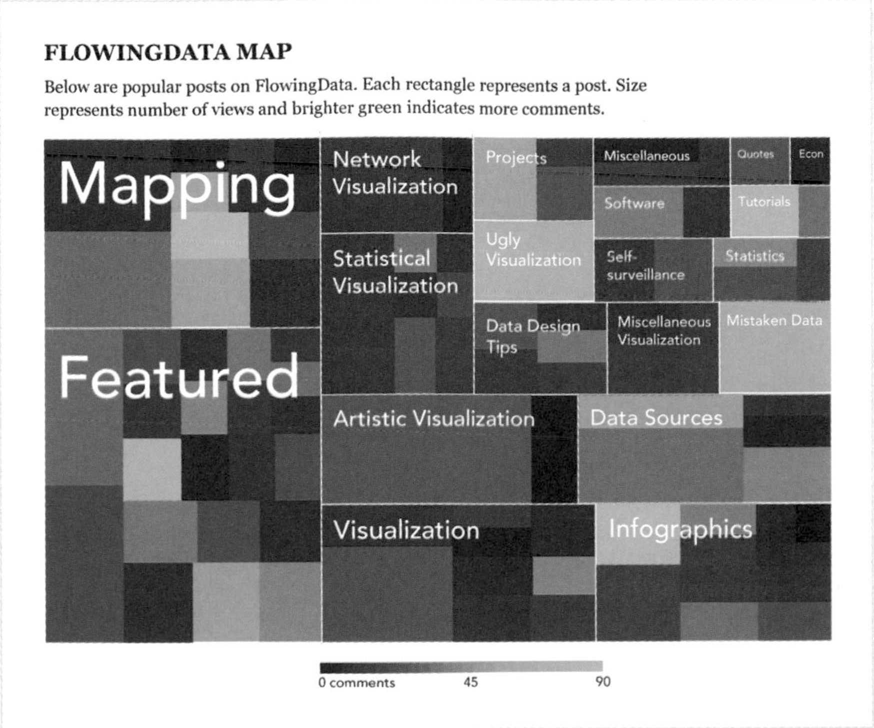

FLOWINGDATA MAP

Below are popular posts on FlowingData. Each rectangle represents a post. Size represents number of views and brighter green indicates more comments.

FIGURE 5-19 Revised treemap from R to Illustrator

Proportions over Time

Often you'll have a set of proportions over time. Instead of results for a series of questions from a single polling session, you might have results from the same poll run every month for a year. You're not just interested in individual poll results; you also want to see how views have changed over time. How has opinion changed from one year ago until now?

This doesn't just apply to polls, of course. There are plenty of distributions that change over time. In the following examples, you take a look at the distribution of age groups in the United States from 1860 to 2005. With improving healthcare and average family size shrinking, the population as a whole is living longer than the generation before.

Stacked Continuous

Imagine you have several time series charts. Now stack each line on top of the other. Fill the empty space. What you have is a stacked area chart, where the horizontal axis is time, and the vertical axis is a range from 0 to 100 percent, as shown in Figure 5-20.

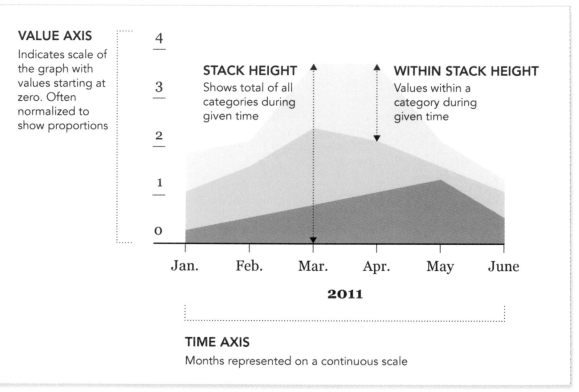

FIGURE 5-20 Stacked area chart generalized

So if you were to take a vertical slice of the area chart, you would get the distribution of that time slice. Another way to look at it is as a series of stacked bar charts connected by time.

CREATE A STACKED AREA CHART

In this example, look at the aging population. Download the data at http://book.flowingdata.com/ch05/data/us-population-by-age.xls. Medicine and healthcare have improved over the decades, and the average lifespan continues to rise. As a result, the percentage of the population in older age brackets has increased. By how much has this age distribution changed over the years? Data from the U.S. Census Bureau can help you see via a stacked area chart. You want to see how the proportion of older age groups has increased and how the proportion of the younger age groups has decreased.

You can do this in a variety of ways, but first use Illustrator. For the stacked area graph, it comes in the form of the Area Graph tool (Figure 5-21).

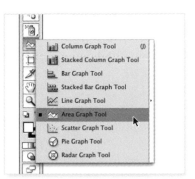

Click and drag somewhere on a new document, and enter the data in the spreadsheet that pops up. You're familiar with the load data, generate graphic, and refine process now, right?

FIGURE 5-21 Area Graph Tool

You can see a stacked area chart, as shown in Figure 5-22, after you enter the data.

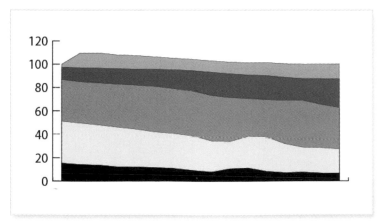

FIGURE 5-22 Default stacked area chart in Illustrator

The top area goes above the 100 percent line. This happened because the stacked area graph is not just for normalized proportions or a set of values that add up to 100 percent. It can also be used for raw values, so if you want each time slice to add up to 100 percent, you need to normalize the data. The above image was actually from a mistake on my part; I entered the data incorrectly. Oops. A quick fix, and you can see the graph in Figure 5-23. Although, you probably entered the data correctly the first time, so you're already here.

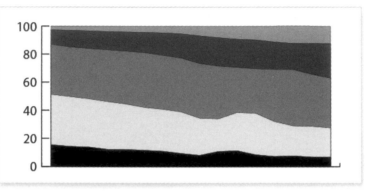

FIGURE 5-23 Fixed area chart

Keep an eye out for stuff like this in your graph design though. It's better to spot typos and small data entry errors in the beginning than it is to finish a design and have to backtrack to figure out where things went wrong.

Now that you have a proper base, clean up the axis and lines. Make use of the Direct Selection tool to select specific elements. I like to remove the vertical axis line and leave thinner tick marks for a cleaner, less clunky look, and add the percentage sign to the numbers because that's what we're dealing with. I also typically change the stroke color of the actual graph fills from the default black to a simpler white. Also bring in some shades of blue. That takes you to Figure 5-24.

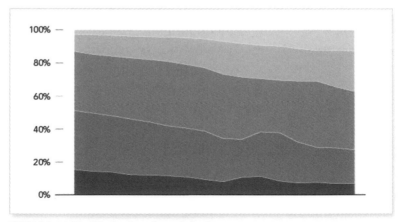

FIGURE 5-24 Modified colors from default

> **TIP**
>
> Be careful when you enter data manually. A lot of silly mistakes come from transferring data from one source to another.

Again, this is just my design taste, and you can do what you want. Color selection can also vary by case. The more graphs that you design, the better feel you'll develop for what you like and what works best.

Are you missing anything else? Well, there are no labels for the horizontal axis. Now put them in. And while you're at it, label the areas to indicate the age groups (Figure 5-25).

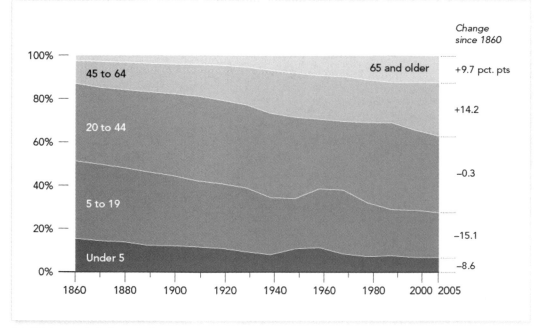

FIGURE 5-25 Labeled stacked area chart

I also added annotation on the right of the graph. What we're most interested in here is the change in age distribution. We can see that from the graph, but the actual numbers can help drive the point home.

Lastly, put in the title and lead-in copy, along with the data source on the bottom. Tweak the colors of the right annotations a little bit to add some more meaning to the display, and you have the final graphic, as shown in Figure 5-26.

AN AGING POPULATION

In 1860, an estimated 13.1 percent of the U.S. population was 45 years or older. In 2005, the estimate is up to 23.9 percent.

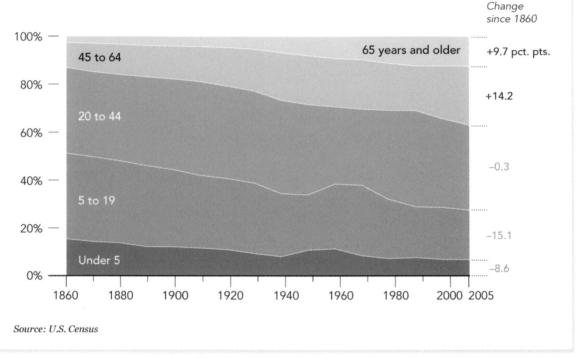

Source: U.S. Census

FIGURE 5-26 Final stacked area chart

CREATE AN INTERACTIVE STACKED AREA CHART

One of the drawbacks to using stacked area charts is that they become hard to read and practically useless when you have a lot of categories and data points. The chart type worked for age breakdowns because there were only five categories. Start adding more, and the layers start to look like thin strips. Likewise, if you have one category that has relatively small counts, it can easily get dwarfed by the more prominent categories. Making the stacked area graph interactive, however, can help solve that problem.

You can provide a way for readers to search for categories and then adjust the axis to zoom in on points of interest. Tooltips can help readers see values in places that are too small to place labels. Basically, you can take data that wouldn't work as a static stacked area chart, but use it with an interactive chart, and make it easy to browse and explore. You could do this in JavaScript with Protovis, but for the sake of learning more tools (because it's super fun), use Flash and ActionScript.

NOTE

Online visualization has slowly been shifting away from Flash toward JavaScript and HTML5, but not all browsers support the latter, namely Internet Explorer. Also, because Flash has been around for years, there are libraries and packages that make certain tasks easier than if you were to try to do it with native browser functionality.

Luckily you don't have to start from scratch. Most of the work has already been done for you via the Flare visualization toolkit, designed and maintained by the UC Berkeley Visualization Lab. It's an ActionScript library, which was actually a port of a Java visualization toolkit called Prefuse. We'll work off one of the sample applications on the Flare site, JobVoyager, which is like NameVoyager, but an explorer for jobs. After you get your development environment set up, it's just a matter of switching in your data and then customizing the look and feel.

You can write the code completely in ActionScript and then compile it into a Flash file. Basically this means you write the code, which is a language that you understand, and then use a compiler to translate the code into bits so that your computer, or the Flash player, can understand what you told it to do. So you need two things: a place to write and a way to compile.

The hard way to do this is to write code in a standard text editor and then use one of Adobe's free compilers. I say hard because the steps are definitely more roundabout, and you have to install separate things on your computer.

The easy way to do this, and the way I highly recommend if you're planning on doing a lot of work in Flash and ActionScript, is to use Adobe Flex Builder. It makes the tedious part of programming with ActionScript quicker, because you code, compile, and debug all in the same place. The downside is that it does cost money, although it's free for students.

▶ The *NameVoyager* by Martin Wattenberg made the interactive stacked area chart popular. It is used to show baby names over time, and the graph automatically updates as you type names in the search box. Try it out at www .babynamewizard .com/voyager.

NOTE

Download Flare for free at http://flare .prefuse.org/.

If you're not sure if it's worth the money, you can always download a free trial and make your decision later. For the stacked area chart example, I'll explain the steps you have to take in Flex Builder.

NOTE

At the time of this writing, Adobe changed the name of Flex Builder to Flash Builder. They are similar but there are some variations between the two. While the following steps use the former, you can still do the same in the latter. Download Flash Builder at www.adobe.com/products/flashbuilder/. Be sure to take advantage of the student discount. Simply provide a copy of your student ID, and you get a free license. Alternatively, find an old, lower-priced copy of Flex Builder.

When you've downloaded and installed Flex Builder, go ahead and open it; you should see a window, as shown in Figure 5-27.

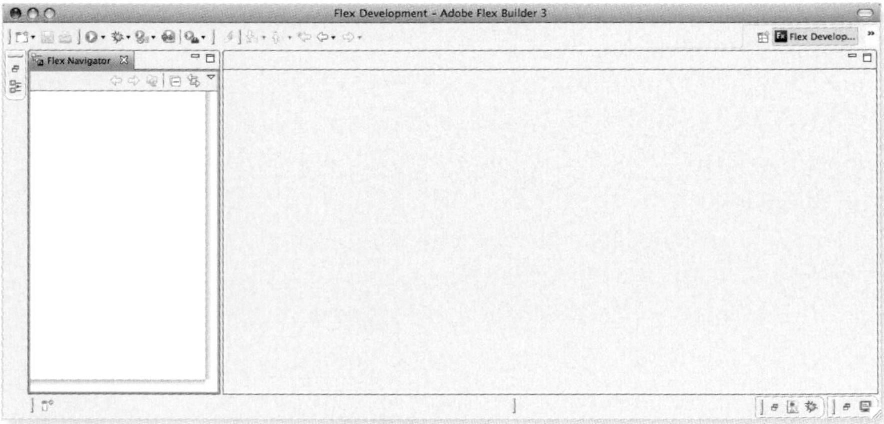

FIGURE 5-27 Initial window on opening Flex Builder

Right-click the Flex Navigator (left sidebar) and click Import. You'll see a pop-up that looks like Figure 5-28.

Select Existing Projects into Workspace and click Next. Browse to where you put the Flare files. Select the flare directory, and then make sure Flare is checked in the project window, as shown in Figure 5-29.

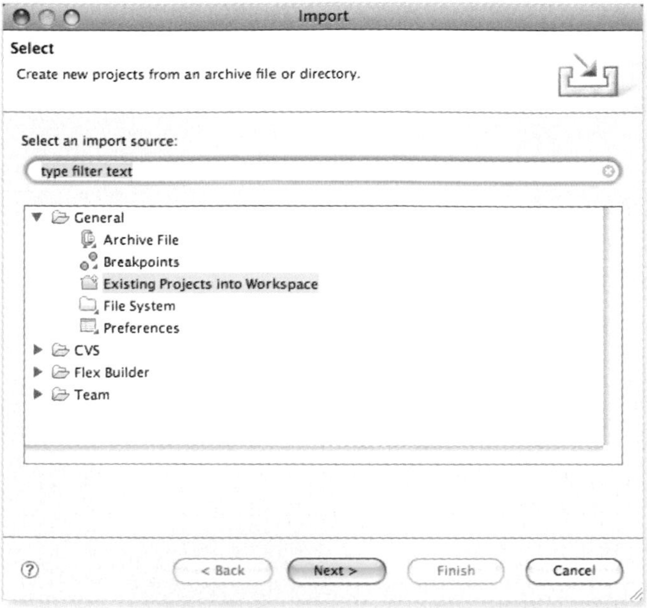

FIGURE 5-28 Import window in Flex Builder

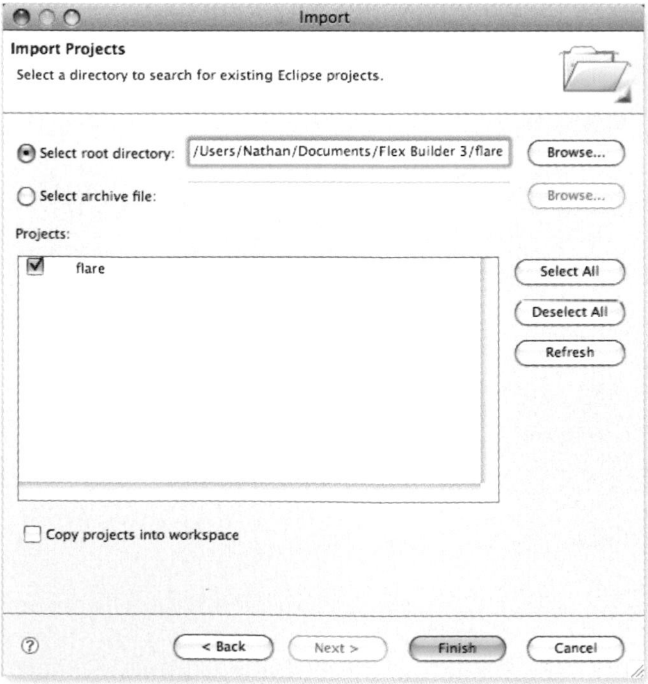

FIGURE 5-29 Existing projects window

Do the same thing with the flare.apps folder. Your Flex Builder window should look like Figure 5-30 after you expand the `flare.apps/flare/apps/` folder and click JobVoyager.as.

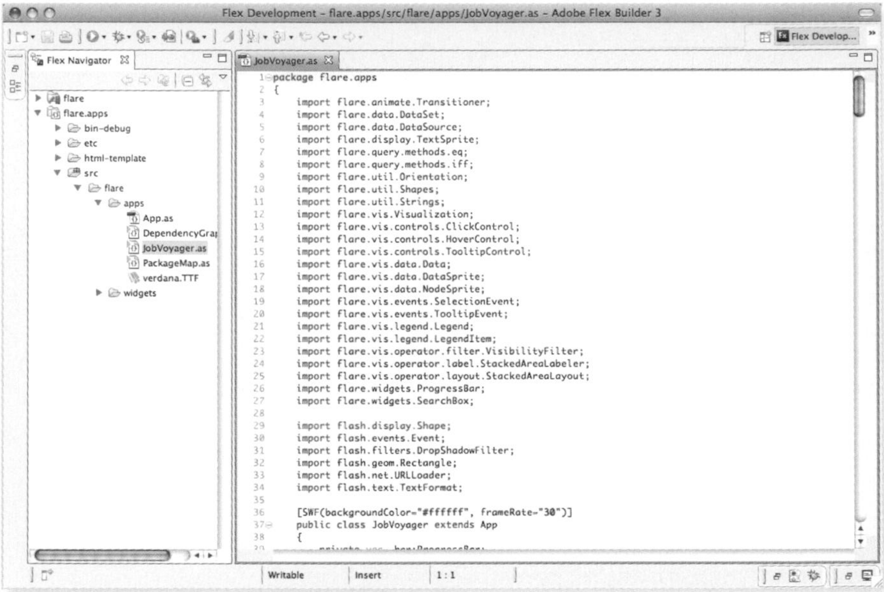

FIGURE 5-30 JobVoyager code opened

If you click the run button right now (the green button with the white play triangle at the top left), you should see the working JobVoyager, as shown in Figure 5-31. Get that working, and you're done with the hardest part: the setup. Now you just need to plug in your own data and customize it to your liking. Sound familiar?

Figure 5-32 shows what you're after. It's a voyager for consumer spending from 1984 to 2008, as reported by the U.S. Census Bureau. The horizontal axis is still years, but instead of jobs, there are spending categories such as housing and food.

Now you need to change the data source, which is specified on line 57 of JobVoyager.as.

```
private var _url:String = "http://flare.prefuse.org/data/jobs.txt";
```

▶ Visit http://datafl.ws/16r to try the final visualization and to see how the explorer works with consumer spending.

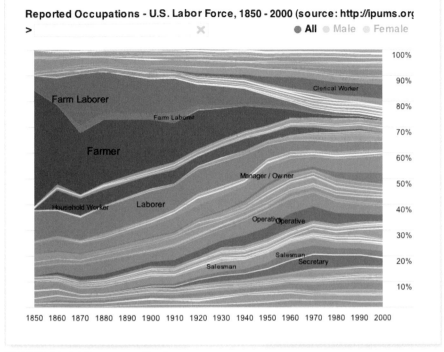

FIGURE 5-31 JobVoyager application

Change the _url to point at the spending data available at http://datasets .flowingdata.com/expenditures.txt. Like jobs.txt, the data is also a tab-delimited file. The first column is year, the second category, and the last column is expenditure.

```
private var _url:String =
    "http://datasets.flowingdata.com/expenditures.txt";
```

Now the file will read in your spending data instead of the data for jobs. Easy stuff so far.

The next two lines, line 58 and 59, are the column names, or in this case, the distinct years that job data was available. It's by decade from 1850 to 2000. You could make things more robust by finding the years in the loaded data, but because the data isn't changing, you can save some time and explicitly specify the years.

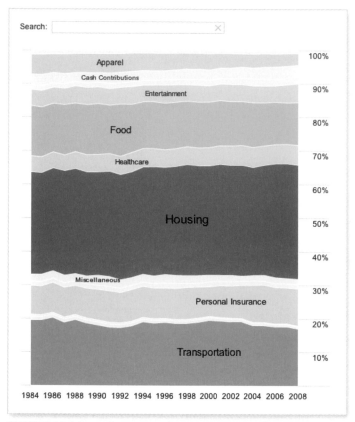

FIGURE 5-32 Interactive voyager for consumer spending

The expenditures data is annual from 1984 to 2008, so Change lines 58–59 accordingly.

```
private var _cols:Array =
    [1984,1985,1986,1987,1988,1989,1990,1991,1992,
    1993,1994,1995,1996,1997,1998,1999,2000,2001,2002,
    2003,2004,2005,2006,2007,2008];
```

Next change references to the data headers. The original data file (jobs.txt) has four columns: year, occupation, people, and sex. The spending data has only three columns: year, category, and expenditure. You need to adapt the code to this new data structure.

Luckily, it's easy. The year column is the same, so you just need to change any people references to expenditure (vertical axis) and any occupation references to category (the layers). Finally, remove all uses of gender.

At line 74 the data is reshaped and prepared for the stacked area chart. It specifies by occupation and sex as the categories (that is, layers) and uses year on the x-axis and people on the y-axis.

```
var dr:Array = reshape(ds.nodes.data, ["occupation","sex"],
    "year", "people", _cols);
```

Change it to this:

```
var dr:Array = reshape(ds.nodes.data, ["category"],
    "year", "expenditure", _cols);
```

You only have one category (sans sex), and that's uh, category. The x-axis is still year, and the y-axis is expenditure.

Line 84 sorts the data by occupation (alphabetically) and then sex (numerically). Now just sort by category:

```
data.nodes.sortBy("data.category");
```

Are you starting to get the idea here? Mostly everything is laid out for you. You just need to adjust the variables to accommodate the data.

Line 92 colors layers by sex, but you don't have that split in the data, so you don't need to do that. Remove the entire row:

```
data.nodes.setProperty("fillHue", iff(eq("data.sex",1), 0.7, 0));
```

We'll come back to customizing the colors of the stacks a little later.

Line 103 adds labels based occupation:

```
_vis.operators.add(new StackedAreaLabeler("data.occupation"));
```

You want to label based on spending category, so change the line accordingly:

```
_vis.operators.add(new StackedAreaLabeler("data.category"));
```

Lines 213–231 handle filtering in JobVoyager. First, there's the male/female filter; then there's the filter by occupation. You don't need the former, so you can get rid of lines 215–218 and then make line 219 a plain if statement.

TIP

There's some great open-source work going on in visualization, and although coding can seem daunting in the beginning, many times you can use existing code with your own data just by changing variables. The challenge is reading the code and figuring out how everything works.

Similarly, lines 264–293 create buttons to trigger the male/female filter. We can get rid of that, too.

You're close to fully customizing the voyager to the spending data. Go back to the `filter()` function at line 213. Again, update the function so that you can filter by the spending category instead of occupation.

Here's line 222 as-is:

```
var s:String = String(d.data["occupation"]).toLowerCase();
```

Change occupation to category:

```
var s:String = String(d.data["category"]).toLowerCase();
```

Next up on the customization checklist is color. If you compiled the code now and ran it, you would get a reddish stacked area graph, as shown in Figure 5-33. You want more contrast though.

Color is specified in two places. First lines 86–89 specify stroke color and color everything red:

```
shape: Shapes.POLYGON,
lineColor: 0,
fillValue: 1,
fillSaturation: 0.5
```

Then line 105 updates saturation (the level of red), by count. The code for the `SaturationEncoder()` is in lines 360–383. We're not going to use saturation; instead, explicitly specify the color scheme.

First, update lines 86–89 to this:

```
shape: Shapes.POLYGON,
lineColor: 0xFFFFFFFF
```

Now make stroke color white with `lineColor`. If there were more spending categories, you probably wouldn't do this because it'd be cluttered. You don't have that many though, so it'll make reading a little easier.

Next, make an array of the colors you want to use ordered by levels. Put it toward the top around line 50:

```
private var _reds:Array = [0xFFFEF0D9, 0xFFFDD49E, 0xFFFDBB84, 0xFFFC8D59,
0xFFE34A33, 0xFFB30000];
```

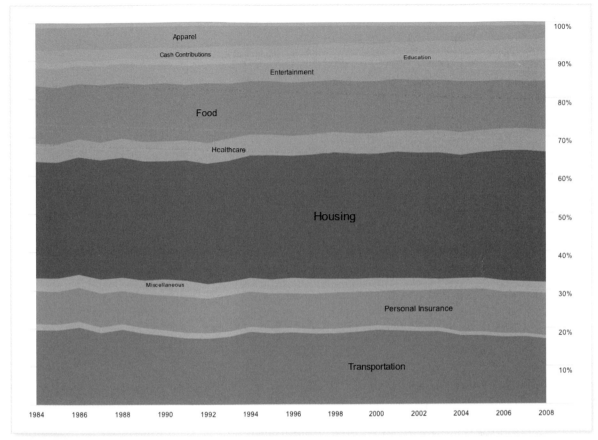

FIGURE 5-33 Stacked area graph with basic coloring

I used the ColorBrewer (referenced earlier) for these colors, which suggests color schemes based on criteria that you set. It's intended to choose colors for maps but works great for general visualization, too.

Now add a new ColorEncoder around line 110:

```
var colorPalette:ColorPalette = new ColorPalette(_reds);
vis.operators.add(new ColorEncoder("data.max", "nodes",
    "fillColor", null, colorPalette));
```

> **NOTE**
>
> If you get an error when you try to compile your code, check the top of JobVoyager.as to see if the following two lines to import the ColorPallete and Encoder objects are specified. Add them if they are not there already.
>
> ```
> import "are.util.palette.*;
> import "are.vis.operator.encoder.*;
> ```

Ta Da! You now have something that looks like what we're after (Figure 5-32). Of course, you don't have to stop here. You can do a lot of things with this. You can apply this to your own data, use a different color scheme, and further customize to fit your needs. Maybe change the font or the tooltip format. Then you can get fancier and integrate it with other tools or add more ActionScript, and so on.

Point-by-Point

One disadvantage of the stacked area graph is that it can be hard to see trends for each group because the placement of each point is affected by the points below it. So sometimes a better way is to plot proportions as a straight up time series like the previous chapter covered.

Luckily, it's easy to switch between the two in Illustrator. The data entry is the same, so you just need to change the graph type. Select the line plot instead of the stacked area in the beginning, and you get this, the default graph in Figure 5-34.

Clean up and format to your liking in the same way you did with the time series examples, and you have the same data from a different point of view (Figure 5-35).

It's easier to see the individual trends in each age group with this time series plot. On the other hand, you do lose the sense of a whole and distributions. The graph you choose should reflect the point you' want to get across or what you want to find in your data. You can even show both views if you have the space.

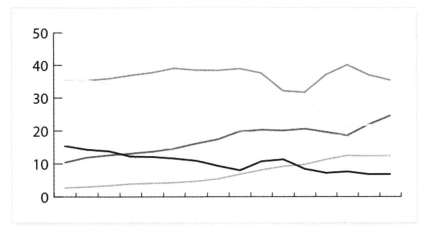

FIGURE 5-34 Default line plot

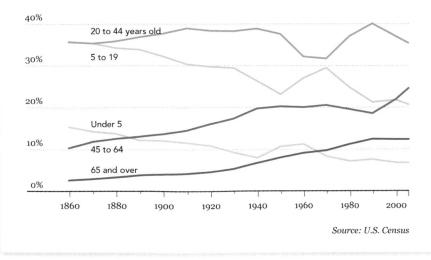

FIGURE 5-35 Labeled line plot cleaned up

Wrapping Up

The main thing that sets proportions apart from other data types is that they represent parts of a whole. Each individual value means something, but so do the sum of all the parts or just a subset of the parts. The visualization you design should represent these ideas.

Only have a few values? The pie chart might be your best bet. Use donut charts with care. If you have several values and several categories, consider the stacked bar chart instead of multiple pie charts. If you're looking for patterns over time, look to your friend the stacked area chart or go for the classic time series. With these steady foundations, your proportions will be good to go.

When it comes time to design and implement, ask yourself what you want to know about your data, and then go from there. Does a static graphic tell your story completely? A lot of the time the answer will be yes, and that's fine. If, however, you decide you need to go with an interactive graphic, map out on paper what should happen when you click objects and what shouldn't. It gets complicated quickly if you add too much functionality, so do your best to keep it simple. Have other people try interacting with your designs to see if they understand what's going on.

Finally, while you're programming—especially if you're new to code—you're undoubtedly going to reach a point where you're not sure what to do next. This happens to me all the time. When you get stuck, there's no better place than the web to find your solution. Look at documentation if it's available or study examples that are similar to what you're trying to do. Don't just look at the syntax. Learn the logic because that's what's going to help you the most. Luckily there are libraries such as Protovis and Flare that have many examples and great documentation.

In the next chapter, we move towards deeper analysis and data interpretation and come back to your good statistical friend. You put R to good use as you study relationships between data sets and variables. Ready? Let's go.

Visualizing Relationships

6

Statistics is about finding relationships in data. What are the similarities between groups? Within groups? Within subgroups? The relationship that most people are familiar with for statistics is correlation. For example, as average height goes up in a population, most likely average weight will go up, too. This is a simple positive correlation. The relationships in your data, just like in real life, can get more complicated though as you consider more factors or find patterns that aren't so linear. This chapter discusses how to use visualization to find such relationships and highlight them for storytelling.

As you get into more complex statistical graphics, you can make heavy use of R in this chapter and the next. This is where the open-source software shines. Like in previous chapters, R does the grunt work, and then you can use Illustrator to make the graphic more readable for an audience.

What Relationships to Look For

So far you looked at basic relationships with patterns in time and proportions. You learned about temporal trends, and compared proportions and percentages to see what's the least and greatest and everything in between. The next step is to look for relationships between different variables. As something goes up, does another thing go down, and is it a causal or correlative relationship? The former is usually quite hard to prove quantitatively, which makes it even less likely you can prove it with a graphic. You can, however, easily show correlation, which can lead to a deeper more exploratory analysis.

You can also take a step back to look at the big picture, or the distribution of your data. Is it actually spaced out or is it clustered in between? Such comparisons can lead to stories about citizens of a country or how you compare to those around you. You can see how different countries compare to one another or general developmental can progress around the world, which can aid in decisions about where to provide aid.

You can also compare multiple distributions for an even wider view of your data. How has the makeup of a population changed over time? How has it stayed the same?

Most important, in the end, when you have all your graphics in front of you, ask what the results mean. Are they what you expected? Does anything surprise you?

This might seem abstract and hand-wavy, so now jump right into some concrete examples on how to look at relationships in your data.

Correlation

Correlation is probably the first thing you think of when you hear about relationships in data. The second thing is probably causation. Now maybe you're thinking about the mantra that correlation doesn't equal causation. The first, correlation, means one thing tends to change a certain way as another thing changes. For example, the price of milk per gallon and the price of gasoline per gallon are positively correlated. Both have been increasing over the years.

Now here's the difference between correlation and causation. If you increase the price of gas, will the price of milk go up by default? More important, if the price of milk did go up, was it because of the increase in the gas price or was it an outside factor, such as a dairy strike?

It's difficult to account for every outside, or confounding factor, which makes it difficult to prove causation. Researchers spend years figuring stuff like that out. You can, however, easily find and see correlation, which can still be useful, as you see in the following sections.

Correlation can help you predict one metric by knowing another. To see this relationship, return to scatterplot and multiple scatterplots.

More with Points

In Chapter 4, "Visualizing Patterns over Time," you used a scatterplot to graph measurements over time, where time was on the horizontal axis and a metric of interest was on the vertical axis. This helped spot temporal changes (or nonchanges). The relationship was between time and another factor, or a variable. As shown in Figure 6-1, however, you can use the scatterplot for variables other than time; you can use a scatterplot to look for relationships between two variables.

If two metrics are positively correlated (Figure 6-2, left), dots move higher up as you read the graph from left to right. Conversely, if a negative correlation exists, the dots appear lower, moving from left to right, as shown in the middle of Figure 6-2.

Sometimes the relationship is straightforward, such as the correlation between peoples' height and weight. Usually, as height increases, weight increases. Other times the correlation is not as obvious, such as that between health and body mass index (BMI). A high BMI typically indicates that someone is overweight; however, muscular people for example, who can be athletically fit, could have a high BMI. What if the sample population were body builders or football players? What would relationships between health and BMI look like?

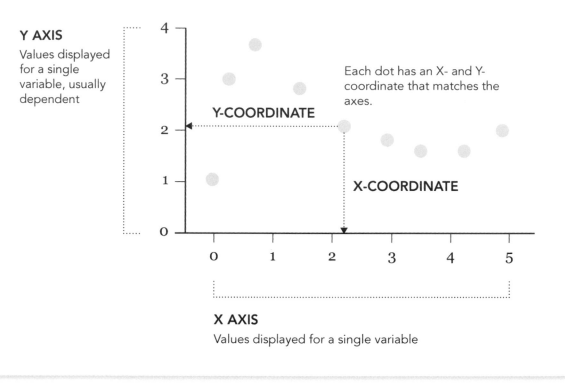

Y AXIS

Values displayed for a single variable, usually dependent

Y-COORDINATE

Each dot has an X- and Y-coordinate that matches the axes.

X-COORDINATE

X AXIS

Values displayed for a single variable

FIGURE 6-1 Scatterplot framework, comparing two variables

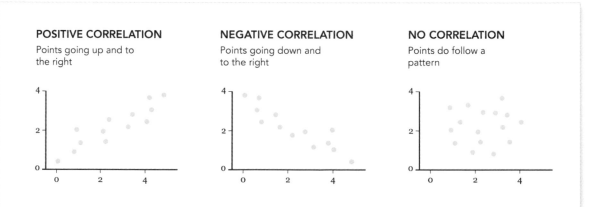

POSITIVE CORRELATION

Points going up and to the right

NEGATIVE CORRELATION

Points going down and to the right

NO CORRELATION

Points do follow a pattern

FIGURE 6-2 Correlations shown in scatterplots

Remember the graph is only part of the story. It's still up to you to inter-pret the results. This is particularly important with relationships. You might be tempted to assume a cause-and-effect relationship, but most of the time that's not the case at all. Just because the price of a gallon of gas and world population have both increased over the years doesn't mean the price of gas should be decreased to slow population growth.

CREATE A SCATTERPLOT

In this example, look at United States crime rates at the state level, in 2005, with rates per 100,000 population for crime types such as murder, robbery, and aggravated assault, as reported by the Census Bureau. There are seven crime types in total. Look at two of them to start: burglary and murder. How do these relate? Do states with relatively high murder rates also have high burglary rates? You can turn to R to investigate.

As always, the first thing you do is load the data into R using read.csv(). You can download the CSV file at http://datasets.flowingdata.com/crimeRatesByState2005.csv, but now load it directly into R via the URL.

```
# Load the data
crime <-
    read.csv('http://datasets.flowingdata.com/crimeRatesByState2005.csv',
    sep=",", header=TRUE)
```

Check out the first few lines of the data by typing the variable, **crime**, fol-lowed by the rows you want to see.

```
crime[1:3,]
```

Following is what the first three rows look like.

	state	murder	forcible_rape	robbery	aggravated_assault	burglary
1	United States	5.6	31.7	140.7	291.1	726.7
2	Alabama	8.2	34.3	141.4	247.8	953.8
3	Alaska	4.8	81.1	80.9	465.1	622.5

	larceny_theft	motor_vehicle_theft	population
1	2286.3	416.7	295753151
2	2650.0	288.3	4545049
3	2599.1	391.0	669488

The first column shows the state name, and the rest are rates for the dif-ferent types of crime. For example, the average robbery rate for the United

States in 2005 was 140.7 per 100,000 population. Use plot() to create the default scatterplot of murder against burglary, as shown in Figure 6-3.

```
plot(crime$murder, crime$burglary)
```

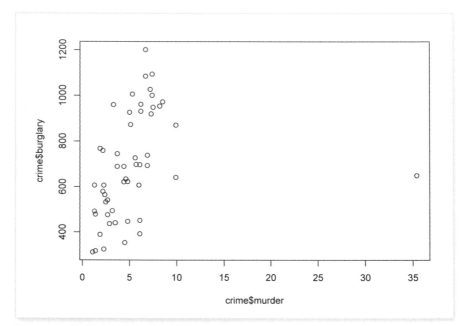

FIGURE 6-3 Default scatterplot of murder against burglary

It looks like there's a positive correlation in there. States that have higher murder rates tend to have higher burglary rates, but it's not so easy to see because of that one dot on the far right. That one dot—that outlier—is forcing the horizontal axis to be much wider. That dot happens to represent Washington, DC, which has a much higher murder rate of 35.4. The states with the next highest murder rates are Louisiana and Maryland, which were 9.9.

For the sake of a graphic that is more clear and useful, take out Washington, DC, and while you're at it, remove the United States averages and place full focus on individual states.

```
crime2 <- crime[crime$state != "District of Columbia",]
crime2 <- crime2[crime2$state != "United States",]
```

The first line stores all rows that aren't for the District of Columbia in *crime2*. Similarly, the second line filters out the United States averages.

Now when you plot murder against burglary, you get a clearer picture, as shown in Figure 6-4.

```
plot(crime2$murder, crime2$burglary)
```

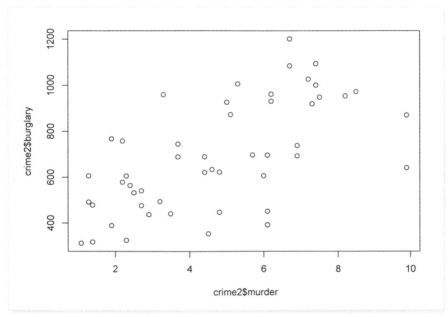

FIGURE 6-4 Scatterplot after filtering data

Although, it could probably be better if the axes started at zero, so do that, too. The x-axis should go from 0 to 10, and the y-axis will go from 0 to 1,200. This shifts the dots up and to the right, as shown in Figure 6-5.

```
plot(crime2$murder, crime2$burglary, xlim=c(0,10), ylim=c(0, 1200))
```

You know what would make this plot even more useful? A LOESS curve like you saw in Chapter 4. This would help you see the relationship between burglary and murder rates. Use scatter.smooth() to make the line with the dots. The result is shown in Figure 6-6.

```
scatter.smooth(crime2$murder, crime2$burglary,
    xlim=c(0,10), ylim=c(0, 1200))
```

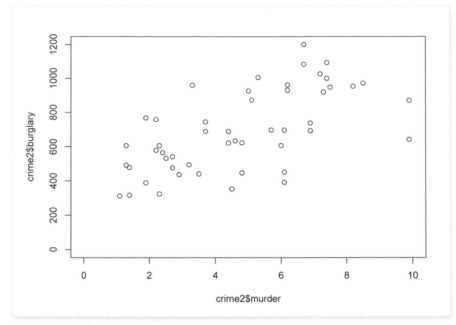

FIGURE 6-5 Scatterplot with axes starting at zero

NOTE

For the sake of simplicity, Washington, DC was removed from the dataset to see the rest of the data better. It is important, however, to consider the importance of the outliers in your data. This is discussed more in Chapter 7, "Spotting Differences."

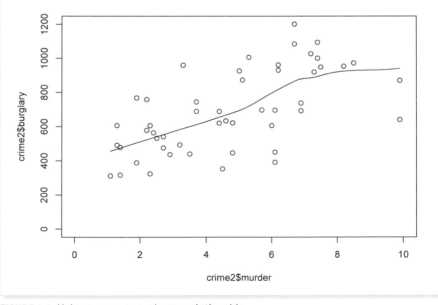

FIGURE 6-6 Using a curve to estimate relationship

It's not bad for a base chart, and if the graphic were just for analysis, you could stop here. However, if you have more than an audience of one, you can improve the readability a lot with a few small changes, as shown in Figure 6-7.

I put less emphasis on the surrounding box by getting rid of the thick border, and direct your attention to the curve by making it thicker and darker than the dots.

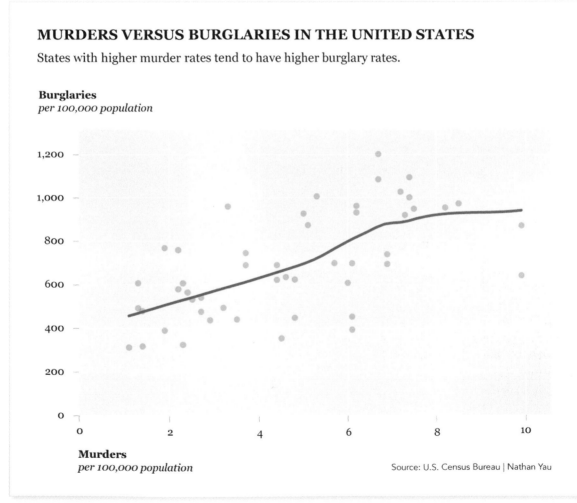

MURDERS VERSUS BURGLARIES IN THE UNITED STATES

States with higher murder rates tend to have higher burglary rates.

Burglaries
per 100,000 population

Murders
per 100,000 population

Source: U.S. Census Bureau | Nathan Yau

FIGURE 6-7 Revised scatterplot on murder versus burglary

Exploring More Variables

Now that you've plotted two variables against each other, the obvious next step is to compare other variables. You could pick and choose the variables you want to compare and make a scatterplot for each pair, but that could easily lead to missed opportunities and ignoring interesting spots in the data. You don't want that. So instead, you can plot every possible pair with a scatterplot matrix, as shown in Figure 6-8.

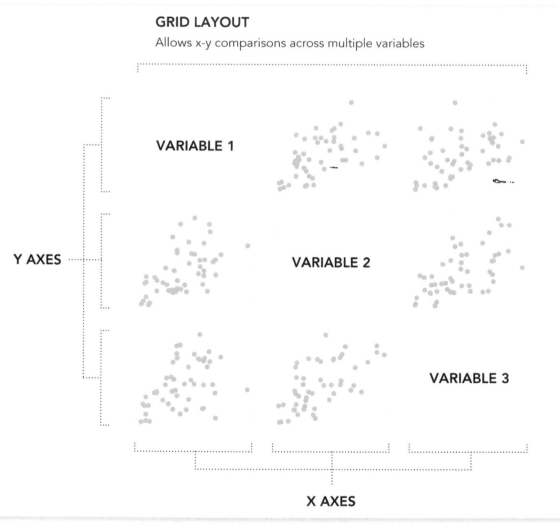

FIGURE 6-8 Scatterplot matrix framework

This method is especially useful during your data exploration phases. You might have a dataset in front of you but have no clue where to start or what it's about. If you don't know what the data is about, your readers won't either.

The scatterplot matrix reads how you expect. It's usually a square grid with all variables on both the vertical and horizontal. Each column represents a variable on the horizontal axis, and each row represents a variable on the vertical axis. This provides all possible pairs, and the diagonal is left for labels because there's no sense in comparing a variable to itself.

CREATE A SCATTERPLOT MATRIX

Now come back to your crime data. You have seven variables, or rates for crime types, but in the previous example, you compared only two: murder and burglary. With a scatterplot matrix, you can compare all the crime types. Figure 6-9 shows what you're making.

As you might expect, a lot of positive correlations can exist. The correlation between burglary and aggravated assault, for example, seems to be relatively high. As the former goes up, the latter also tends to increase, and vice versa; however, the relationship between murder and larceny theft is not so clear. You shouldn't make any assumptions, but it should be easy to see how the scatterplot matrix can be useful. At first glance, it can look confusing with all the lines and plots, but read from left to right and top to bottom, and you can take away a lot of information.

Luckily, R makes creating a scatterplot matrix as easy as it is to make a single scatterplot, albeit creation of the matrix is not as robust. Again, use the plot() function, but instead of passing two columns, pass the whole data frame, minus the first column because that's just state names.

```
plot(crime2[,2:9])
```

This gives you a matrix as shown in Figure 6-10, which is almost what you want. It's still missing fitted curves though that can help you see relationships a bit better.

> **TIP**
>
> To tell a complete story, you have to understand your data. The more you know about your data, the better the story you can tell.

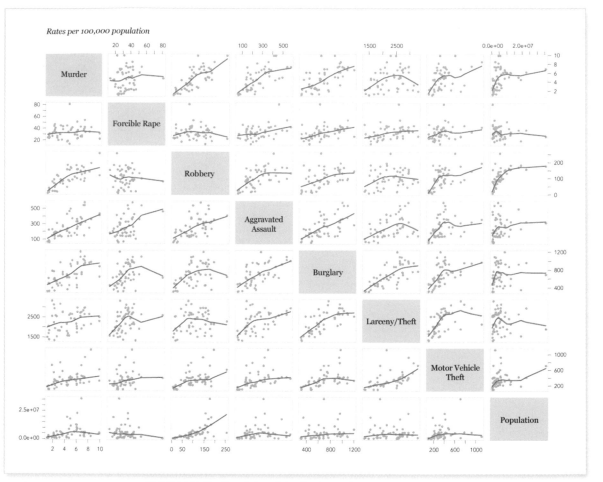

Rates per 100,000 population

FIGURE 6-9 Scatterplot matrix of crime rates

To create a scatterplot matrix with fitted LOESS curves, you can use the pairs() function instead, but it's equally as simple to call. The result is shown in Figure 6-11.

```
pairs(crime2[,2:9], panel=panel.smooth)
```

TIP The panel argument in pairs() takes a function of x and y. In this example, you use panel.smooth(), which is a native function in R and results in a LOESS curve. You can also specify your own function.

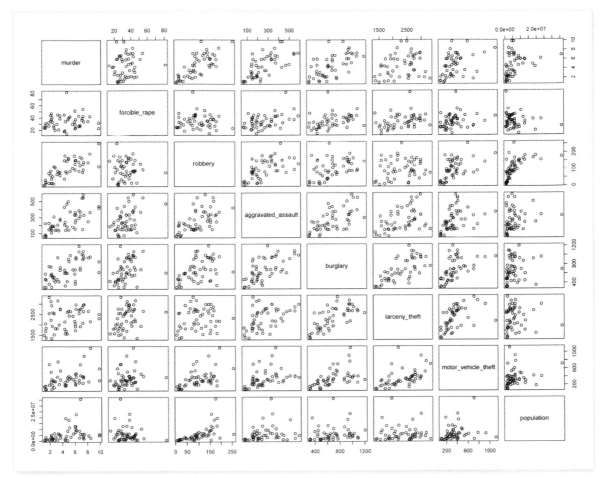

FIGURE 6-10 Default scatterplot matrix in R

Now you have a nice framework to work off of, and you can edit it further to make it more readable (refer to Figure 6-9). Save the graphic as a PDF and open the file in Illustrator.

Mainly, you need to get rid of clutter and make it easier to see what's important. That's the crime types and trend lines first, the points second, and the axes last, and you should see that order in the choice of color and sizes. The size of the labels across the diagonal increase, and the boxes are grayed out. Then make the trend lines thicker and provide more contrast between the lines and the dots. Finally, the borders and grid lines are made more subtle with a thinner stroke width and lighter gray. Compare Figure 6-9 to Figure 6-11. There's a lot less visual vibration in Figure 6-9, right?

TIP

Decide what part of the story you want to tell and design your graphic to emphasize those areas, but also take care not to obscure facts.

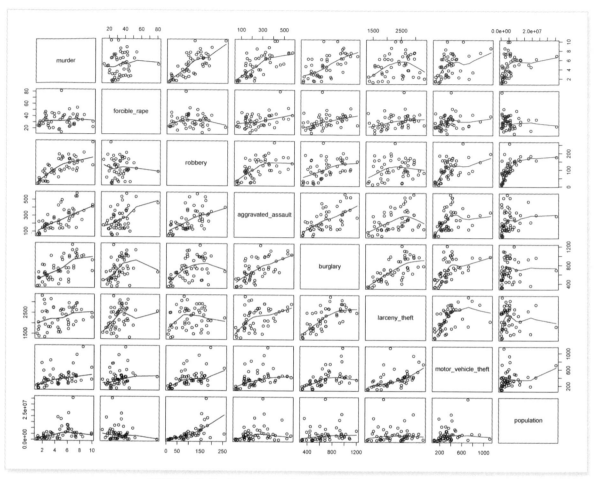

FIGURE 6-11 Scatterplot matrix with LOESS curves

Bubbles

▶ Check out Hans Rosling's now famous talks on the Gapminder site at `www.gapminder.org`, including a BBC documentary on the joy of statistics.

Ever since Hans Rosling, Professor of International Health at Karolinska Institute and chairman of the Gapminder Foundation, presented a motion chart to tell his story of the wealth and health of nations, there has been an affinity for proportional bubbles on an x-y axis. Although the motion chart is animated to show changes over time, you can also create a static version: the bubble chart.

A bubble chart can also just be straight up proportionally sized bubbles, but now consider how to create the variety that is like a scatterplot with a third, bubbly dimension.

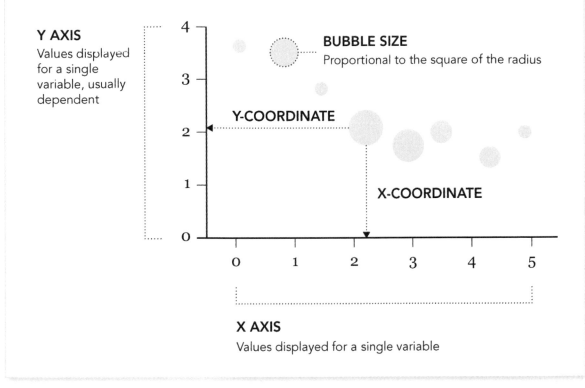

FIGURE 6-12 Bubble chart framework

The advantage of this chart type is that it enables you to compare three variables at one time, as shown in Figure 6-12. One variable is on the x-axis, one is on the y-axis, and the third is represented by the area size of the bubbles.

Take note of that last part because people often size the bubbles incorrectly. As discussed in Chapter 1, "Telling Stories with Data," bubbles should be sized by area. They should not be sized by radius, diameter, or circumference, which can easily happen. If you go with software defaults, you might end up with circles that are too big and too small.

Now look at a quick example to emphasize this point. Imagine you run ad sales for your company, and you're testing two banner ads on a site. You want to know which ad converts better. Over the course of a month, both ads run the same number of times; however, the number of clicks is different. The first banner was clicked 150 times, whereas the second banner

TIP

When using circles to represent data, size by the area rather than the diameter, radius, or circumference.

was clicked 100 times. So the first banner performed 50 percent better than the second. Figure 6-13 shows a circle, sized by area, for each banner. The circle for the first banner is 50 percent bigger than the second.

FIGURE 6-13 Bubbles sized by area

In Figure 6-14, you see how the bubbles compare to each other if they are sized by radius.

FIGURE 6-14 Bubbles sized by radius

The radius for the first circle, representing the first banner, is 50 percent larger than the radius for the second banner, which makes the area of the first circle more than twice that of the second. Although this doesn't seem like a huge deal with only two data points, which are easy to compare, the challenge becomes more obvious when you use more data.

CREATE A BUBBLE CHART

Look at the final chart in Figure 6-15 to see what you're making. It's the same crime data relating murder and burglary rate by state, but population is added as a third dimension. Do states with more people have higher crime rates? It's not clear-cut (as is usually the case). Large states such as California, Florida, and Texas are near the top-right quadrant, but New York and Pennsylvania have relatively low burglary rates. Similarly, Louisiana and Maryland, which have smaller populations, are far on the right.

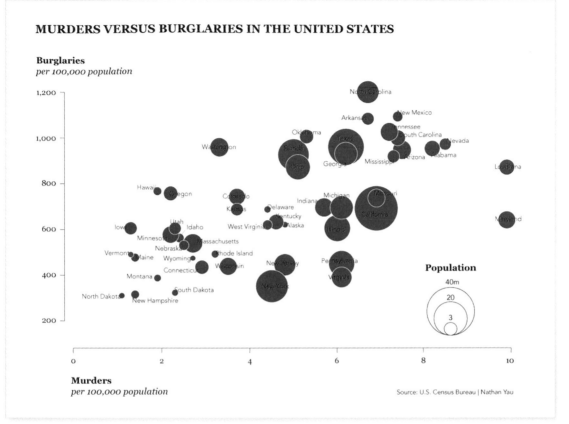

MURDERS VERSUS BURGLARIES IN THE UNITED STATES

FIGURE 6-15 Bubble plot showing crime in the United States

To start, load the data in R with read.csv(). This is the same data that you just used, except a column for population was added, and Washington, DC is not included. It's also tab-delimited instead of comma-delimited. No biggie. Simply change the *sep* argument in the function.

```
crime <-
    read.csv("http://datasets.flowingdata.com/crimeRatesByState2005.tsv",
    header=TRUE, sep="\t")
```

Then jump right into drawing some bubbles with the symbols() function. The x-axis is murder rate, the y-axis is burglary rate, and radius of bubbles is sized proportionally to population. Figure 6-16 shows the result. Want to do try more with symbols()? You'll get to that soon.

```
symbols(crime$murder, crime$burglary, circles=crime$population)
```

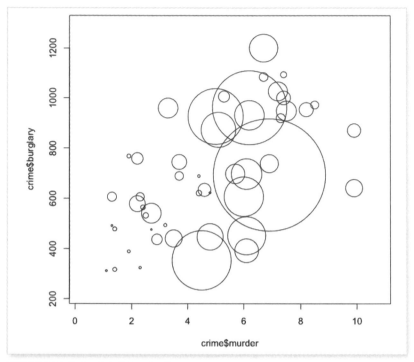

FIGURE 6-16 Default bubble chart

All done, right? Wrong. That was a test. The preceding sizes the circles such that population is proportional to the radius. You need to size the circles proportional to the area. The relative proportions are all out of whack if you size by radius. Is California's population, represented by that giant circle in the middle, that much higher than that of all of the other states?

To size radiuses correctly, look to the equation for the area of a circle.

Area of circle = πr^2

The area of each bubble represents population. What you need to find out is how to size the radius, so isolate the radius to find that it should be proportional to the square root of the area.

$r = \sqrt{(\text{Area of circle} / \pi)}$

You can actually get rid of the π altogether because it's a constant, but leave it in there for the sake of clarity. Now instead of using *crime$population* to size the circle radiuses, find the square root and then plug it into symbols().

```
radius <- sqrt( crime$population/ pi )
symbols(crime$murder, crime$burglary, circles=radius)
```

The first row of code simply creates a new vector of square root values stored in *radius*. Figure 6-17 shows the bubble plot with radiuses sized correctly, but it's a mess because the states with populations smaller than California are a little bigger now.

You need to scale down all circles to see what's going on. The *inches* argument of symbols() sets the size of the largest circle in, well, inches. By default it's 1 inch, so in Figure 6-17 California is sized at 1 inch, and the rest of the circles are scaled accordingly. You can make the maximum smaller, say 0.35 inches, while still maintaining the right proportions. You also can change color using *fg* and *bg* to change stroke color and fill color, respectively. You can also add your own labels to the axes. Figure 6-18 shows the output.

```
symbols(crime$murder, crime$burglary, circles=radius, inches=0.35,
    fg="white", bg="red", xlab="Murder Rate", ylab="Burglary Rate")
```

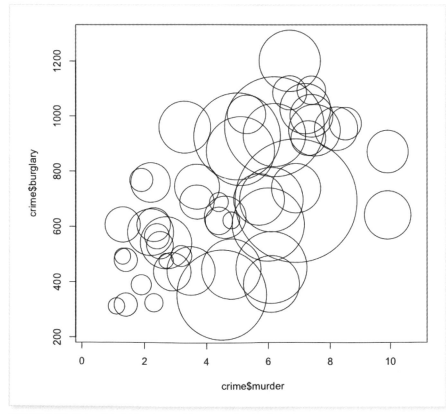

FIGURE 6-17 Default bubble chart with correctly sized circles

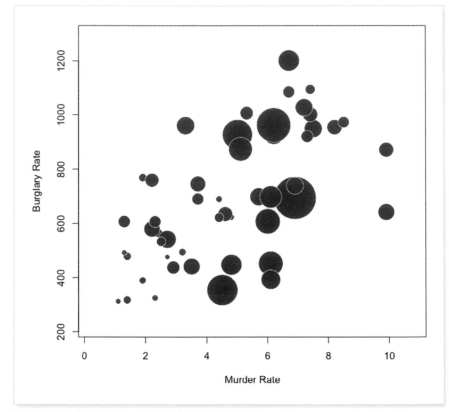

FIGURE 6-18 Bubble chart with bubbles scaled down

Now you're getting somewhere.

You also can make a chart with other shapes, too, with symbols()—you can make squares, rectangles, thermometers, boxplots, and stars. They take different arguments than the circle. The squares, for example, use side length to size; however, like with bubbles, you want the squares to be sized by area. In other words, you need to size the square sides by the square root of the area.

Figure 6-19 shows what squares look like using the following line of code:

```
symbols(crime$murder, crime$burglary,
    squares=sqrt(crime$population), inches=0.5)
```

Stick with circles for now. The chart in Figure 6-18 shows some sense of distribution, but you don't know which circle represents each state. So now add labels. with text(), whose arguments are x-coordinates, y-coordinates, and the actual text to print—you have all of these. Like the bubbles, the *x* is murders and the *y* is burglaries. The actual labels are state names, which is the first column in your data frame.

```
text(crime$murder, crime$burglary, crime$state, cex=0.5)
```

The *cex* argument controls text size, which is 1 by default. Values greater than one can make the labels bigger and the opposite for less than one. The labels can center on the x- and y-coordinates, as shown in Figure 6-20.

At this point, you don't need to make a ton of changes to get your graphic to look like the final one in Figure 6-15. Save the chart you made in R as a PDF, and open it in your favorite illustration software to refine the graphic to what you want it to look and read like. You can thin the axis lines and remove the surrounding box to simplify a bit. You can also move around some of the labels, particularly in the bottom left, so that you can actually read the state names; then bring the bubble for Georgia to the front— before it was hidden by the larger Texas bubble.

There you go. Type in ?symbols in R for more plotting options. Go wild.

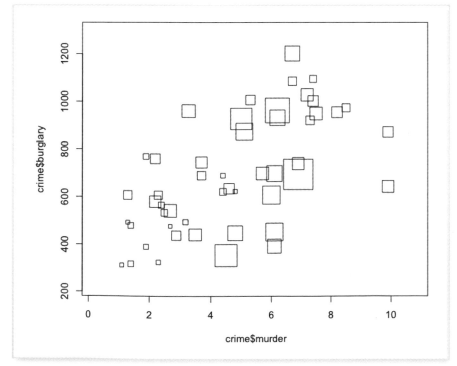

FIGURE 6-19 Using squares instead of circles

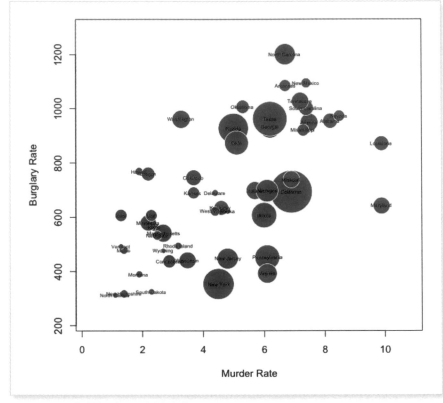

FIGURE 6-20 Bubble chart with labels

Distribution

You've probably heard of mean, median, and mode. Schools teach you this stuff in high school; although they should teach it much sooner. The mean is the sum of all data points divided by the number of points. To find the median, you order your data from least to greatest and mark the halfway point. The mode is the number that occurs the most. These are well and good and super easy to find, but they don't give you the whole story. They describe how parts of your data are distributed. If you visualize everything though, you can see the full distribution.

A skew to the left means most of your data is clustered in the lower side of the full range. A skew to the right means the opposite. A flat line means a uniform distribution, whereas the classic bell curve shows a clustering at the mean and a gradual decrease in both directions.

Next take a look at a classic plot, mainly to get a feel for distribution, and then move on to the more practical histogram and density plot.

Old School Distribution

In the 1970s, when computers weren't so popular, most data graphics were drawn by hand. Some of the tips offered by famed statistician John Tukey, in his book *Exploratory Data Analysis*, were centered around using pen and pencil to vary darkness of lines and shades. You could also use hash patterns as a fill to differentiate between variables.

The stem-and-leaf plot, or stemplot, was designed in a similar manner. All you have to do is write the numbers using an ordered method, and the end result is a rough view of the distribution. The method was particularly popular in the 1980s (when using statistical graphics for analysis was gaining momentum), because it was easy to include the graphic—even if you were writing with a typewriter.

Although there are easier and faster ways to look at distributions today, it's useful to take a look because you can still apply the same principles making a stem-and-leaf plot as you would a histogram.

CREATE A STEM-AND-LEAF

If you want to live on the wild side, you can draw a stem-and-leaf plot with pen and paper, but you can make one much quicker in R. Figure 6-21 shows a stem-and-leaf plot for worldwide birth rates in 2008, as estimated by the World Bank.

As you can see, it's basic. Base numbers are on the left and trailing numbers are on the right. In this case, the decimal point is at the bar (|), so the interval with the most countries in it is the one that ranges from 10 to 12 live births per 1,000 population. There's also one country, Niger, with a birth rate between 52 and 54.

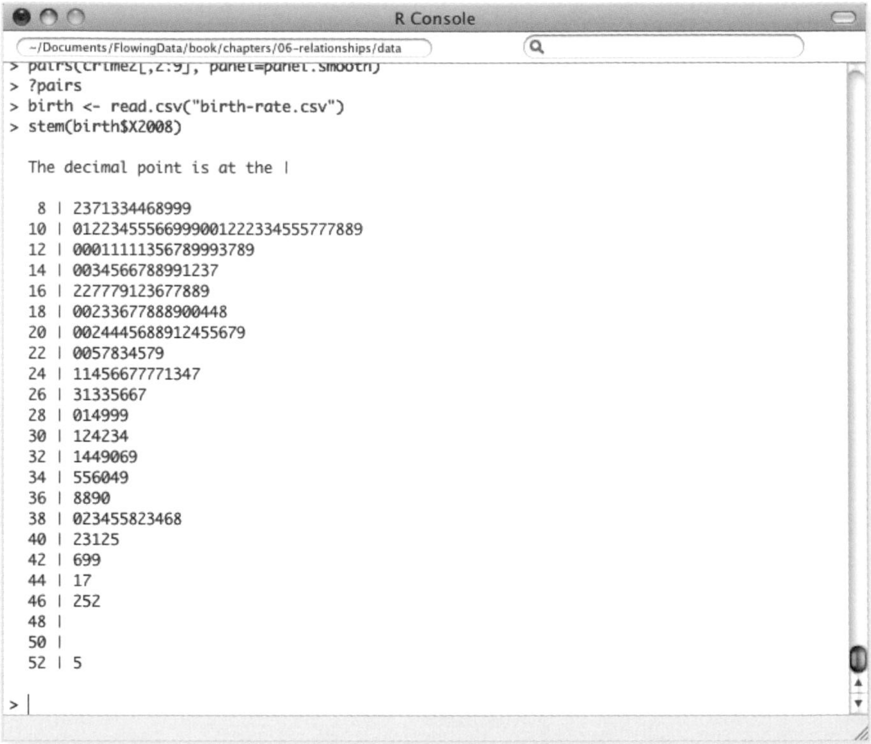

FIGURE 6-21 Stem-and-leaf plot showing worldwide birth rates

Here's how you would draw this by hand. Write numbers 8 to 52 in intervals of 2, top to bottom. Draw a line to the right of the column of numbers. Then go down each row of your data and add numbers accordingly. If a country has a birth rate of 8.2, you add a 2 to the right of the 8. If there is a country with a rate of 9.9, it also goes in the row with an 8. You write a 9.

This can obviously get tedious if you have a lot of data, so here's how to make a stemplot in R. After you load your data, simply use the stem() function.

```
birth <- read.csv("http://datasets.flowingdata.com/birth-rate.csv")
stem(birth$X2008)
```

That's all there is to it. If you want to style it, as shown in Figure 6-22, you can copy the text in R, and paste it elsewhere—but this method is outdated and probably better off with a histogram. The histogram is basically the more graphical version of the stem-and-leaf.

8	2371334468999
10	012234555669990012223345555777889
12	00011111356789993789
14	0034566788991237
16	227779123677889
18	00233677888900448
20	0024445688912455679
22	0057834579
24	11456677771347
26	31335667
28	014999
30	124234
32	1449069
34	556049
36	8890
38	023455823468
40	23125
42	699
44	17
46	252
48	
50	
52	5

FIGURE 6-22 Revised stem-and-leaf plot

Distribution Bars

Looking at the steam-and-leaf plot in Figure 6-22, you can spot frequency in specific ranges. The more countries with a birth rate in a range, the more numbers that are drawn, and the longer the row will be. Now flip the plot on its side so that the rows become columns. The higher the column, the more countries there are in that range. Now change the column of numbers into a simple bar or rectangle. Now you have a histogram, as shown in Figure 6-23.

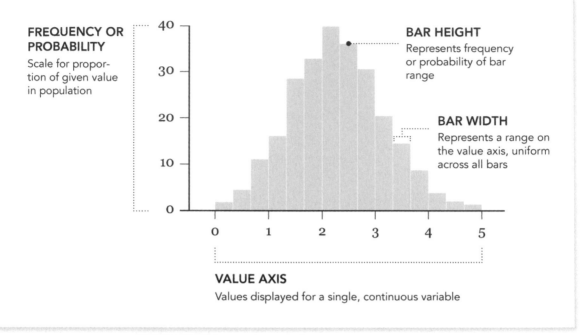

FREQUENCY OR PROBABILITY

Scale for propor-
tion of given value
in population

BAR HEIGHT
Represents frequency
or probability of bar
range

BAR WIDTH
Represents a range on
the value axis, uniform
across all bars

VALUE AXIS
Values displayed for a single, continuous variable

FIGURE 6-23 Histogram framework

Bar height represents frequency, and bar width does not represent anything. The horizontal and vertical axes are continuous. In contrast, the
horizontal axis of a bar chart is discrete. You have set categories and usually space in between each bar when you use a bar chart.

Often, people who don't read data graphics on a regular basis mistake the
horizontal axis to be time. It can be time, but there's no restriction. This is
especially important when you consider your audience. If your graphic is
for a more general readership, you need to explain how to read the graph
and what important points to note. Also keep in mind that a lot of people
aren't familiar with the concept of distributions. But design your graphic
clearly, and you can teach them.

CREATE A HISTOGRAM

Like the stem-and-leaf, the histogram is just as easy to create in R. Using
the hist() function, again plot the distribution of birth rates worldwide, as
shown in Figure 6-24. Notice how the shape is similar to the stem-and-leaf
in Figure 6-22?

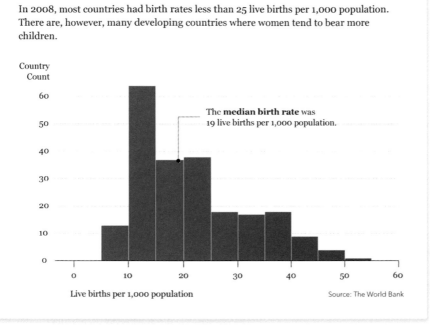

GLOBAL DISTRIBUTION OF BIRTH RATES

In 2008, most countries had birth rates less than 25 live births per 1,000 population. There are, however, many developing countries where women tend to bear more children.

Country Count

The **median birth rate** was 19 live births per 1,000 population.

Live births per 1,000 population

Source: The World Bank

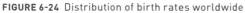

FIGURE 6-24 Distribution of birth rates worldwide

Assuming you've already loaded the data from your previous example, run the hist() function with the same numbers from 2008.

```
hist(birth$X2008)
```

This is the default histogram shown in Figure 6-25.

There are ten bars or ranges in the default histogram, but you can change that to what you like with the *breaks* argument. For example, you could have fewer, wider bars, as shown in Figure 6-26. It has only five breaks.

```
hist(birth$X2008, breaks=5)
```

You can also go the other way and make a histogram with more skinny bars, say 20 of them (Figure 6-27).

```
hist(birth$X2008, breaks=20)
```

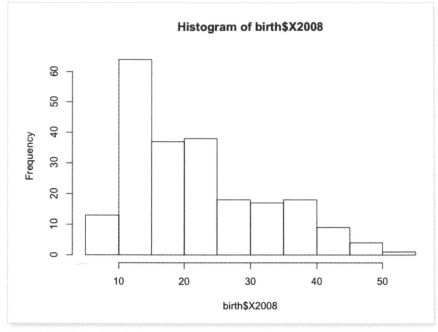

FIGURE 6-25 Default histogram

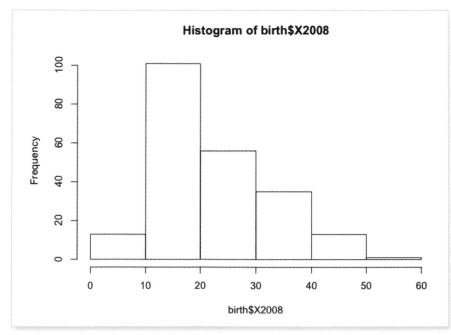

FIGURE 6-26 Histogram with five breaks

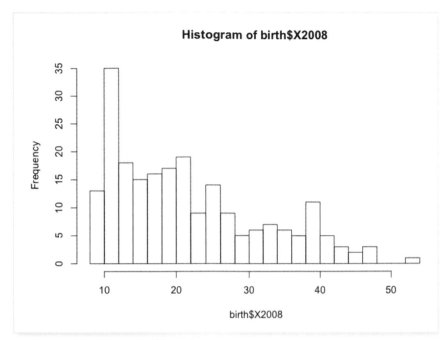

FIGURE 6-27 Histogram with 20 breaks

The number of breaks you should choose depends on the data that you visualize. If most of your data is clustered toward the beginning, you might want to have more breaks so that you can see the variations instead of one high bar. On the other hand, if you don't have that much data or the numbers are evenly distributed, thicker bars could be more appropriate. The good news is that it's easy to change and experiment.

For the purposes of the birth rate data, the default number of breaks is fine. You can see that there are some countries with birth rates under 10, but most countries have birth rates between 10 and 25 live births per 1,000 population. A number of countries are also above the 25 mark, but relatively fewer compared to the lower groups.

At this point, you can save the output as a PDF and make further edits in Illustrator. Most of the edits will be similar to what you did with the bar charts in Chapter 4, but a few things are specific to the histogram that you can add to make it read better and to explain to readers what the graphic is about.

TIP

The default number of breaks for your histogram isn't always the best choice. Play around with the options and decide what makes the most sense for your particular dataset.

TIP

You can find mean, median, maximum, and quartiles easily with the summary() function in R.

In the final graphic in Figure 6-24, you can see some of the important facets of the distribution, namely the median, maximum, and minimum. The lead-in copy, of course, is another opportunity to explain, and you can add a little bit of color so that the histogram doesn't look like a wireframe.

Continuous Density

Although the value axis is continuous, the distribution is still broken up into a discrete number of bars. Each bar represents a collection of items, or in the case of the previous examples, countries. What sort of variation is occurring within each bin? With the stem-and-leaf plot, you could see every number, but it's still hard to gauge the magnitude of differences, which is similar to how you used Cleveland and Devlin's LOESS in Chapter 4 to see trends better; you can use a density plot to visualize the smaller variations within a distribution.

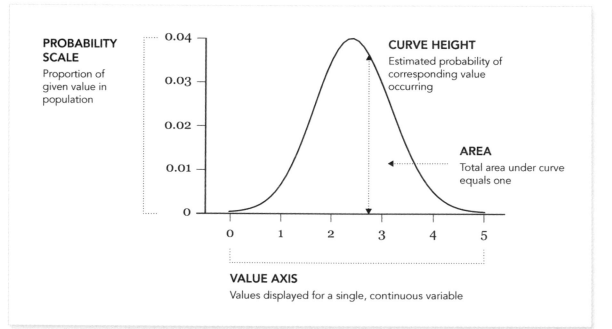

FIGURE 6-28 Density plot framework

Figure 6-28 shows the use of a curve instead of bars. The total area under the curve is equal to one, and the vertical axis represents the probability or a proportion of a value in the sample population.

CREATE A DENSITY PLOT

Returning to the birth rates data, you need to take one extra step to make a density plot. It's a small step. You need to use the density() function to estimate the points for the curve; however, the data can't have any missing values. Actually 15 rows are in the 2008 data without any values.

In R these spots with missing values are labeled as *NA*. Luckily, it's easy to filter those spots out.

```
birth2008 <- birth$X2008[!is.na(birth$X2008)]
```

This line of code retrieves the 2008 column from the birth data frame, and then basically you request only the rows that don't have missing values and store it in *birth2008*. More technically speaking, is.na() checks each item in the *birth$X2008* vector and returns an equal-length vector of true and false values known as *booleans*. When you pass a vector of booleans into the index of a vector, only the items that correspond to true values are returned. Don't worry if this confuses you. You don't have to know the technical details to get it to work. If, however, you plan on writing your own functions, it helps to know the language. It can also make documentation easier to read, but you'll tend to pick it up with practice.

Now you have the clean birth rate data stored in *birth2008*, so you can pass it into the density() function to estimate a curve and store the results in *d2008*.

```
d2008 <- density(birth2008)
```

This gives the x- and y-coordinates for the curve. The cool thing about this is that you can save the coordinates into a text file in case you want to use a different program to make the plot. Type **d2008** in the R console to see what's stored in the variable. Here's what you get.

```
Call:
    density.default(x = birth2008)

Data: birth2008 (219 obs.);    Bandwidth 'bw' = 3.168
```

> **NOTE**
>
> In this example, missing values are removed for the sake of simplicity. When you visualize and explore your own data, you should look more closely at missing values. Why are the values missing? Should they be set to zero or removed completely?

NOTE

The `write.table()` function saves new files in your current working directory. Change your working directory via the main menu or with `setwd()`.

```
            x                    y
Min.    :-1.299    Min.    :6.479e-06
1st Qu.:14.786    1st Qu.:1.433e-03
Median :30.870    Median :1.466e-02
Mean    :30.870    Mean    :1.553e-02
3rd Qu.:46.954    3rd Qu.:2.646e-02
Max.    :63.039    Max.    :4.408e-02
```

The main thing you care about is the x and y. That shows the breakdown of the coordinates, but if you want to access all of them you could enter the following.

```
d2008$x
d2008$y
```

Then to store them in a text file, use `write.table()`. As arguments, it takes the data you want to save, the filename you want to save it as, the separator you want to use (for example, comma or tab), and some others. To save the data as a basic tab-delimited text file, do the following.

```
d2008frame <- data.frame(d2008$x, d2008$y)
write.table(d2008frame, "birthdensity.txt", sep="\t")
```

The file `birthdensity.txt` should now be available in your working directory. If you don't want the rows to be numbered and a comma as the separator instead of tabs, you can do that just as easily.

```
write.table(d2008frame, "birthdensity.txt", sep=",", row.names=FALSE)
```

TIP

If you like to do your plotting with different software other than R but want to make use of R's computing functionality, you can save any or all of your results with `write.table()`.

Now you can load that data into Excel, Tableau, Protovis, or whatever you want that accepts delimited text, which is just about everything.

Back to the actual density plot. Remember, you already have the coordinates for your density plot. You just have to put them in graph form with, naturally, the `plot()` function. Figure 6-29 shows the result.

```
plot(d2008)
```

You can also make a filled density plot if you want, using `plot()` along with `polygon()`, as shown in Figure 6-30. You use the former to set the axes, but with the *type* set to "n" for no plotting. Then use the latter to actually draw the shape; set the fill color to a dark red and the border to a light gray.

```
plot(d2008, type="n")
polygon(d2008, col="#821122", border="#cccccc")
```

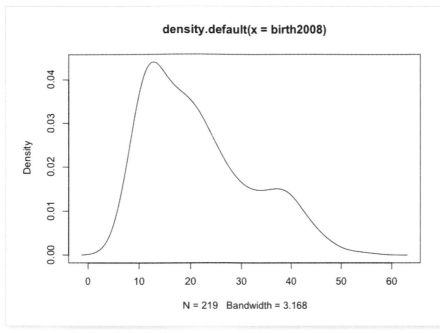

FIGURE 6-29 Density plot for birth rate

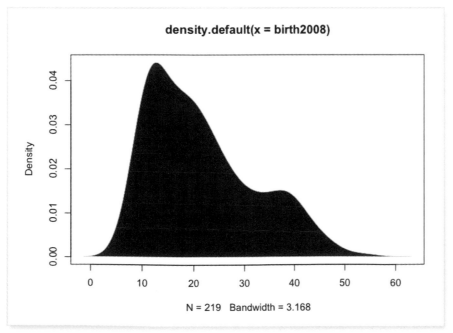

FIGURE 6-30 Filled density plot

No need to stop here though. You can plot the histogram and density plot together to get the exact frequencies represented by the bars and the estimated proportions from the curve, as shown in Figure 6-31. Use the histogram() (from the lattice package) and lines() functions. The former creates a new plot whereas the latter adds lines to an existing plot.

```
library(lattice)
histogram(birth$X2008, breaks=10)
lines(d2008)
```

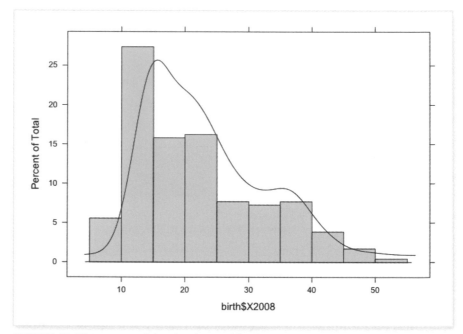

FIGURE 6-31 Histogram and density plot combined

So there's a lot you can do and plenty of variations, but the math and geometry are still the same as the old-school stem-and-leaf plot. You're counting, aggregating, and grouping. The best variation can vary based on what data you have. Figure 6-32 shows a more finished graphic. I de-emphasized the axis lines, rearranged the labels, and added a pointer for median. The vertical axis, which represents density, isn't especially useful in this graphic, but I left it in there for the sake of completeness.

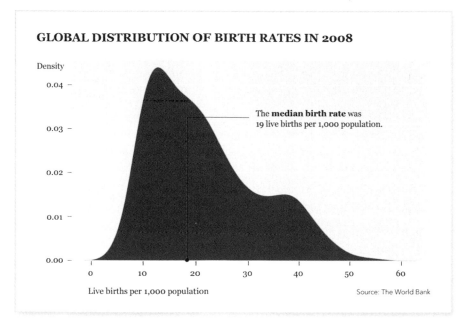

GLOBAL DISTRIBUTION OF BIRTH RATES IN 2008

The **median birth rate** was 19 live births per 1,000 population.

Live births per 1,000 population

Source: The World Bank

FIGURE 6-32 Density plot for worldwide birth rates in 2008

Comparison

Often it's useful to compare multiple distributions rather than just the mean, median, and mode. These summary statistics are after all descriptors of the big picture. They tell you only part of a story.

For example, I could tell you that the average birth rate for the world in 2008 was 19.98 live births per 1,000 population and 32.87 in 1960, so the birth rate was about 39 percent lower in 2008 than it was in 1960. That only tells you what's going on in the center of the distribution though. Or is it even the center? Are there only a few countries that had high birth rates in 1960, bringing up the average? Did differences in birth rate increase or decrease over the past few decades?

You can make comparisons in lots of ways. You could go entirely analytical and not use visualization at all. (I spent a year learning about statistical methods in graduate school, and that was just the tip of the iceberg.) You could also go the other way and use visualization. Your results won't be an exact answer offered by a thorough statistical analysis, but they could be good enough to make an informed decision about whatever you're looking into. Obviously you're going to go the visualization route, or I would have named this book *Analyze This*.

Multiple Distributions

So far you've looked at only single distributions, namely birth rates for 2008. But if you looked at the data file or the data frame in R, you know that you have annual birth rates all the way back to 1960. If you didn't look, then um, you still have annual birth rates all the way back to 1960. Like I said earlier, the world birth rate has decreased significantly, but how has the entire distribution changed?

Now take the straightforward route to create a histogram for every year and lay them out nicely organized as a matrix. It's a similar idea to the scatterplot matrix designed at the beginning of this chapter.

CREATE A HISTOGRAM MATRIX

The lattice package in R makes it easy to create a whole bunch of histograms with just one line of code, but there's a small catch. You have to give it the data in the format that the function wants it. Following is a snippet of the originally loaded text file.

```
Country,1960,1961,1962,1963...
Aruba,36.4,35.179,33.863,32.459...
Afghanistan,52.201,52.206,52.208,52.204...
...
```

There's a row for each country. The first column is the country name, and then there's a column for each year, so there are 30 columns and 234 rows of data, plus the header. You need the data to be in two columns though, one for the year and the other for the birth rate. You don't actually need country names for this, so the first few rows should look like this.

```
year,rate
1960,36.4
1961,35.179
1962,33.863
1963,32.459
1964,30.994
1965,29.513
...
```

If you compare the snippet you want to the current snippet, you should notice that the values in the second snippet match the values for Aruba. So there's a row for every birth rate value that is accompanied by the year. This results in 9,870 rows of data, plus a header.

How do you get the data into the format you want? Remember what you did with Python in Chapter 2, "Handling Data"? You loaded the CSV file in Python, and then iterated over each row, printing the values into the format that you wanted. You can do the same thing here. Start a new file in your favorite text editor called transform-birth-rate.py. Make sure it's in the same directory as birth-rate.csv. Then enter the following script.

```python
import csv

reader = csv.reader(open('birth-rate.csv', 'r'), delimiter=",")

rows_so_far = 0
print 'year,rate'
for row in reader:
    if rows_so_far == 0:
        header = row
        rows_so_far += 1
    else:

        for i in range(len(row)):
            if i > 0 and row[i]:
                print header[i] + ',' + row[i]

        rows_so_far += 1
```

This should look familiar, but now break it down. You import the csv package and then load birth-rate.csv. Then print the header, and iterate through each row and column so that the script outputs the data in the format you want. Run the script in your console and save the output in a new CSV file named birth-rate-yearly.csv.

```
python transform-birth-rate.py > birth-rate-yearly.csv
```

Great. Now use histogram() for that matrix; go back to R and load the new data file with read.csv(). In case you skipped all the data formatting stuff (to save for later), the new data file is online so that you can load it from a URL.

```
birth_yearly <-
    read.csv("http://datasets.flowingdata.com/birth-rate-yearly.csv")
```

> **TIP**
>
> If you want to keep all your coding in R, you can try using Hadley Wickham's reshape package. It helps you shift data frames into the format you want.

Now plug the data into `histogram()` to make a 10 by 5 matrix, with rate categorized by year. The output is shown in Figure 6-33.

```
histogram(~ rate | year, data=birth_yearly, layout=c(10,5))
```

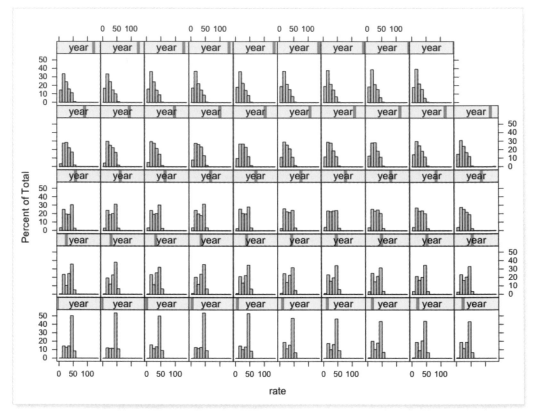

FIGURE 6-33 Default histogram matrix

Okay, not bad, but you can improve it. First, there is an outlier on the far right that's pushing all the bars to the left. Second, an orange bar shifts left and right according to the year for each cell of the matrix, but it'd be easier to read if those were actually labels that showed the year number. Finally, it's hard to tell because there are no year labels, but the order of the histograms isn't actually working. The first year, 1960, is at the bottom left, and 1969 is at the bottom right. The cell above 1960 is the one for 1970. So the order is going bottom to top and left to right. Weird.

To find the outlier, use summary() again on *birth_yearly*.

```
      year              rate
 Min.   :1960    Min.    :   6.90
 1st Qu.:1973    1st Qu.:  18.06
 Median :1986    Median :  29.61
 Mean   :1985    Mean    :  29.94
 3rd Qu.:1997    3rd Qu.:  41.91
 Max.   :2008    Max.    : 132.00
```

The maximum rate is 132. That seems off. No other rates even come close to 100. What's going on? It turns out that the rate recorded for Palau in 1999 is 132. This is most likely a typo because the rates for Palau before and after 1999 are no greater than 20. It's probably supposed to be 13.2, but you'd have to look into that deeper. For now, temporarily remove that mistake.

```
birth_yearly.new <- birth_yearly[birth_yearly$rate < 132,]
```

On to the labels for the years. When the values used for labels are stored as numeric, the lattice function automatically uses the orange bar to indicate value. If, however, the labels are characters, the function uses strings, so now do that.

```
birth_yearly.new$year <- as.character(birth_yearly.new$year)
```

You still need to update the order, but create the histogram matrix first and store it in a variable.

```
h <- histogram(~ rate | year, data=birth_yearly.new, layout=c(10,5))
```

Now use the update() function to change the order of the histograms.

```
update(h, index.cond=list(c(41:50, 31:40, 21:30, 11:20, 1:10)))
```

This basically reverses the order of all the rows. As shown in Figure 6-34, you get a nicely labeled histogram matrix—and a better sense of the distributions after removing the typo. Plus the histograms are arranged more logically so that you can read from left to right, top to bottom. Read just one cell from each row, and move your eyes top to bottom so that you can see how the distribution has changed by decade.

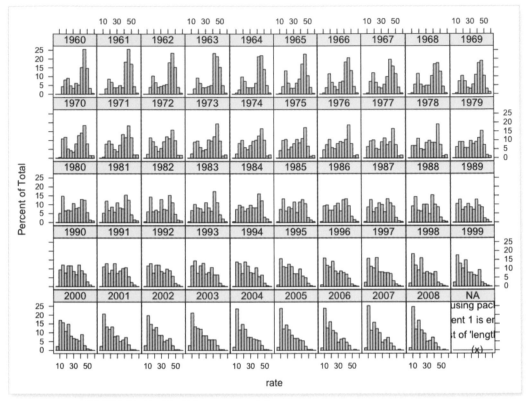

FIGURE 6-34 Modified histogram matrix

At this point, the layout is good. If you were to refine the graphic in Illustrator, you could make the labels smaller, change the border and fill colors, and do some general cleanup, as shown in Figure 6-35. It's more readable this way. To make it even clearer, and to complete the story, you can also add a proper lead-in, include the source, and point out how the distribution is shifting left toward lower birth rates worldwide. This could be too complex as a standalone graphic. You'd need to provide a lot of context for readers to fully appreciate the data.

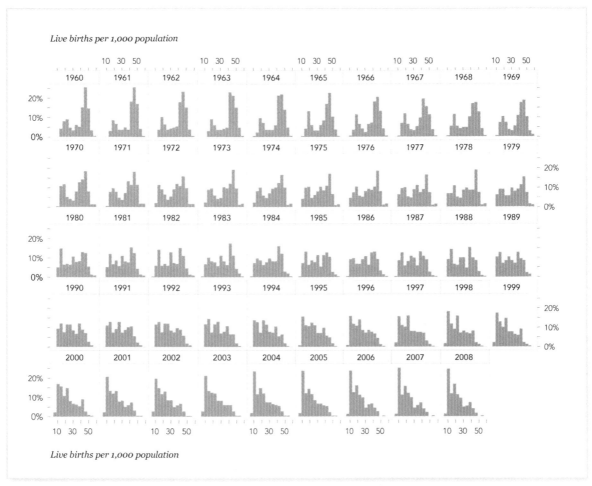

FIGURE 6-35 Histogram matrix refined in Illustrator

This isn't the only way to do things. You could create the same matrix with Processing, Protovis, PHP, or anything that draws bars. There are even multiple ways to make the same type of matrix within R. For example, I made a graphic for FlowingData on the changing distribution of television sizes from 2002 through 2009, as shown in Figure 6-36.

Television Size Over the Years

A quick search for 'average TV size' quotes Sharp as saying average TV size could be up to 60 inches by 2015. (Although I can't find the actual source.) So by how much has that magical entertainment screen grown during the past 8 years? Probably not as much as you think.

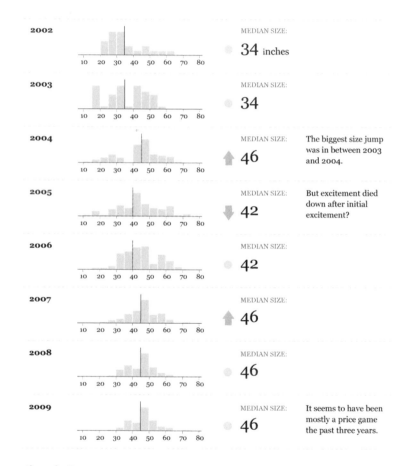

2002 MEDIAN SIZE: **34** inches

2003 MEDIAN SIZE: **34**

2004 MEDIAN SIZE: ▲ **46** The biggest size jump was in between 2003 and 2004.

2005 MEDIAN SIZE: ▼ **42** But excitement died down after initial excitement?

2006 MEDIAN SIZE: **42**

2007 MEDIAN SIZE: ▲ **46**

2008 MEDIAN SIZE: **46**

2009 MEDIAN SIZE: **46** It seems to have been mostly a price game the past three years.

About the Data

The numbers come from the past 745 dated CNet television reviews. While reviews aren't a direct indicator of what televisions people buy, they do show what's on the market.

Data from CNet / *Created by* FlowingData

FIGURE 6-36 Distribution of television size over the years

The code looks different from what you just did, but the logic is similar. I loaded the data, applied some filters for outliers, and then drew a bunch of histograms. The difference is that I didn't use histogram() from the lattice package. Instead, I set the layout with par(), which you use to set universal parameters in R, and then used hist() to draw each histogram.

```
# Load data
tvs <- read.table('http://datasets.flowingdata.com/tv_sizes.txt',
    sep="\t", header=TRUE)

# Filter outliers
tvs <- tvs[tvs$size < 80, ]
tvs <- tvs[tvs$size > 10, ]

# Set breaks for histograms
breaks = seq(10, 80, by=5)

# Set the layout
par(mfrow=c(4,2))

# Draw histograms, one by one
hist(tvs[tvs$year == 2009,]$size, breaks=breaks)
hist(tvs[tvs$year == 2008,]$size, breaks=breaks)
hist(tvs[tvs$year == 2007,]$size, breaks=breaks)
hist(tvs[tvs$year == 2006,]$size, breaks=breaks)
hist(tvs[tvs$year == 2005,]$size, breaks=breaks)
hist(tvs[tvs$year == 2004,]$size, breaks=breaks)
hist(tvs[tvs$year == 2003,]$size, breaks=breaks)
hist(tvs[tvs$year == 2002,]$size, breaks=breaks)
```

The graphic output of this code is shown in Figure 6-37. It has four rows and two columns, which was specified in the *mfrow* argument of par(). For the final graphic, I ended up putting them all in one column, but the important part is that I didn't have to do a bunch of data entry in Illustrator or Excel to manually make eight graphs.

SMALL MULTIPLES

The technique of putting a bunch of small graphs together in a single graphic is more commonly referred to as small multiples. It encourages readers to make comparisons across groups and categories, and within them. Plus, you can fit a lot in one space if your graphic is organized.

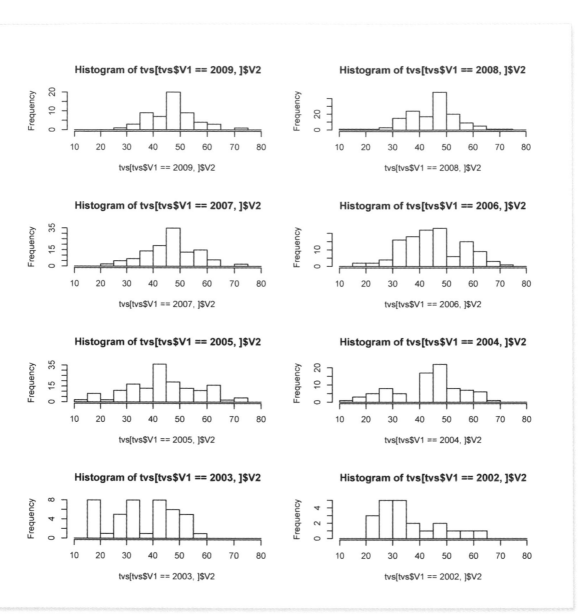

FIGURE 6-37 Grid layout for histograms

For example, I looked at movie ratings on the site Rotten Tomatoes for trilogies. In case you're unfamiliar, Rotten Tomatoes aggregates movie reviews and marks them as positive and negative. When at least 60 percent of reviewers say they like a film, it is marked fresh. Otherwise, it's rotten.

I wanted to know how sequels compared to their originals in freshness. It turns out not very well, as shown in Figure 6-38. The median rating of finales was 37 percentage points lower than the median of the originals. In other words, most originals were fresh, and most finales were rotten.

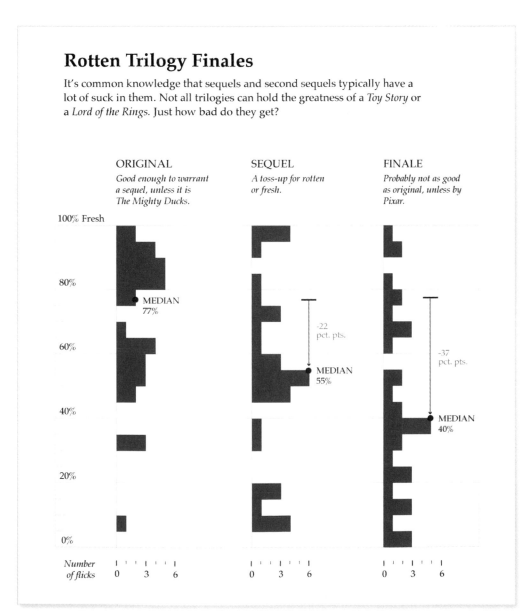

FIGURE 6-38 How trilogies rate from original to finale

This was actually just three histograms flipped on their sides. Figure 6-39 shows the original histograms in R. I just gussied them up a bit in Illustrator.

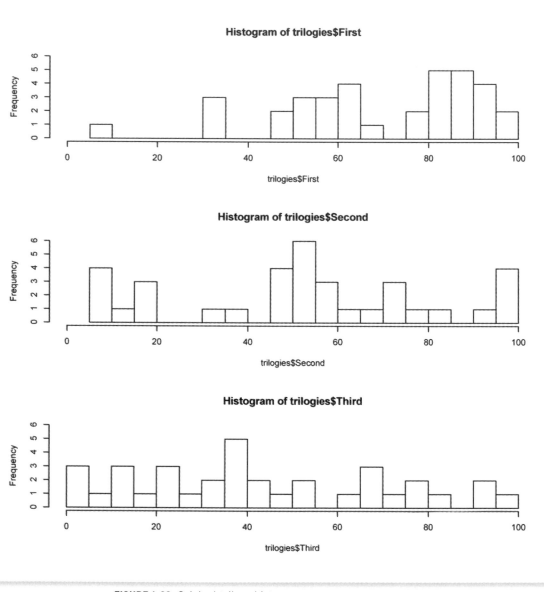

FIGURE 6-39 Original trilogy histograms

In any case, FlowingData readers understood the graphic for the most part—they're a data savvy bunch, naturally. However, the graphic was later linked from IMDB, also known as the Internet Movie Database. IMDB has a much more general audience, and judging by the comments after that link-back, the less data savvy readers had trouble interpreting the distributions.

However, the second part of the graphic, as shown in Figure 6-40, seemed much easier to understand. It's a use of small multiples where each bar represents the rating for a movie. Bars were colored red for rotten and green for fresh.

FIGURE 6-40 Small multiples for ratings of trilogies

In case you're wondering how to do this, it's just a bunch of bar charts, so you could change the *mfrow* parameter like you did before and use the plot() or polygon() functions. I did this using the Column Graph tool in Illustrator though, because I happened to already have it open.

I learned a couple of things after posting this graphic. The first and most important is that aggregates and distributions are not something everybody deals with on a regular basis, so you need to do your best to explain the data and take extra care in telling the story. The second is that people love their movies, and when you say that their favorite movies of all time are horrible, they sort of take it to heart.

Wrapping Up

Looking for relationships in your data can be challenging at times and requires more critical thinking than blindly graphing numbers, but it can also be the most rewarding and informative. It's how your data, or rather, how the things that your data represents relate and interact with each other that's interesting—that's what makes for the best stories.

This chapter covered how to look for correlations between multiple variables, but explained relationships in a more general sense, too. Look at how everything relates to each other as a whole through distributions. Look within the distributions for outliers or patterns, and then think about the context of what you see. Then if you find something interesting, ask why. Think about the context of the data and possible explanations.

This is the best part about playing with data because you get to explore what the data is about and maybe dig up something interesting. Then when you dig enough, you can explain to readers what you find. Remember, not everyone speaks the language of numbers, so keep it at a human level for the general audience. Don't be afraid to turn it up to nerd level though, if you have the right audience.

Spotting Differences 7

Sports commentators like to classify a select few athletes as super-stars or as part of an elite group, while the rest are designated aver-age or role players. These classifications usually aren't so much from sports statistics as they are from watching a lot of games. It's the know-it-when-I-see-it mentality. There's nothing wrong with this. The commentators (usually) know what they're talking about and are always considering the context of the numbers. It always makes me happy when a group of sports analysts look at performance metrics, and almost without fail someone will say, "You can't just look at the numbers. It's the intangibles that make so and so great." That's statis-tics right there.

Obviously this doesn't apply to just sports. Maybe you want to find the best restaurants in an area or identify loyal customers. Rather than categorizing units, you could look for someone or something that stands out from the rest. This chapter looks at how to spot groups within a population and across multiple criteria, and spot the outliers using common sense.

What to Look For

It's easy to compare across a single variable. One house has more square feet than another house, or one cat weighs more than another cat. Across two variables, it is a little more difficult, but it's still doable. The first house has more square feet, but the second house has more bathrooms. The first cat weighs more and has short hair, whereas the second cat weighs less and has long hair.

What if you have one hundred houses or one hundred cats to classify? What if you have more variables for each house, such as number of bedrooms, backyard size, and housing association fees? You end up with the number of units times the number of variables. Okay, now it is more tricky, and this is what we focus on.

Perhaps your data has a number of variables, but you want to classify or group units (for example, people or places) into categories and find the outliers or standouts. You want to look at each variable for differences, but you also want to see differences across all variables. Two basketball players could have completely different scoring averages, but they could be almost identical in rebounds, steals, and minutes played per game. You need to find differences but not forget the similarities and relationships, just like, oh yes, the sports commentators.

Comparing across Multiple Variables

One of the main challenges when dealing with multiple variables is to determine where to begin. You can look at so many variations and subsets that it can be overwhelming if you don't stop to think about what data you have. Sometimes, it's best to look at all the data at once, and interesting points could point you in the next interesting direction.

Getting Warmer

One of the most straightforward ways to visualize a table of data is to show it all at once. Instead of the numbers though, you can use colors to indicate values, as shown in Figure 7-1.

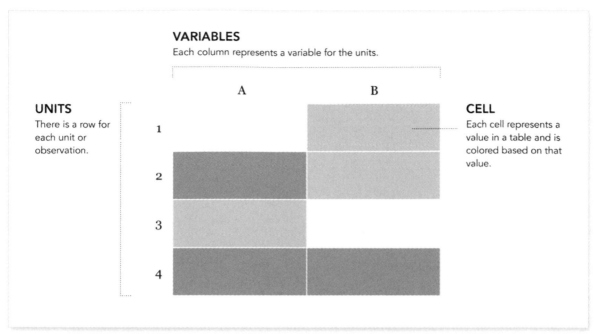

VARIABLES
Each column represents a variable for the units.

A   B

UNITS
There is a row for
each unit or
observation.

1
2
3
4

CELL
Each cell represents a
value in a table and is
colored based on that
value.

FIGURE 7-1 Heatmap framework

You end up with a grid the same size of the original data table, but you can easily find relatively high and low values based on color. Typically, dark colors mean greater values, and lighter colors represent lower values but that can easily change based on your application.

You also read the heatmap (or heat matrix) the same way you would a table. You can read a row left to right to see the values of all variables for a single unit, or you can see how all the units compare across a single variable.

This layout can still confuse you, especially if you have a large table of data, but with the right color scheme and some sorting, you can make a useful graphic.

CREATE A HEATMAP

It's easy to make heatmaps in R. There's a `heatmap()` function that does all the math work, which leaves you with picking colors best suited for your data and organizing labels so that they're still readable, even if you have a lot of rows and columns. In other words, R sets up the framework, and you handle the design. That should sound familiar by now.

In this example, take a look at NBA basketball statistics for 2008. You can download the data as a CSV file at http://datasets.flowingdata.com/ppg2008 .csv. There are 22 columns, the first for player names, and the rest for stats such as points per game and field goal percentage. You can use read .csv() to load the data into R. Now look at the first five rows to get a sense of the data's structure (Figure 7-2).

```
bball <-
    read.csv("http://datasets.flowingdata.com/ppg2008.csv",
    header=TRUE)
bball[1:5,]
```

```
> bball <- read.csv("http://datasets.flowingdata.com/ppg2008.csv", header=TRUE)
> bball[1:5,]
          Name  G  MIN  PTS  FGM   FGA   FGP FTM FTA   FTP X3PM X3PA  X3PP
1  Dwyane Wade 79 38.6 30.2 10.8 22.0 0.491 7.5 9.8 0.765  1.1  3.5 0.317
2  LeBron James 81 37.7 28.4  9.7 19.9 0.489 7.3 9.4 0.780  1.6  4.7 0.344
3   Kobe Bryant 82 36.2 26.8  9.8 20.9 0.467 5.9 6.9 0.856  1.4  4.1 0.351
4 Dirk Nowitzki 81 37.7 25.9  9.6 20.0 0.479 6.0 6.7 0.890  0.8  2.1 0.359
5 Danny Granger 67 36.2 25.8  8.5 19.1 0.447 6.0 6.9 0.878  2.7  6.7 0.404
  ORB DRB TRB AST STL BLK  TO  PF
1 1.1 3.9 5.0 7.5 2.2 1.3 3.4 2.3
2 1.3 6.3 7.6 7.2 1.7 1.1 3.0 1.7
3 1.1 4.1 5.2 4.9 1.5 0.5 2.6 2.3
4 1.1 7.3 8.4 2.4 0.8 0.8 1.9 2.2
5 0.7 4.4 5.1 2.7 1.0 1.4 2.5 3.1
>
```

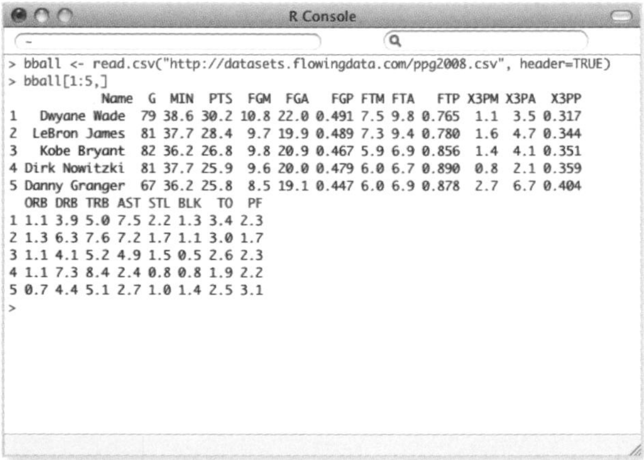

FIGURE 7-2 Structure of the first five rows of data

TIP

The *decreasing* argument in order() specifies whether you want the data to be sorted in ascending or descending order.

Players are currently sorted by points per game, greatest to least, but you could order players by any column, such as rebounds per game or field goal percentage, with order().

```
bball_byfgp <- bball[order(bball$FGP, decreasing=TRUE),]
```

Now if you look at the first five rows of *bball_byfgp*, you see the list is led by Shaquille O'Neal, Dwight Howard, and Pau Gasol instead of Dwyane Wade, Lebron James, and Kobe Bryant. For this example, reverse the order on points per game.

```
bball <- bball[order(bball$PTS, decreasing=FALSE),]
```

As is, the column names match the CSV file's header. That's what you want. But you also want to name the rows by player name instead of row number, so shift the first column over to row names.

```
row.names(bball) <- bball$Name
bball <- bball[,2:20]
```

The first line changes row names to the first column in the data frame. The second line selects columns 2 through 20 and sets the subset of data back to *bball*.

The data also has to be in matrix format rather than a data frame. You'd get an error if you tried to use a data frame with the heatmap() function. Generally speaking, a data frame is like a collection of vectors where each column represents a different metric. Each column can have different formats such as numeric or a string. A matrix on the other hand is typically used to represent a two-dimensional space and the data type has to be uniform across all cells.

```
bball_matrix <- data.matrix(bball)
```

The data is ordered how you want it and formatted how you need it to be, so you can plug it into heatmap() to reap the rewards. By setting the *scale* argument to "column," you tell R to use the minimum and maximum of each column to determine color gradients instead of the minimum and maximum of the entire matrix.

```
bball_heatmap <- heatmap(bball_matrix, Rowv=NA,
    Colv=NA, col = cm.colors(256), scale="column", margins=c(5,10))
```

Your result should resemble Figure 7-3. Using cm.colors(), you specified a color range from cyan to magenta. The function creates a vector of hexadecimal colors with a cyan-to-magenta range by default with *n* shades in between (in this case, 256). So notice the third column, which is for points per game, starts at magenta, indicating the highest values for Dwyane Wade and Lebron James, and then shifts toward a darker cyan hue to the bottom for Allen Iverson and Nate Robinson. You can also quickly find other magenta spots representing leading rebounder Dwight Howard or assist leader Chris Paul.

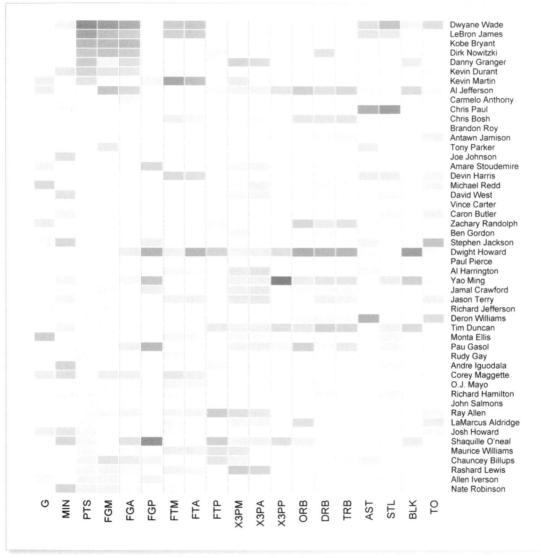

FIGURE 7-3 Default heatmap ordered by points per game

Maybe you want a different color scheme. Just change the *col* argument, which is cm.colors(256) in the line of code you just executed. Type **?cm.colors** for help on what colors R offers. For example, you could use more heat-looking colors, as shown in Figure 7-4.

```
bball_heatmap <- heatmap(bball_matrix,
    Rowv=NA, Colv=NA, col = heat.colors(256), scale="column",
    margins=c(5,10))
```

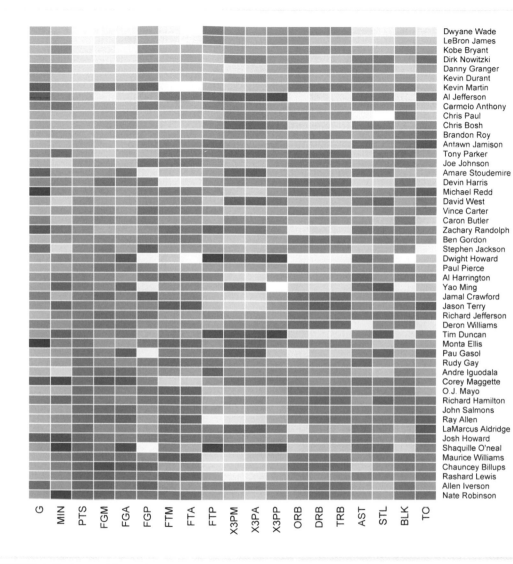

FIGURE 7-4 Heatmap with a red-yellow color scale

If you typed cm.colors(10) in the R console, you'd get an array of ten colors
that range from cyan to magenta. Then heatmap() automatically chooses
the color that corresponds to each value based on a linear scale.

```
[1]  "#80FFFFFF"  "#99FFFFFF"  "#B3FFFFFF"  "#CCFFFFFF"  "#E6FFFFFF"
[6]  "#FFE6FFFF"  "#FFCCFFFF"  "#FFB3FFFF"  "#FF99FFFF"  "#FF80FFFF"
```

This is great, because you can easily create your own color scale. For example, you could go to 0to255.com and pick out the base color and go from there. Figure 7-5 shows a gradient with a red base. You can pick a handful of colors, from light to dark, and then easily plug them into heatmap(), as shown in Figure 7-6. Instead of using R to create a vector of colors, you define your own in the *red_colors* variable.

```
red_colors <- c("#ffd3cd", "#ffc4bc", "#ffb5ab",
    "#ffa69a", "#ff9789", "#ff8978", "#ff7a67", "#ff6b56",
    "#ff5c45", "#ff4d34")
bball_heatmap <- heatmap(bball_matrix, Rowv=NA,
    Colv=NA, col = red_colors, scale="column", margins=c(5,10))
```

TIP

Choose your colors wisely because they also set the tone for the context of your story. For example, if you deal with a somber topic, it's probably better to stay with more neutral, muted tones, whereas you can use vibrant colors for a more uplifting or casual topic.

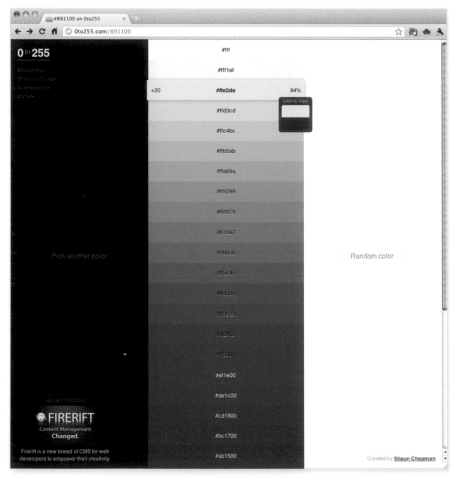

FIGURE 7-5 Red gradient from 0to255.com

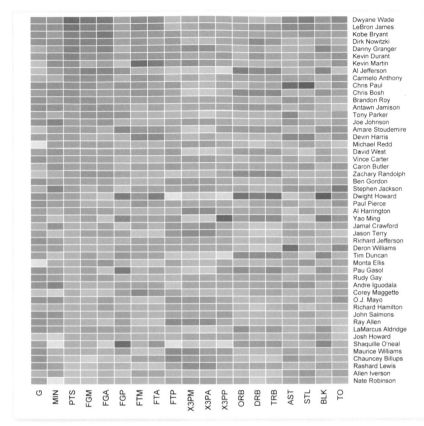

FIGURE 7-6 Heatmap using custom red color scale

If you don't want to pick your own colors, you can also use the RColorBrewer package. The package is not installed by default, so you need to download and install it via the Package Installer if you haven't already. ColorBrewer was designed by cartographer Cynthia Brewer and was originally intended for maps, but it can help you create data graphics in general. You can choose from a variety of options, such as a sequential or divergent color palette and number of shades. For the purposes of this example, go with a simple blue palette. Enter **?brewer.pal** in the R console for more options—it's fun to play with. Assuming you installed RColorBrewer, enter the following for a heatmap using a blue palette with nine shades. The result is shown in Figure 7-7.

▶ Visit the interactive version of Colorbrewer at http:// colorbrewer2.com. You can select options from drop-down menus to see how color schemes look in a sample map.

```
library(RColorBrewer)
bball_heatmap <- heatmap(bball_matrix, Rowv=NA,
    Colv=NA, col = brewer.pal(9, "Blues"),
    scale="column", margins=c(5,10))
```

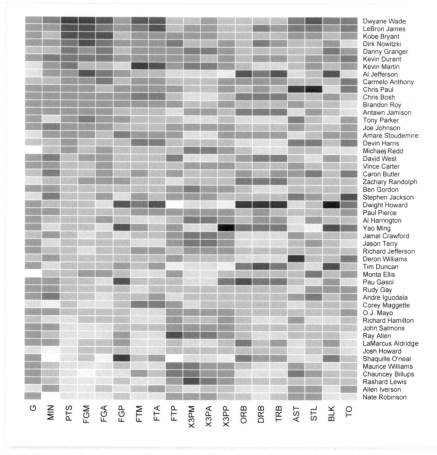

FIGURE 7-7 Heatmap using RColorBrewer for color palette

Check out Figure 7-7, which you can bring into Illustrator to spruce up. The graphic doesn't need a ton of edits, but you can make the labels more readable and soften the colors so that the graphic is easier to scan.

Addressing the former, it'd be better if the labels were the full descriptions. As a basketball fan, I know what each abbreviation stands for, but someone not so familiar with the sport would be confused. As for the latter, you can tone down the contrast by using transparency, available in the Color Window in Illustrator. Cell borders can also provide more definition to each cell so that the graphic is easier to scan left to right and top to bottom. Figure 7-8 shows the finished graphic.

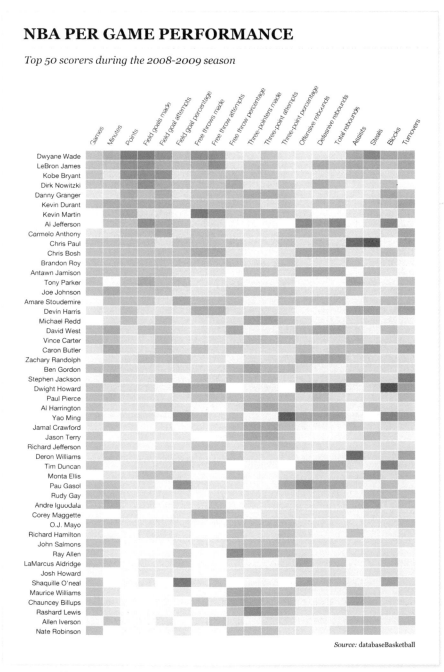

NBA PER GAME PERFORMANCE

Top 50 scorers during the 2008-2009 season

Source: databaseBasketball

FIGURE 7-8 Heatmap showing NBA per game performance for the top 50 scorers during the 2008–2009 season

▶ Mike Bostock ported this example to Protovis, which you can find in the Protovis examples section. The aesthetic is the same, but it has the added bonus of tooltips as you mouse over each cell.

See It in His Face

The good thing about a heatmap is that it enables you to see all your data at once; however, the focus is on individual points. You can easily spot highs and lows for points or rebounds per game, but it's more challenging to compare one player to another.

Often you want to see each unit as a whole instead of split up by several metrics. Chernoff Faces is one way to do this; however the method isn't an exact one, and it's possible a general audience might become confused. That said, Chernoff Faces can be useful from time to time, it's good data nerd fun, which makes it totally worth it.

The point of Chernoff Faces is to display multiple variables at once by positioning parts of the human face, such as ears, hair, eyes, and nose, based on numbers in a dataset (Figure 7-9). The assumption is that you can read people's faces easily in real life, so you should recognize small differences when they represent data. That's a big assumption, but roll with it.

As you see in the following example, larger values stand out in the form of big hair or big eyes, whereas smaller values tend to shrink facial features. In addition to size, you can also adjust features such as the curve of the lips or shape of the face.

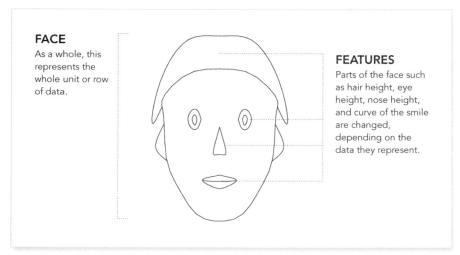

FACE
As a whole, this represents the whole unit or row of data.

FEATURES
Parts of the face such as hair height, eye height, nose height, and curve of the smile are changed, depending on the data they represent.

FIGURE 7-9 Chernoff Faces framework

CREATE CHERNOFF FACES

Go back to the basketball data, which represents the top 50 scorers in the NBA, during the 2008–2009 season. There will be one face per player. Don't worry—you don't have to create each face manually. The aplpack in R provides a faces() function to help get you to where you want.

If you haven't already, go ahead and install aplpack with install.packages() or via the Package Installer. The package name stands for "another plotting package" in case you were wondering, and it was designed by Hans Peter Wolf. When installed, the package is usually automatically loaded, but if not, you should do that, too.

```
library(aplpack)
```

You should have also already loaded the basketball data while creating a heatmap. If not, again use read.csv() to load the data directly from a URL.

```
bball <- read.csv("http://datasets.flowingdata.com/ppg2008.csv",
header=TRUE)
```

After you load the package and data, it's straightforward to make Chernoff Faces with the faces() function, as shown in Figure 7-10.

```
faces(bball[,2:16], ncolors=0)
```

Your dataset has 20 variables, plus player names; however, the faces() function offered by the aplpack enables only a maximum of 15 variables, because there are only so many facial features you can change. This is why you subset the data on columns 2 to 16.

What does each face represent? The faces() function changes features in the following order, matching the order of the data columns.

1. Height of face
2. Width of face
3. Shape of face
4. Height of mouth
5. Width of mouth
6. Curve of smile
7. Height of eyes
8. Width of eyes
9. Height of hair
10. Width of hair
11. Styling of hair
12. Height of nose
13. Width of nose
14. Width of ears
15. Height of ears

> **NOTE**
>
> The newest version of the aplpack lets you add color with the faces() function. In this example, you set *ncolors* to 0 to use only black and white. See **?faces** to see how you can use color vectors in the same way you used them with the previous heatmap example.

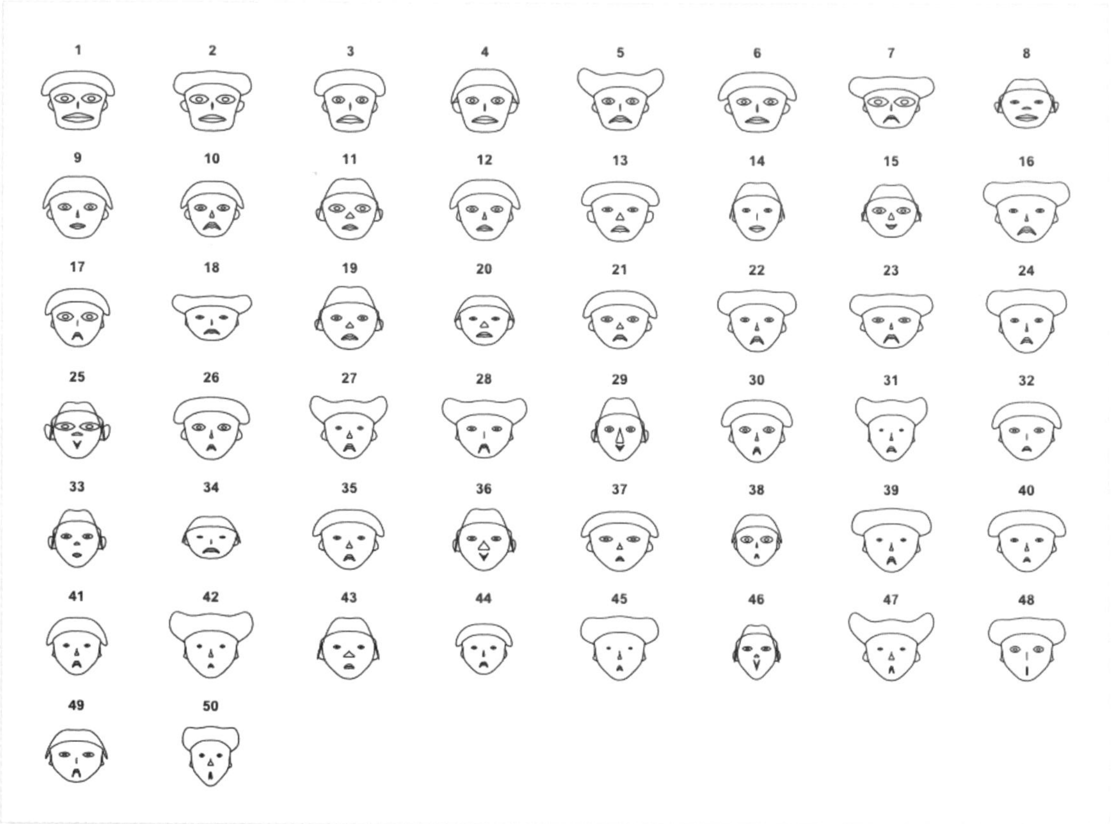

FIGURE 7-10 Default Chernoff Faces

> **TIP**
>
> When you have a lot of individuals, it can be useful to cluster by category so that the faces are easier to scan. For this example, you could separate faces by position: guards, forwards, and centers.

So for example, the height of a face represents the number of games played, and the height of a mouth represents field goals made per game. This is kind of useless as it is because you don't have any names to the faces, but you can see that the first few have more well-rounded gameplay than the others, whereas player 7, for instance, has relatively wide hair, which corresponds to three-pointers made.

Use the *labels* argument in `faces()` to add names to the faces, as shown in Figure 7-11.

```
faces(bball[,2:16], labels=bball$Name)
```

That's better. Now you can see which face corresponds to which player. To identify the point guards, you can start with say, Chris Paul, and look for similar faces such as the one for Devin Harris or Deron Williams. Chauncey Billups, in the bottom-right corner is also a point guard, but the face looks different than the others. The hair is higher and mouth width is narrow, which corresponds to high free throw percentage and field goal attempts, respectively.

To make the graphic more readable, you can add some more spacing between rows, and at the least, provide a description of what feature provides what, as shown in Figure 7-12. Normally, I'd use a graphical legend, but we used every facial feature, so it's a challenge to provide that many pointers on a single face.

Again, the usefulness of Chernoff Faces can vary by dataset and audience, so you can decide whether you want to use the method. One thing though, is that people who aren't familiar with Chernoff Faces, tend to take the faces somewhat literally, as if the face that represents Shaquille O'Neal is actually supposed to look like the player. Most of you know that O'Neal is one of the physically biggest players of all time.

TIP

White space in your graphics can make them more readable, especially when there is a lot to look at and evaluate.

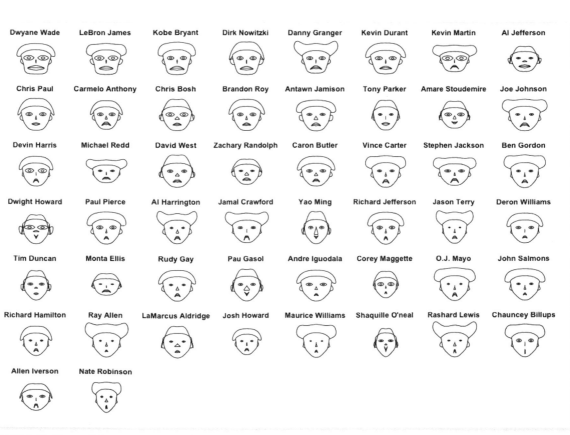

FIGURE 7-11 Chernoff Faces with names for players

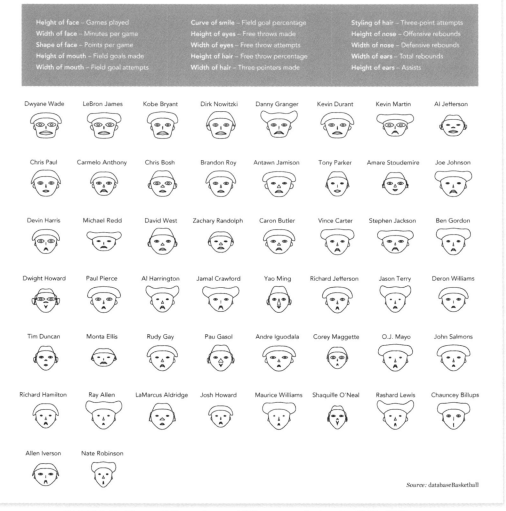

FIGURE 7-12 Chernoff Faces for top NBA scorers during the 2008–2009 season

Along the same lines, I designed a graphic for crime in the United States (Figure 7-13) using Chernoff Faces, and someone actually commented that it was racist because of how the face looked for states with high crime rates. That never crossed my mind because changing a facial feature was like changing the length of a bar on a graph for me, but hey, it's something to think about.

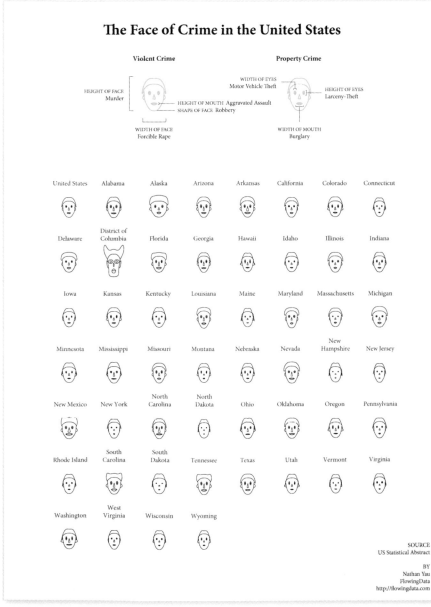

FIGURE 7-13 Crime in the United States represented by a face for each state

Starry Night

Instead of using faces to show multivariate data, you can use the same idea but abstract on it by using a different shape. Instead of changing facial features, you can modify the shape to match data values. This is the idea for star charts, also known as radar or spider charts.

As shown in Figure 7-14, you can draw several axes, one for each variable, starting from the middle and equally spaced in a circle. The center is the minimum value for each variable, and the ends represent the maximums. So if you draw a chart for a single unit, start at a variable and draw a connecting line to the corresponding spot on the next axis. Then you end up with something that looks like a star (or a radar or spider web).

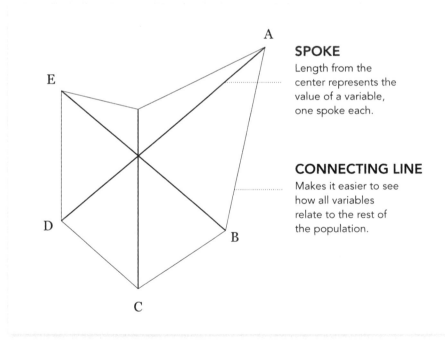

SPOKE
Length from the center represents the value of a variable, one spoke each.

CONNECTING LINE
Makes it easier to see how all variables relate to the rest of the population.

FIGURE 7-14 Star chart framework

You can represent several units on a single chart, but it'll become useless in a hurry, which makes for a poorly told story. So stick to separate star charts and compare.

CREATE STAR CHARTS

Now use the same crime data used for Figure 7-13 to see if it makes any difference to use these star charts. First things first. Load the data into R.

```
crime <- read.csv("http://datasets.flowingdata.com/
crimeRatesByState-formatted.csv")
```

Now it's as straightforward to make star charts as it was to make Chernoff Faces. Use the stars() function, which comes packaged with base R.

```
stars(crime)
```

The default charts are shown in Figure 7-15. Hopefully, these won't offend anyone. Of course, you still need state labels, but you also need a key to tell you which dimension is which. A certain order is followed, like with faces(), but you don't know where the first variable starts. So take care of both in one swoop. Notice that you can change to first column to row names just like you did with the heatmap. You can also set flip.labels to *FALSE*, because you don't want the labels to alternate heights. Figure 7-16 shows the results.

```
row.names(crime) <- crime$state
crime <- crime[,2:7]
stars(crime, flip.labels=FALSE, key.loc = c(15, 1.5))
```

It's relatively easy to spot the differences and similarities now. In the Chernoff version, the District of Columbia looked like a wild-eyed clown compared to all the other states, but with the star version, you see that yes, it does have high rates of crime in some categories, but relatively lower rates of forcible rape and burglary. It's also easy to find the states with relatively low crime rates such as New Hampshire and Rhode Island. Then there are states such as North Carolina that are high in just a single category.

For this dataset, I'm satisfied with this format, but there are two variations that you might want to try with your own data. The first restricts all data to the top half of the circle, as shown in Figure 7-17.

```
stars(crime, flip.labels=FALSE, key.loc = c(15, 1.5), full=FALSE)
```

The second variation uses the length of the segments instead of placement of points, as shown in Figure 7-18. These are actually Nightingale charts (also known as polar area diagrams) more than they are star charts, but there you go. If you do go with this option, you might want to try a different color scheme other than this crazy default one.

```
stars(crime, flip.labels=FALSE, key.loc = c(15, 1.5), draw.segments=TRUE)
```

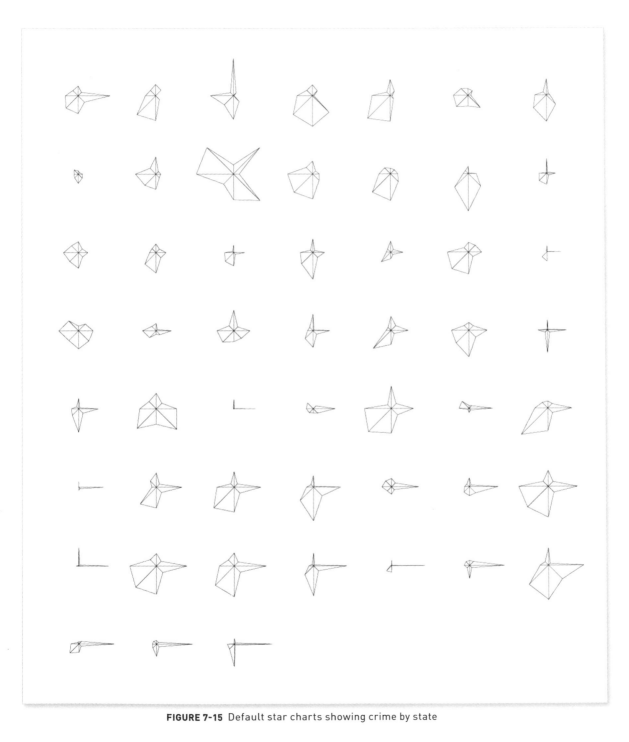

FIGURE 7-15 Default star charts showing crime by state

FIGURE 7-16 Star charts with labels and key

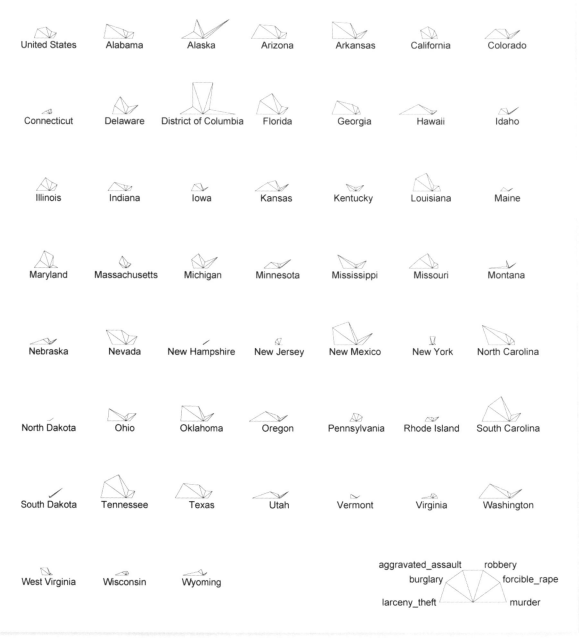

FIGURE 7-17 Star charts restricted to top half of circle

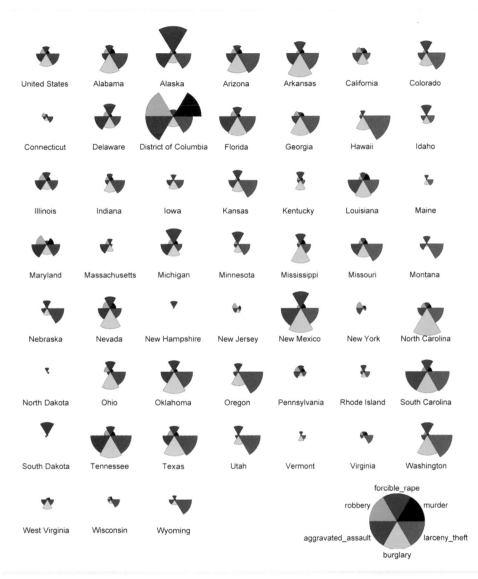

FIGURE 7-18 Crime displayed as Nightingale charts

Like I said though, I'm good with the original format in Figure 7-16, so you can take that into Illustrator to do some cleanup. It doesn't need a whole lot of modification. More white space between the rows could make the labels less ambiguous, and you can place the key on top so that readers know what they're getting into (Figure 7-19). Other than that, it's good to go.

FIGURE 7-19 Series of star charts showing crime by state

Running in Parallel

Although star charts and Chernoff Faces can make it easier to spot units that are different from the rest of the pack, it's a challenge to identify groups or how variables could be related. Parallel coordinates, which were invented in 1885 by Maurice d'Ocagne, can help with this.

As shown in Figure 7-20, you place multiple axes parallel to each other. The top of each axis represents a variable's maximum, and the bottom represents the minimum. For each unit, a line is drawn from left to right, moving up and down, depending on the unit's values.

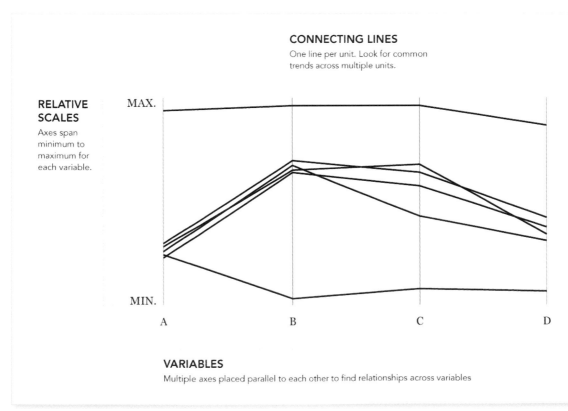

FIGURE 7-20 Parallel coordinates framework

For example, imagine you made a plot using the basketball data from earlier in the chapter. For the sake of simplicity, you only plot points, rebounding, and fouls, in that order. Now imagine a player who was a top scorer, a weak rebounder, and fouled a lot. A line in the parallel coordinates plot for that player would start high, go low, and then come back up again.

When you plot more units, this method helps to spot groups and tendencies. In the following example, you can use parallel coordinates on data from the National Center for Education Statistics.

CREATE A PARALLEL COORDINATES PLOT

You have several interactive options for parallel coordinates. You can build it in Protovis if you want to make a custom graphic, or you can plug your data into an exploratory tool such as GGobi. These implementations enable you to filter and highlight the data points you're interested in; however, I still like to go with static parallel coordinates plots, namely because you can compare different filters all at once. With interactive versions, you have only one plot, and it's tough to make sense of what you're looking at when you have a bunch of highlighting all in one place.

▶ Download GGobi for free at http://ggobi.org.

You know the first step. Before doing any visualizing, you need data. Load our education data into R with read.csv().

```
education <- read.csv("http://datasets.flowingdata.com/education.csv",
header=TRUE)
education[1:10,]
```

There are seven columns. The first is for state name, including "United States" for the national average. The next three are average reading, mathematics, and writing SAT scores. The fifth column is percentage of graduates who actually take the SAT, and the last two columns are pupil-to-staff ratio and high school dropout rate. What you're interested in is whether any of these variables are related and if there are any clear groupings. For example, do states with high dropout rates tend to have low SAT scores on average?

The base distribution of R doesn't supply a straightforward way to use parallel coordinates, but the lattice package does, so use that. Go ahead and load the package (or install if you haven't already).

```
library(lattice)
```

Great, now this will be super easy. The lattice package provides a parallel() function that you can quickly use.

```
parallel(education)
```

This produces the plot shown in Figure 7-21. Okay, that's quite useless, actually. There are a bunch of lines all over the place, and the variables go top to bottom instead of left to right. It looks like rainbow spaghetti at this point.

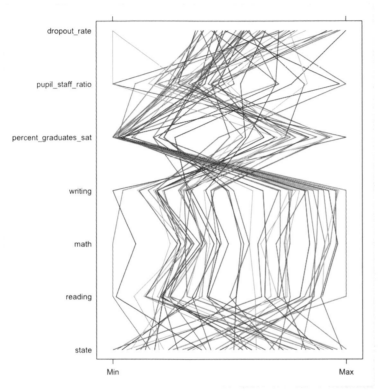

FIGURE 7-21 Default parallel coordinates plot with the lattice package

How can you modify this parallel coordinates plot so that you can actually get some information out of it? For starters, flip it on its side. This is more of a personal preference than it is a rule, but parallel coordinates left to right makes more sense, as shown in Figure 7-22.

```
parallel(education, horizontal.axis=FALSE)
```

You also don't need to include the *state* column, because for one, it's categorical, and second, every state has a different name. Now change the color of the lines to black—I'm all for color, but it's too much as-is. Execute the line of code below and you get Figure 7-23.

```
parallel(education[,2:7], horizontal.axis=FALSE, col="#000000")
```

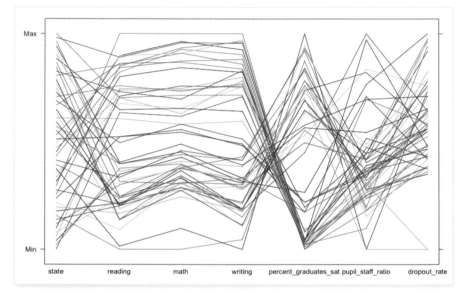

FIGURE 7-22 Horizontal parallel coordinates

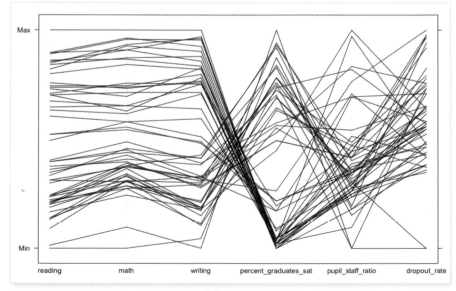

FIGURE 7-23 Parallel coordinates, simplified

That's a little better. The lines from reading, to math, to writing seldom criss-cross and almost run parallel. This makes sense that states with high reading scores also have math and writing scores. Similarly, states with low reading scores tend to have low math and writing scores.

Then something interesting happens as you go from SAT scores to percentage of graduates who take the SAT. It looks like the states with higher SAT score averages tend to have a lower percentage of graduates who take the test. It's the opposite for states with lower SAT averages. My specialty isn't in education, but my best bet is that in some states everyone takes the SAT, whereas in others people don't take the test if they're not planning to go to college. Thus, the average comes down when you require people who don't care about the results to take the test.

You can make this point more obvious by offering some contrasting colors. The parallel() function gives you full control over the colors with the col argument. Previously, you used only a single color (#000000), but you can also pass it an array of colors, a color value for each row of data. Now make the states in the 50th percentile of reading scores black and the bottom half gray. Use summary() to find the medians in the education data. Simply enter summary(education) in the console. This actually gives you summary stats for all columns, but it's a quick way to find that the median for reading is 523.

```
          state          reading            math             writing
Alabama    : 1   Min.   :466.0   Min.   :451.0   Min.    :455.0
Alaska     : 1   1st Qu.:497.8   1st Qu.:505.8   1st Qu.:490.0
Arizona    : 1   Median :523.0   Median :525.5   Median :510.0
Arkansas   : 1   Mean   :533.8   Mean   :538.4   Mean    :520.8
California : 1   3rd Qu.:571.2   3rd Qu.:571.2   3rd Qu.:557.5
Colorado   : 1   Max.   :610.0   Max.   :615.0   Max.    :588.0
(Other)    :46
percent_graduates_sat  pupil_staff_ratio  dropout_rate
Min.   : 3.00          Min.   : 4.900     Min.   :-1.000
1st Qu.: 6.75          1st Qu.: 6.800     1st Qu.: 2.950
Median :34.00          Median : 7.400     Median : 3.950
Mean   :37.35          Mean   : 7.729     Mean   : 4.079
3rd Qu.:66.25          3rd Qu.: 8.150     3rd Qu.: 5.300
Max.   :90.00          Max.   :12.100     Max.   : 7.600
```

Now iterate through each row of the data; check if it's above or below and specify the colors accordingly. The c() directive creates an empty vector, which you add to in each iteration.

```
reading_colors <- c()
for (i in 1:length(education$state)) {

    if (education$reading[i] > 523) {
        col <- "#000000"
    } else {
        col <- "#cccccc"
    }
    reading_colors <- c(reading_colors, col)
}
```

Then pass the reading_colors array into parallel instead of the lone "#000000". This gives you Figure 7-24, and it's much easier to see the big move from high to low.

```
parallel(education[,2:7], horizontal.axis=FALSE, col=reading_colors)
```

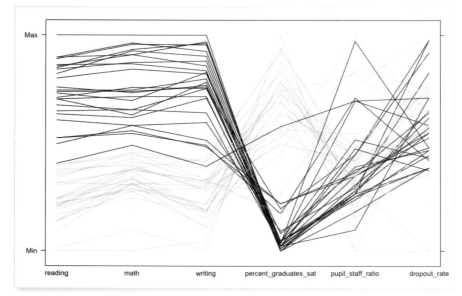

FIGURE 7-24 States with top reading scores highlighted

What about dropout rates? What if you do the same thing with dropout rates that you just did with reading scores, except you use the third
quartile instead of the median? The quartile is 5.3 percent. Again, you iterate over each row of data, but this time check the dropout rate instead of
reading score.

```
dropout_colors <- c()
for (i in 1:length(education$state)) {

    if (education$dropout_rate[i] > 5.3) {
        col <- "#000000"
    } else {
        col <- "#cccccc"
    }
    dropout_colors <- c(dropout_colors, col)
}
parallel(education[,2:7], horizontal.axis=FALSE, col=dropout_colors)
```

Figure 7-25 shows what you get, and it's not nearly as compelling as the
previous graphic. Visually speaking, there aren't any obvious groupings
across all of the variables.

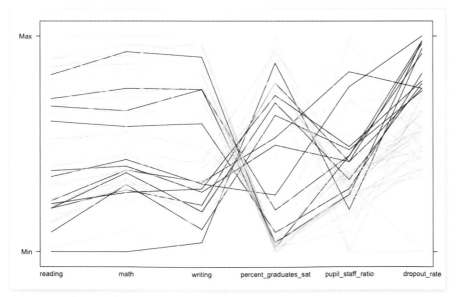

FIGURE 7-25 States with highest dropout rates highlighted

You can do more exploring on your own. Now go back to Figure 7-24 and tighten it up. Better looking labels that are more obvious would be good. Maybe add some color instead of all grayscale? How about a short blurb about why the top 50 percent of states are highlighted? What do you get? Figure 7-26.

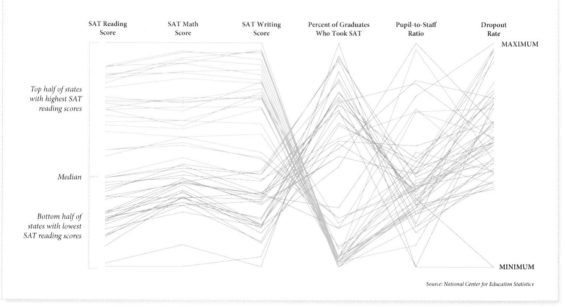

FIGURE 7-26 Standalone parallel coordinates plot on SAT scores

Reducing Dimensions

When you use Chernoff Faces or parallel coordinates, your main goal is to reduce. You want to find groups within the dataset or population. The challenge is that you don't always know where to start looking in the faces or the connecting lines, so it'd be nice if you could cluster objects, based on several criteria. This is one of the goals of multidimensional scaling (MDS). Take everything into account, and then place units that are more similar closer together on a plot.

Entire books are written on this topic, so explanations can get technical, but for the sake of simplicity, I'll keep it at a high level and leave the math for another day. That said, MDS is one of the first concepts I learned in graduate school, and it is worth learning the mechanics behind it, if you're into that sort of thing.

Imagine that you're in an empty, square-shaped room and there are two other people there. It's your job to tell those people where to stand in the room, based on their height. The more similar their height, the closer they should stand, and the more different their height, the farther away they should stand. One is really short. The other is really tall. Where should they go? The two people should stand at opposite corners, because they are complete opposites.

Now a third person comes in, and he's medium height. Sticking with the arrangement scheme, the new person should stand in the center of the room, right in between the first two. He's equally different from the tall and the short, so he's equal distance from each. At the same time, the tall and short people are still maximum distance from each other.

Okay, now introduce another variable: weight. You know the height and weight of all three people. The short and medium height people are actually the exact same weight whereas the tall person is, say, a third heavier. How can you, based on height and weight, place the three people in the room? Well, if you keep the first two people (short and tall) in their opposite positions, the third person (medium height) would need to move closer to the shorter person, because their weights are the same.

Do you get what is occurring? The more similar two people are, the closer they should stand to each other. In this simple case, you have only three people and two variables, so it's easy to work this out manually, but imagine you have 50 people, and you have to place them in the room based on say, five criteria. It's trickier. And that's what multidimensional scaling is for.

▶ For more details on the method, look up multidimensional scaling or principal components analysis.

Make Use of Multidimensional Scaling

Multidimensional scaling is much easier to understand with a concrete example, so jump right in. Come back to the education data, so if you haven't loaded it in R already, go ahead and do that first.

```
education <-
    read.csv("http://datasets.flowingdata.com/education.csv",
    header=TRUE)
```

Remember, there is a row for each state, which includes the District of Columbia and more rows for the United States averages. There are six variables for each state: reading, math, and writing SAT scores; percentage of graduates who took the SAT; pupil-to-staff ratio; and dropout rate.

It's just like the room metaphor, but instead of a square room, it's a square plot; instead of people, there are states; and instead of height and weight, you have education-related metrics. The goal is the same. You want to place the states on an x-y plot, so that similar states are closer together.

First step: Figure out how far each state should be from every other state. Use the dist() function, which does just that. You use only columns 2 through 7 because the first column is state names, and you know all those are different.

```
ed.dis <- dist(education[,2:7])
```

If you type **ed.dis** in the console, you see a series of matrices. Each cell represents how far one state should be from another (by Euclidean pixel distance). For example, the value in the second row, second column over is the distance Alabama should be from Alaska. The units aren't so important at this point. Rather it's the relative differences that matter.

How do you plot this 51 by 51 matrix on an x-y plot? You can't yet, until you have an x-y coordinate for each state. That's what cmdscale() is for. It takes a distance matrix as input and returns a set of points so that the differences between those points are about the same as specified in the matrix.

```
ed.mds <- cmdscale(ed.dis)
```

Type ed.mds in the console, and you see you now have x-y coordinates for each row of data. Store these in the variables *x* and *y*, and toss them into plot() to see what it looks like (Figure 7-27).

```
x <- ed.mds[,1]
y <- ed.mds[,2]
plot(x,y)
```

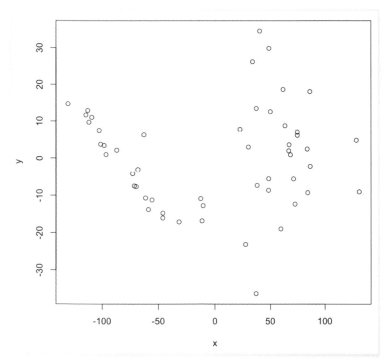

FIGURE 7-27 Dot plot showing results of multidimensional scaling

Not bad. Each dot represents a state. One problem, though: You don't
know what state is which. You need labels, so like before use text() to put
state names in place of the dots, as shown in Figure 7-28.

```
plot(x, y, type="n")
text(x, y, labels=education$state)
```

That's kind of cool. You see a couple of clusters emerge, with one on the
left and the other on the right. United States is on the bottom of the right
cluster, toward the middle, which seems about right. At this point, it's up
to you to figure what the clusters mean, but it's a good jumping off point in
your data exploration escapades.

You could, for example, color the states by dropout_colors like you did with
the parallel coordinates, as shown in Figure 7-29. It doesn't tell you much,
but it does confirm what you saw in Figure 7-25.

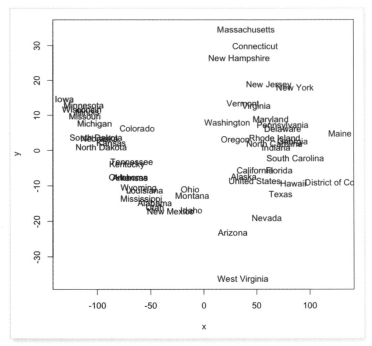

FIGURE 7-28 Using state names instead of dots to see where each state was placed

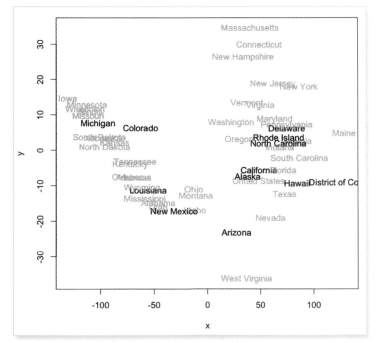

FIGURE 7-29 States colored by dropout rates

What about states colored by reading scores? Yeah, you can do that, too, as shown in Figure 7-30. Ah, it looks like there's a clear pattern there. High scores are on the left and lower scores are on the right? What makes Washington different? Look into that—you can tell me later.

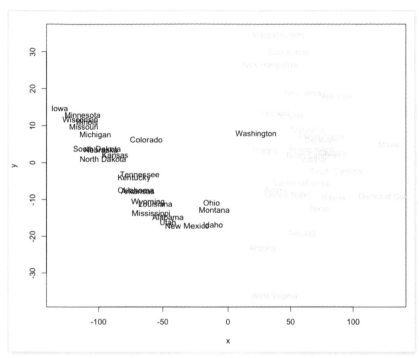

FIGURE 7-30 States colored by reading scores

If you want to be fancy, you can try something called model-based clustering. I'm not going to get into the details of it. I'll just show you how to do it, and you can take my word for it that we're not doing any magic here. There's actual math involved. Basically, use the mclust package to identify clusters in your MDS plot. Install mclust if you haven't already. Now run the following code for the plots in Figure 7-31.

```
library(mclust)
ed.mclust <- Mclust(ed.mds)
plot(ed.mclust, data=ed.mds)
```

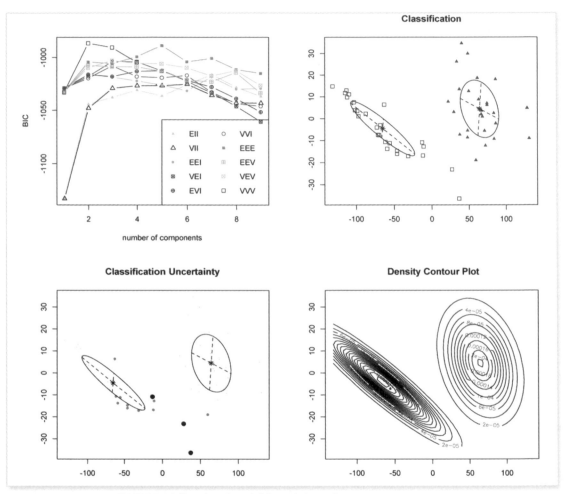

FIGURE 7-31 Results of model-based clustering

That first plot on the top left shows the results of running an algorithm to find the ideal number of clusters in the data. The remaining three plots show the clusters. Pretty awesome. You get the two clusters, now more well defined, showing high and low states.

This is usually when I tell you to bring your PDF files into Illustrator and apply some touchups, but I'm not so sure I'd ever publish these for a general audience. It's too abstract for the nontechnically minded to figure out what's going on. They're good for data exploration; however, if you were so inclined, all standard design principles apply. Figure out what you need to tell a clear story, and strip out the rest.

Searching for Outliers

Rather than looking for how units of data belong in certain groups, you should also be interested in how they don't belong in groups. That is, there will often be data points that stand out from the rest, which are called, you guessed it, *outliers*. These are data points that are different from the rest of the population. Sometimes they could be the most interesting part of your story, or they could just be boring typos with a missing zero. Either way, you need to check them out to see what's going on. You don't want to make a giant graphic on the premise of an outlier, only to find out later from a diligent reader that your hard work makes no sense.

Graphic types have been designed specifically to highlight outliers, but in my experience, nothing beats basic plots and common sense. Learn about the context of your data, do your homework, and ask experts about the data when you're not sure about something. Once you find the outliers, you can use the same graphical techniques that we've used so far to highlight them for readers: Use varied colors, provide pointers, or use thicker borders.

Now look at a simple example. Figure 7-32 shows a time series plot that shows weather data scraped from Weather Underground (like you did in Chapter 2, "Handling Data"), from 1980 to 2005. There are seasonal cycles like you'd expect, but what's going on in the middle? It seems to be unusually smooth, whereas the rest of the data has some noise. This is nothing to go crazy over, but if you happen to run weather models on this data, you might want to know what has been estimated and what's real data.

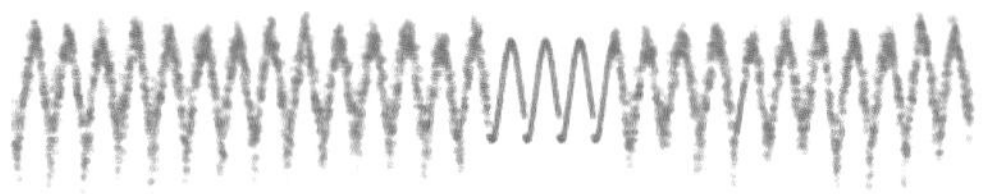

FIGURE 7-32 Estimated weather data from Weather Underground

Similarly, looking at the star charts you made that show crime, you can see the District of Columbia stands out. You could have seen this just as easily with a basic bar chart, as shown in Figure 7-33. Is it fair to compare Washington, DC to the states, considering it has more of a city makeup? You be the judge.

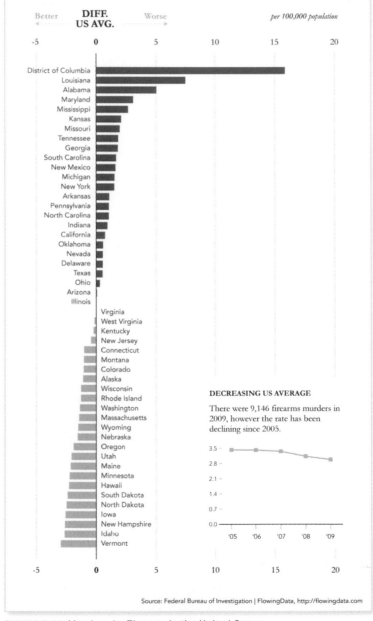

FIGURE 7-33 Murders by Firearm in the United States

How about the subscriber counts from Chapter 3, "Choosing Tools to Visualize Data," shown in Figure 7-34? There's that big dip in the middle where it looks like more than half of FlowingData's readership is lost.

You can also look at the distribution as a whole via a histogram, as shown in Figure 7-35. All counts are sitting on the right, except for a couple all the way to the left with nothing in the middle.

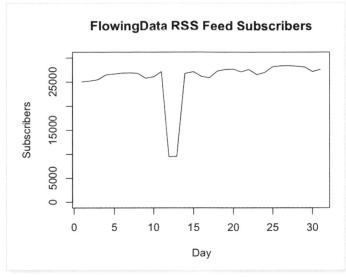

FIGURE 7-34 FlowingData subscriber counts over time

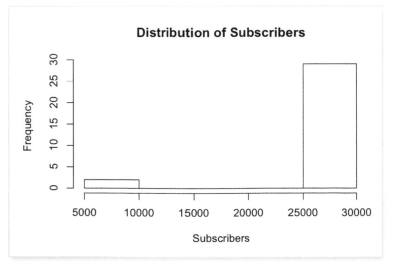

FIGURE 7-35 Histogram showing distribution of subscriber counts

More concretely, you can use a boxplot, which shows quartiles in a distribution. Boxplots generated in R with the `boxplot()` function can automatically highlight points that are more than 1.5 times more or less than the upper and lower quartiles, respectively (Figure 7-36).

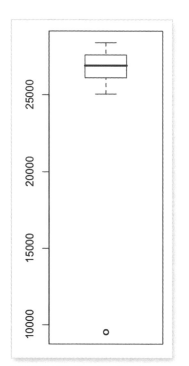

FIGURE 7-36 Boxplot showing distribution of subscriber counts

▶ A *quartile* is one of three points in a dataset, which marks quarter spots. The middle quartile is the median or the halfway point; the upper quartile marks the spot where 25 percent of the data is greater than that value; and the lower quartile marks the bottom 25 percent.

If I had a small number of subscribers in the single digits, then sure, such a big percentage-wise decrease could be possible, but it's unlikely that I said something so offensive to compel tens of thousands of readers to defect (and then come back a couple of days later). It's much more likely that Feedburner, the feed delivery service I use, made a reporting error.

These outliers in these datasets are obvious because you know a little bit about the data. It could be less obvious if you use datasets you're not familiar with. When that happens, it can be helpful to go directly to the source and just ask whoever is in charge. The person or group curating the data is usually happy that you're making use of it and will offer some quick advice. If you can't find out any more details, you can at least say you tried, and make a note of the ambiguity in your explanation of your graphic.

Wrapping Up

For beginners, one of the hardest parts to design data graphics is to figure out where to start. You have all this data in front of you without a clue about what it is or what to expect. Usually, you should start with a question about the data and work off of that question, but what if you don't know what to ask? The methods described in this chapter can help a lot with this. They help you see all the data at once, which makes it easier to figure out what part of the data to explore next.

However, don't stop here. Use these as jumping off points to narrow down to spots that look interesting. This, in addition to what previous chapters cover should be enough to help you dig deep into your data, no matter what type of data you deal with. Well, except for one. The next chapter covers one more data type: spatial data. Get ready to make some maps.

Visualizing Spatial Relationships

8

Maps are a subcategory of visualization that have the added benefit of being incredibly intuitive. Even as a kid, I could read them. I remember sitting in the passenger seat of my dad's car and sounding off directions as I read the fantastically big unfolded map laid out in front of me. An Australian lady with a robotic yet calming voice spits out directions from a small box on the dash nowadays.

In any case, maps are a great way to understand your data. They are scaled down versions of the physical world, and they're everywhere. In this chapter you dive into several spatial datasets, looking for patterns over space and time. You create some basic maps in R and then jump to more advanced mapping with Python and SVG. Finally, you round it up with interactive and animated maps in ActionScript and Flash.

What to Look For

You read maps much the same way that you read statistical graphics. When you look at specific locations on a map, you still look for clustering in specific regions or for example, compare one region to the rest of a country. The difference is that instead of x- and y-coordinates, you deal with latitude and longitude. The coordinates on a map actually relate to each other in the same way that one city relates to another. Point A and Point B are a specific number of miles away, and it takes an estimated time to get there. In contrast, the distance on a dot plot is abstract and (usually) has no units.

This difference brings with it a lot of subtleties to maps and cartography. There's a reason *The New York Times* has a group of people in its graphics department who exclusively design maps. You need to make sure all your locations are placed correctly, colors make sense, labels don't obscure locations, and that the right projection is used.

This chapter covers only a handful of the basics. These can actually take you pretty far in terms of finding stories in your data, but keep in mind there's a whole other level of awesome that you can strive for.

Things can get especially interesting when you introduce time. One map represents a slice in time, but you can represent multiple slices in time with several maps. You can also animate changes to, say, watch growth (or decline) of a business across a geographic region. Bursts in specific areas become obvious, and if the map is interactive, readers can easily focus in on their area to see how things have changed. You don't get the same effect with bar graphs or dot plots, but with maps, the data can become instantly personal.

Specific Locations

A list of locations is the easiest type of spatial data you'll come across. You have the latitude and longitude for a bunch places, and you want to map them. Maybe you want to show where events, such as crime, occurred, or you want to find areas where points are clustered. This is straightforward to do, and there are a lot of ways to do it.

On the web, the most common way to map points is via Google or Microsoft Maps. Using their mapping APIs, you can have an interactive map that you can zoom and pan in no time with just a few lines of JavaScript. Tons of tutorials and excellent documentation are online on how to make use of these APIs, so I'll leave that to you.

NOTE

Google and Microsoft provide super straightforward tutorials that start with their mapping APIs, so be sure to check those out if you're interested in taking advantage of some basic mapping functionality.

However, there is a downside. You can only customize the maps so much, and in the end you'll almost always end up with something that still looks like a Google or Microsoft map. I'm not saying they're ugly, but when you're developing an application or designing a graphic that fits into a publication, it's often more fitting to have a map that matches your design scheme. There are sometimes ways to get around these barriers, but it's not worth the effort if you can just do the same thing but better, with a different tool.

Find Latitude and Longitude

Before you do any mapping, consider the available data and the data that you actually need. If you don't have the data you need, then there's nothing to visualize, right? In most practical applications, you need latitude and longitude to map points, and most datasets don't come like that. Instead, you most likely will have a list of addresses.

As much as you might want to, you can't just plug in street names and postal codes and expect a pretty map. You have to get latitude and longitude first, and for that, turn to *geocoding*. Basically, you take an address, give it to a service, the service queries its database for matching addresses, and then you get latitude and longitude for where the service thinks your address is located in the world.

As for which service to use, well, there are many. If you have only a few locations to geocode, it's easy to just go to a website and manually enter them. Geocoder.us is a good free option for that. If you don't need your locations to be exact, you can try Pierre Gorissen's *Google Maps Latitude Longitude Popup*. It's a simple Google Maps interface that spits out latitude and longitude for anywhere you click on the map.

If, however, you have a lot of locations to geocode, then you should do it programmatically. You don't need to waste your time copying and pasting. Google, Yahoo!, Geocoder.us, and Mediawiki all provide APIs for gecoding; and Geopy, a geocoding toolbox for Python, wraps them all up into one package.

USEFUL GEOCODING TOOLS

- Geocoder.us, **http://geocoder.us**—Provides a straightforward interface to copy and paste location to get latitude and longitude. Also provides an API.
- Latitude Longitude Popup, **www.gorissen.info/Pierre/maps/**—Google Maps' mashup. Click a location on the map, and it gives you latitude and longitude.
- Geopy, **http://code.google.com/p/geopy/**—Geocoding toolbox for Python. Wraps up multiple geocoding APIs into a single package.

Visit the Geopy project page for instructions on how to install the package. There are also lots of straightforward examples on how to start. The following example assumes you have already installed the package on your computer.

After you install Geopy, download location data at `http://book.flowingdata` `.com/ch08/geocode/costcos-limited.csv`. This is a CSV file that contains the address of every Costco warehouse in the United States, but it doesn't have latitude or longitude coordinates. That's up to you.

Open a new file and save it as `geocode-locations.py`. As usual, import the packages that you need for the rest of the script.

```
from geopy import geocoders
import csv
```

You also need an API key for each service you want to use. For the purposes of this example, you only need one from Google.

Store your API key in a variable named g_api_key, and then use it when you instantiate the geocoder.

```
g_api_key = 'INSERT_YOUR_API_KEY_HERE'
g = geocoders.Google(g_api_key)
```

Load the `costcos-limited.csv` data file, and then loop. For each row, you piece together the full address and then plug it in for geocoding.

```
costcos = csv.reader(open('costcos-limited.csv'), delimiter=',')
next(costcos) # Skip header

# Print header
```

> **NOTE**
>
> Visit `http://code` `.google.com/apis/` `maps/signup.html` to sign up for a free API key for the Google Maps API. It's straightforward and takes only a couple of minutes.

```
print "Address,City,State,Zip Code,Latitude,Longitude"
for row in costcos:

    full_addy = row[1] + "," + row[2] + "," + row[3] + "," + row[4]
    place, (lat, lng) = list(g.geocode(full_addy, exactly_one=False))[0]
    print full_addy + "," + str(lat) + "," + str(lng)
```

That's it. Run the Python script, and save the output as costcos-geocoded.csv. Here's what the first few lines of the data looks like:

```
Address,City,State,Zip Code,Latitude,Longitude
1205 N. Memorial Parkway,Huntsville,Alabama,35801-5930,34.7430949,-86
.6009553
3650 Galleria Circle,Hoover,Alabama,35244-2346,33.377649,-86.81242
8251 Eastchase Parkway,Montgomery,Alabama,36117,32.363889,-86.150884
5225 Commercial Boulevard,Juneau,Alaska,99801-7210,58.3592,-134.483
330 West Dimond Blvd,Anchorage,Alaska,99515-1950,61.143266,-149.884217
...
```

Pretty cool. By some stroke of luck, latitude and longitude coordinates are found for every address. That usually doesn't happen. If you do run into that problem, you should add error checking at the second to last line of the preceding script.

```
    try:
        place, (lat, lng) = list(g.geocode(full_addy, exactly_one=False))
[0]
        print full_addy + "," + str(lat) + "," + str(lng)
    except:
        print full_addy + ",NULL,NULL"
```

This tries to find the latitude and longitude coordinates, and if it fails, it prints the row with the address and null coordinate values. Run the Python script and save the output as a file, and you can go back and look for the nulls. You can either try a different service for the missing addresses via Geopy, or you can just manually enter the addresses in Geocoder.us.

Just Points

Now that you have points with latitude and longitude, you can map them. The straightforward route is to do the computer equivalent of putting pushpins in a paper map on a billboard. As shown in the framework in Figure 8-1, you place a marker for each location on the map.

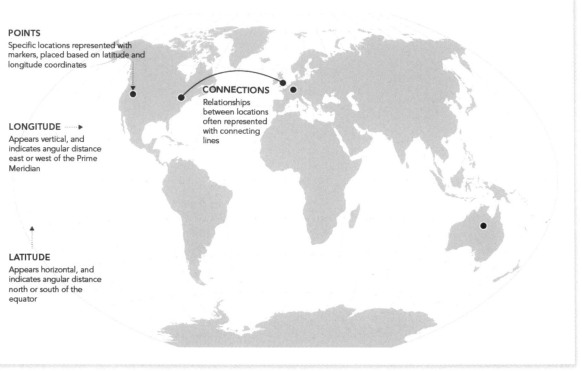

POINTS
Specific locations represented with markers, placed based on latitude and longitude coordinates

CONNECTIONS
Relationships between locations often represented with connecting lines

LONGITUDE ┈┈▶
Appears vertical, and indicates angular distance east or west of the Prime Meridian

LATITUDE
Appears horizontal, and indicates angular distance north or south of the equator

FIGURE 8-1 Mapping points framework

Although a simple concept, you can see features in the data such as clustering, spread, and outliers.

MAP WITH DOTS

R, although limited in mapping functionality, makes placing dots on a map easy. The maps package does most of the work. Go ahead and install it via the Package Installer, or use `install.packages()` in the console. When installed, load it into the workspace.

```
library(maps)
```

Next step: Load the data. Feel free to use the Costco locations that you just geocoded, or for convenience, I've put the processed dataset online, so you can load it directly from the URL.

```
costcos <-
  read.csv("http://book.flowingdata.com/ch08/geocode/costcos-geocoded
  .csv", sep=",")
```

Now on to mapping. When you create your maps, it's useful to think of them as layers (regardless of the software in use). The bottom layer is usually the base map that shows geographical boundaries, and then you place data layers on top of that. In this case the bottom layer is a map of the United States, and the second layer is Costco locations. Here's how to make the first layer, as shown in Figure 8-2.

```
map(database="state")
```

FIGURE 8-2 Plain map of the United States

The second layer, or Costco's, are then mapped with the symbols() function. This is the same function you used to make the bubble plots in Chapter 6, "Visualizing Relationships," and you use it in the same way, except you pass latitude and longitude instead of x- and y-coordinates. Also set *add* to *TRUE* to indicate that you want symbols to be added to the map rather than creating a new plot.

```
symbols(costcos$Longitude, costcos$Latitude,
    circles=rep(1, length(costcos$Longitude)), inches=0.05, add=TRUE)
```

Figure 8-3 shows the results. All the circles are the same size because you set *circles* to an array of ones with the length equal to the number of locations. You also set *inches* to 0.05, which sizes the circles to that number. If you want smaller markers, all you need to do is decrease that value.

FIGURE 8-3 Map of Costco locations

As before, you can change the colors of both the map and the circles so that the locations stand out and boundary lines sit in the background, as shown in Figure 8-4. Now change the dots to a nice Costco red and the state boundaries to a light gray.

```
map(database="state", col="#cccccc")
symbols(costcos$Longitude, costcos$Latitude, bg="#e2373f", fg="#ffffff",
  lwd=0.5, circles=rep(1, length(costcos$Longitude)),
  inches=0.05, add=TRUE)
```

FIGURE 8-4 Using color with mapped locations

In Figure 8-3, the unfilled circles and the map were all the same color and line width, so everything blended together, but with the right colors, you can make the data sit front and center.

It's not bad for a few lines of code. Costco has clearly focused on opening locations on the coasts with clusters in southern and northern California, northwest Washington, and in the northeast of the country.

However, there is a glaring omission here. Well, two of them actually. Where are Alaska and Hawaii? They're part of the United States, too, but are nowhere to be found even though you use the "state" database with map(). The two states are actually in the "world" database, so if you want to see Costco locations in Alaska in Hawaii, you need to map the entire world, as shown in Figure 8-5.

```
map(database="world", col="#cccccc")
symbols(costcos$Longitude, costcos$Latitude, bg="#e2373f", fg="#ffffff",
    lwd=0.3, circles=rep(1, length(costcos$Longitude)),
    inches=0.03, add=TRUE)
```

FIGURE 8-5 World map of Costco locations

It's a waste of space, I know. There are options that you can mess around with, which you can find in the documentation, but you can edit the rest in Illustrator to zoom in on the United States or remove the other countries from view.

> **TIP**
>
> With R, when in doubt, always jump to the documentation for the function or package you're stuck on by preceding the name with a question mark.

Taking the map in the opposite direction, say you want to only map Costco locations for a few states. You can do that with the *region* argument.

```
map(database="state", region=c("California", "Nevada", "Oregon",
    "Washington"), col="#cccccc")
symbols(costcos$Longitude, costcos$Latitude, bg="#e2373f", fg="#ffffff",
    lwd=0.5, circles=rep(1, length(costcos$Longitude)), inches=0.05,
    add=TRUE)
```

As shown in Figure 8-6, you create a bottom layer with California, Nevada, Oregon, and Mexico. Then you create the data layer on top of that. Some dots are not in any of those states, but they're in the plotting region, so they still appear. Again, it's trivial to remove those in your favorite vector editing software.

MAP WITH LINES

In some cases it could be useful to connect the dots on your map if the order of the points have any relevance. With online location services such as Foursquare growing in popularity, location traces aren't all that rare. An easy way to draw lines is, well, with the lines() function. To demonstrate, look at locations I traveled during my seven days and nights as a spy for the fake government of Fakesville. Start with loading the data (as usual) and drawing a base world map.

```
faketrace <-
    read.csv("http://book.flowingdata.com/ch08/points/fake-trace.txt",
    sep="\t")
map(database="world", col="#cccccc")
```

Take a look at the data frame by entering **faketrace** in your R console. You see that it's just two columns for latitude and longitude and eight data points. You can assume that the points are already in the order that I traveled during those long seven nights.

```
    latitude    longitude
1   46.31658     3.515625
2   61.27023    69.609375
3   34.30714   105.468750
4  -26.11599   122.695313
5  -30.14513    22.851563
6  -35.17381   -63.632813
7   21.28937   -99.492188
8   36.17336  -115.180664
```

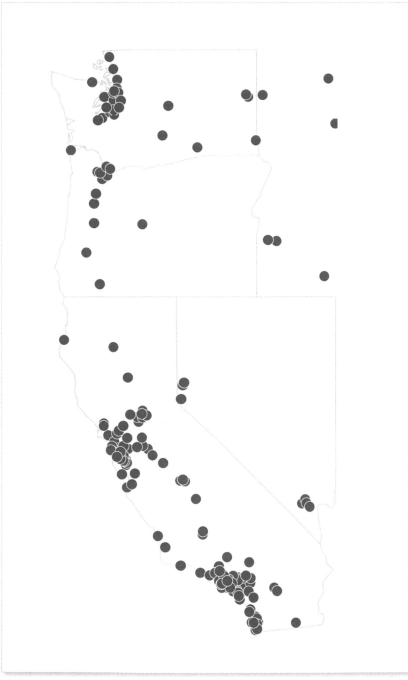

FIGURE 8-6 Costco locations in selected states

Draw the lines by simply plugging in the two columns into lines(). Also specify color (*col*) and line width (*lwd*).

```
lines(faketrace$longitude, faketrace$latitude, col="#bb4cd4", lwd=2)
```

Now also add dots, exactly like you just did with the Costco locations, for the graphic in Figure 8-7.

```
symbols(faketrace$longitude, faketrace$latitude, lwd=1, bg="#bb4cd4",
fg="#ffffff", circles=rep(1, length(faketrace$longitude)), inches=0.05,
add=TRUE)
```

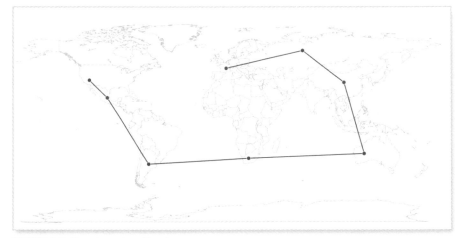

FIGURE 8-7 Drawing a location trace

After those seven days and nights as a spy for the Fakesville government, I decided it wasn't for me. It's just not as glamorous as James Bond makes it out to be. However, I did make connections in all the countries I visited. It could be interesting to draw lines from my location to all the others, as shown in Figure 8-8.

```
map(database="world", col="#cccccc")
for (i in 2:length(faketrace$longitude)-1) {
        lngs <- c(faketrace$longitude[8], faketrace$longitude[i])
        lats <- c(faketrace$latitude[8], faketrace$latitude[i])
        lines(lngs, lats, col="#bb4cd4", lwd=2)
}
```

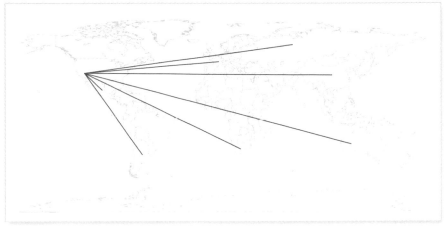

FIGURE 8-8 Drawing worldwide connections

After you create the base map, you can loop through each point and draw a line from the last point in the data frame to every other location. This isn't incredibly informative, but maybe you can find a good use for it. The point here is that you can draw a map and then use R's other graphics functions to draw whatever you want using latitude and longitude coordinates.

By the way, I wasn't actually a spy for Fakesville. I was just kidding about that.

Scaled Points

Switching gears back to real data and a more interesting topic than my fake spy escapades, more often than not, you don't just have locations. You also have another value attached to locations such as sales for a business or city population. You can still map with points, but you can take the principles of the bubble plot and use it on a map.

I don't have to explain how bubbles should be sized by area and not radius again, right? Okay, cool.

MAP WITH BUBBLES

In this example, look at adolescent fertility rate as reported by the United Nations Human Development Report—that is, the number of births per 1,000 women aged 15 to 19 in 2008. The geo-coordinates were provided by GeoCommons. You want to size bubbles in proportion to these rates.

The code is almost the same as when you mapped Costco locations, but remember you just passed a vector of ones for circle size in the symbols() function. Instead, we use the sqrt() of the rates to indicate size.

```
fertility <-
    read.csv("http://book.flowingdata.com/ch08/points/adol-fertility.csv")
map('world', fill = FALSE, col = "#cccccc")
symbols(fertility$longitude, fertility$latitude,
    circles=sqrt(fertility$ad_fert_rate), add=TRUE,
    inches=0.15, bg="#93ceef", fg="#ffffff")
```

FIGURE 8-9 Adolescent fertility rate worldwide

Figure 8-9 shows the output. Immediately, you should see that African countries tend to have the highest adolescent fertility rates, whereas European countries have relatively lower rates. From the graphic alone, it's not clear what value each circle represents because there is no legend. A quick look with summary() in R can tell you more.

```
summary(fertility$ad_fert_rate)
```

Min.	1st Qu.	Median	Mean	3rd Qu.	Max.	NA's
3.20	16.20	39.00	52.89	78.20	201.40	1.00

That's fine for us, an audience of one, but you need to explain more if you want others, who haven't looked at the data, to understand the graphic. You can add annotation to highlight countries with the highest and lowest fertility rates, point out the country where most readers will be from (in this case, the United States), and provide a lead-in to set up readers for what they're going to look at. Figure 8-10 shows these changes.

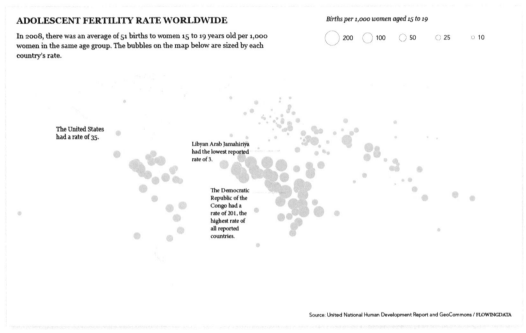

ADOLESCENT FERTILITY RATE WORLDWIDE

In 2008, there was an average of 51 births to women 15 to 19 years old per 1,000 women in the same age group. The bubbles on the map below are sized by each country's rate.

Births per 1,000 women aged 15 to 19

200   100   50   25   10

The United States had a rate of 35.

Libyan Arab Jamahiriya had the lowest reported rate of 3.

The Democratic Republic of the Congo had a rate of 201, the highest rate of all reported countries.

Source: United National Human Development Report and GeoCommons / FLOWINGDATA

FIGURE 8-10 Rates more clearly explained for a wider audience

Regions

Mapping points can take you only so far because they represent only single locations. Counties, states, countries, and continents are entire regions with boundaries, and geographic data is usually aggregated in this way. For example, it's much easier to find health data for a state or a country than it is for individual patients or hospitals. This is usually done for privacy, whereas other times aggregated data is just easier to distribute. In any case, this is usually how you're going to use your spatial data, so now learn to visualize it.

Color by Data

Choropleth maps are the most common way to map regional data. Based on some metric, regions are colored following a color scale that you define, as shown in Figure 8-11. The areas and location are already defined, so your job is to decide the appropriate color scales to use.

SHADED REGIONS
Areas on the map are shaded according to a color scheme. Darker regions usually indicate higher values.

FIGURE 8-11 Choropleth map framework

As touched on in a previous chapter, Cynthia Brewer's ColorBrewer is a great way to pick your colors, or at least a place to start to design a color palette. If you have continuous data, you might want a similarly continuous color scale that goes from light to dark, but all with the same hue (or multiple similar hues), as shown in Figure 8-12.

A diverging color scheme, as shown in Figure 8-13, might be good if your data has a two-sided quality to it, such as good and bad or above and below a threshold.

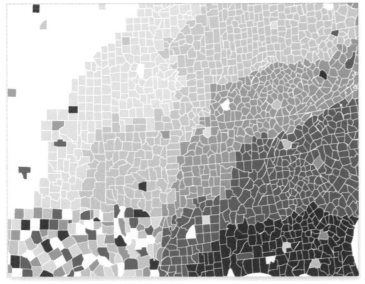

FIGURE 8-12 Sequential color schemes with ColorBrewer

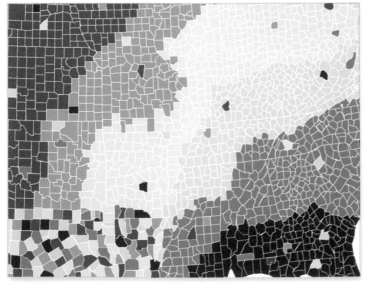

FIGURE 8-13 Diverging color schemes with ColorBrewer

Finally, if your data is qualitative with classes or categories, then you might want a unique color for each (Figure 8-14).

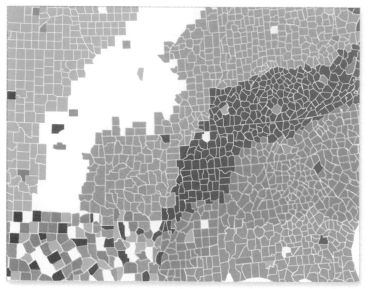

FIGURE 8-14 Qualitative color scheme with ColorBrewer

When you have your color scheme, you have two more things to do. The first is to decide how the colors you picked match up to the data range, and the second is to assign colors to each region based on your choice. You can do both with Python and Scalable Vector Graphics (SVG) in the following examples.

MAP COUNTIES

The U.S. Bureau of Labor Statistics provides county-level unemployment data every month. You can download the most recent rates or go back several years from its site. However, the data browser it provides is kind of outdated and roundabout, so for the sake of simplicity (and in case the BLS site changes), you can download the data at http://book.flowingdata.com/ ch08/regions/unemployment-aug2010.txt. There are six columns. The first is a code specific to the Bureau of Labor Statistics. The next two together are a unique id specifying county. The fourth and fifth columns are the county name and month the rate is an estimate of, respectively. The last column is the estimated percentage of people in the county who are unemployed. For the purposes of this example, you care only about the county id (that is, FIPS codes) and the rate.

Now for the map. In previous examples, you generated base maps in R, but now you can use Python and SVG to do this. The former is to process the data, and the latter is for the map itself. You don't need to start completely from scratch, though. You can get a blank map from Wikimedia Commons found here: http://commons.wikimedia.org/wiki/File:USA_Counties_with_FIPS_and_names.svg, as shown in Figure 8-15. The page links to the map in four sizes in PNG format and then one in SVG. You want the SVG one. Download the SVG file and save it as counties.svg, in the same directory that you save the unemployment data.

FIGURE 8-15 Blank U.S. county map from Wikimedia Commons

The important thing here, if you're not familiar with SVG, is that it's actually an XML file. It's text with tags, and you can edit it in a text editor like you would an HTML file. The browser or image viewer reads the XML, and the XML tells the browser what to show, such as the colors to use and shapes to draw.

TIP

SVG files are XML files, which are easy to change in a text editor. This also means that you can parse the SVG code to make changes programmatically.

To drive the point home, open the map SVG file in a text editor to see what you're dealing with. It's mostly SVG declarations and boiler plate stuff, which you don't totally care about right now.

Scroll down some more to start to see some `<path>` tags, as shown in Figure 8-16. All those numbers in a single tag specify the boundaries of a county. You're not going to touch those. You're interested in changing the fill color of each county to match the corresponding unemployment rate. To do that, you need to edit the *style* in the path.

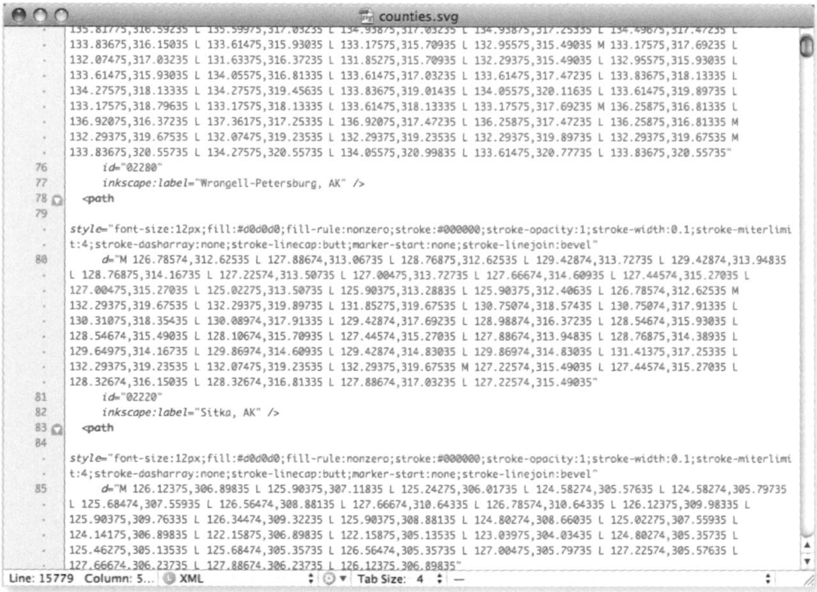

FIGURE 8-16 Paths specified in SVG file

Notice how each `<path>` starts with *style*? Those who have written CSS can immediately recognize this. There is a *fill* attribute followed by a hexadecimal color, so if you change that in the SVG file, you change the color of the output image. You could edit each one manually, but there are more than 3,000 counties. That would take way too long. Instead, come back to your old friend Beautiful Soup, the Python package that makes parsing XML and HTML relatively easy.

Open a blank file in the same directory as your SVG map and unemployment data. Save it as `colorize_svg.py`. You need to import the CSV data file and parse the SVG file with Beautiful Soup, so start by importing the necessary packages.

```
import csv
from BeautifulSoup import BeautifulSoup
```

Then open the CSV file and store it so that you can iterate through the rows using `csv.reader()`. Note that the "r" in the `open()` function just means that you want to open the file to read its contents, as opposed to writing new rows to it.

```
reader = csv.reader(open('unemployment-aug2010.txt', 'r'), delimiter=",")
```

Now also load the blank SVG county map.

```
svg = open('counties.svg', 'r').read()
```

Cool, you loaded everything you need to create a choropleth map. The challenge at this point is that you need to somehow link the data to the SVG. What is the commonality between the two? I'll give you a hint. It has to do with each county's unique id, and I mentioned it earlier. If you guessed FIPS codes, then you are correct!

Each path in the SVG file has a unique id, which happens to be the combined FIPS state and county FIPS code. Each row in the unemployment data has the state and county FIPS codes, too, but they're separate. For example, the state FIPS code for Autauga County, Alabama, is 01, and its county FIPS code is 001. The path id in the SVG are those two combined: 01001.

You need to store the unemployment data so that you can retrieve each county's rate by FIPS code, as we iterate through each path. If you start to become confused, stay with me; it'll be clearer with actual code. But the main point here is that the FIPS codes are the common bond between your SVG and CSV, and you can use that to your advantage.

> **TIP**
>
> Paths in SVG files, geographic ones in particular, usually have a unique id. It's not always FIPS code, but the same rules apply.

To store the unemployment data so that it's easily accessible by FIPS code later, use a construct in Python called a dictionary. It enables you to store and retrieve values by a keyword. In this case, your keyword is a combined state and county FIPS code, as shown in the following code.

```
unemployment = {}
min_value = 100; max_value = 0
for row in reader:
```

```
try:
    full_fips = row[1] + row[2]
    rate = float( row[8].strip() )
    unemployment[full_fips] = rate
except:
    pass
```

Next parse the SVG file with BeautifulSoup. Most tags have an opening and closing tag, but there are a couple of self-closing tags in there, which you need to specify. Then use the findAll() function to retrieve all the paths in the map.

```
soup = BeautifulSoup(svg, selfClosingTags=['defs','sodipodi:namedview'])
paths = soup.findAll('path')
```

Then store the colors, which I got from ColorBrewer, in a Python list. This is a sequential color scheme with multiple hues ranging from purple to red.

```
colors = ["#F1EEF6", "#D4B9DA", "#C994C7", "#DF65B0", "#DD1C77", "#980043"]
```

You're getting close to the climax. Like I said earlier, you're going to change the style attribute for each path in the SVG. You're just interested in fill color, but to make things easier, you can replace the entire style instead of parsing to replace only the color. I changed the hexadecimal value after stroke to #ffffff, which is white. This changes the borders to white instead of the current gray.

```
path_style = 'font-size:12px;fill-rule:nonzero;stroke:#fffff;stroke-
opacity:1;stroke-width:0.1;stroke-miterlimit:4;stroke-
dasharray:none;stroke-linecap:butt;marker-start:none;stroke-
linejoin:bevel;fill:'
```

I also moved fill to the end and left the value blank because that's the part that depends on each county's unemployment rate.

Finally, you're ready to change some colors! You can iterate through each path (except for state boundary lines and the separator for Hawaii and Alaska) and color accordingly. If the unemployment rate is greater than 10, use a darker shade, and anything less than 2 has the lightest shade.

```
for p in paths:

    if p['id'] not in ["State_Lines", "separator"]:
        # pass
```

```
try:
    rate = unemployment[p['id']]
except:
    continue

if rate > 10:
    color_class = 5
elif rate > 8:
    color_class = 4
elif rate > 6:
    color_class = 3
elif rate > 4:
    color_class = 2
elif rate > 2:
    color_class = 1
else:
    color_class = 0

color = colors[color_class]
p['style'] = path_style + color
```

The last step is to print out the SVG file with prettify(). The function converts your soup to a string that your browser can interpret.

```
print soup.prettify()
```

Now all that's left to do is run the Python script and save the output as a new SVG file named, say, colored_map.svg (Figure 8-17).

▶ You can grab the script in its entirety here:
http://book
.flowingdata.com/
ch08/regions/
colorize_svg
.py.txt

FIGURE 8-17 Running Python script and saving output as a new SVG file

Open your brand spanking new choropleth map in Illustrator or a modern browser such as Firefox, Safari, or Chrome to see the fruits of your labor, as shown in Figure 8-18. It's easy to see now where in the country there were higher unemployment rates during August 2010. Obviously a lot of the west coast and much of the southeast had higher rates, as did Alaska and Michigan. There are a lot of counties in middle America with relatively lower unemployment rates.

With the hard part of this exercise done, you can customize your map to your heart's content. You can edit the SVG file in Illustrator, change border colors and sizes, and add annotation to make it a complete graphic for a larger audience. (Hint: It still needs a legend.)

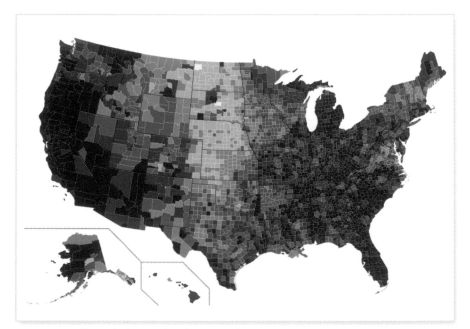

FIGURE 8-18 Choropleth map showing unemployment rates

The best part is that the code is reusable, and you can apply it to other datasets that use the FIPS code. Or even with this same dataset, you can mess around with color scheme to design a map that fits with the theme of your data.

Depending on your data, you can also change the thresholds for how to color each region. The examples so far used equal thresholds where regions were colored with six shades, and every 2 percentage points was a new class. Every county with an unemployment rate greater than 10 percent was one class; then counties with rates between 8 and 10, then 6 and 8, and so forth. Another common way to define thresholds is by quartiles, where you use four colors, and each color represents a quarter of the regions.

For example, the lower, middle, and upper quartiles for these unemployment rates are 6.9, 8.7, and 10.8 percent, respectively. This means that a quarter of the counties have rates below 6.9 percent, another quarter between 6.9 and 8.7, one between 8.7 and 10.8, and the last quarter is greater than 10.8 percent. To do this, change the colors list in your script to something like the following. It's a purple color scheme, with one shade per quarter.

```python
colors = ["#f2f0f7", "#cbc9e2", "#9e9ac8", "#6a51a3"]
```

Then modify the color conditions in the for loop, using the preceding quartiles.

```python
        if rate > 10.8:
            color_class = 3
        elif rate > 8.7:
            color_class = 2
        elif rate > 6.9:
            color_class = 1
        else:
            color_class = 0
```

Run the script and save like before, and you get Figure 8-19. Notice how there are more counties colored lightly.

To increase the usability of your code, you can calculate quartiles programmatically instead of hard-coding them. This is straightforward in Python. You store a list of your values, sort them from least to greatest, and find the values at the one-quarter, one-half, and three-quarters marks. More concretely, as it pertains to this example, you can modify the first loop in colorize_svg.py to store just unemployment rates.

```python
unemployment = {}
rates_only = [] # To calculate quartiles
min_value = 100; max_value = 0; past_header = False
for row in reader:
    if not past_header:
```

```
            past_header = True
            continue

    try:
        full_fips = row[1] + row[2]
        rate = float( row[5].strip() )
        unemployment[full_fips] = rate
        rates_only.append(rate)
    except:
        pass
```

Then you can sort the array, and find the quartiles.

```
# Quartiles
rates_only.sort()
q1_index = int( 0.25 * len(rates_only) )
q1 = rates_only[q1_index]      # 6.9

q2_index = int( 0.5 * len(rates_only) )
q2 = rates_only[q2_index]      # 8.7

q3_index = int( 0.75 * len(rates_only) )
q3 = rates_only[q3_index]      # 10.8
```

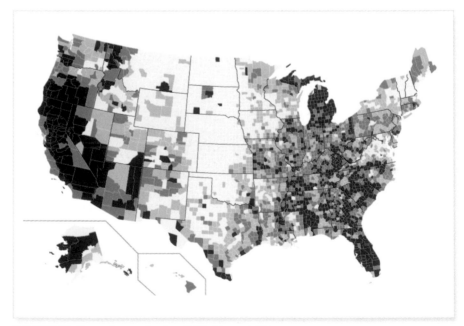

FIGURE 8-19 Unemployment rates divided by quartiles

Instead of hard-coding the values 6.9, 8.7, and 10.8 in your code, you can replace those values with *q1*, *q2*, and *q3*, respectively. The advantage of calculating the values programmatically is that you can reuse the code with a different dataset just by changing the CSV file.

Which color scale you choose depends on that data you have and what message you want to convey. For this particular dataset, I prefer the linear scale because it represents the distribution better and highlights the relatively high unemployment rates across the country. Working from Figure 8-18, you can add a legend, a title, and a lead-in paragraph for a more finalized graphic, as shown in Figure 8-20.

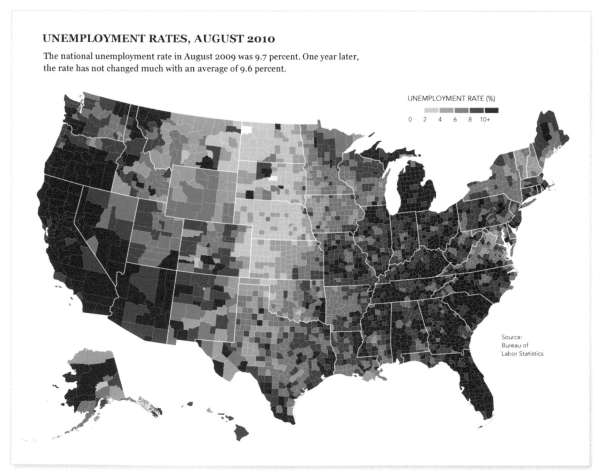

UNEMPLOYMENT RATES, AUGUST 2010

The national unemployment rate in August 2009 was 9.7 percent. One year later, the rate has not changed much with an average of 9.6 percent.

UNEMPLOYMENT RATE (%)

0   2   4   6   8   10+

Source:
Bureau of
Labor Statistics

FIGURE 8-20 Finished map with title, lead-in, and legend

TIP

World Bank is one of the most complete resources for country-specific demographic data. I usually go here first.

MAP COUNTRIES

The process to color counties in the previous example isn't exclusive to these regions. You can use the same steps to color states or countries. All you need is an SVG file with unique ids for each region you want to color (which are easily accessible on Wikipedia) and data with ids to match. Now try this out with open data from the World Bank.

Look at percentages of urban populations with access to an improved water source, by country, in 2008. You can download the Excel file from the World Bank data site here: `http://data.worldbank.org/indicator/SH.H2O.SAFE.UR.ZS/countries`. For convenience, you can also download the stripped down data as a CSV file here: Full URL is: `http://book.flowingdata.com/ch08/worldmap/water-source1.txt`. There are some countries with missing data, which is common with country-level data. I've removed those rows from the CSV file.

There are seven columns. The first is the country name; the second is a country code (could this be your unique id?); and the last five columns are percentages for 1990 to 2008.

For the base map, again go to Wikipedia. You can find a lot of versions when you search for the SVG world map, but use the one found here: `http://en.wikipedia.org/wiki/File:BlankMap-World6.svg`. Download the full resolution SVG file, and save it in the same directory as your data. As shown in Figure 8-21, it's a blank world map, colored gray with white borders.

FIGURE 8-21 Blank world map

Open the SVG file in a text editor. It is of course all text formatted as XML, but it's formatted slightly differently than your counties example. Paths don't have useful ids and the *style* attribute is not used. The paths do, however, have classes that look like country codes. They have only two letters, though. The country codes used in the World Bank data have three letters.

According to World Bank documentation, it uses ISO 3166-1 alpha 3 codes. The SVG file from Wikipedia, on the other hand, uses ISO 3166-1 alpha 2 codes. The names are horrible, I know, but don't worry; you don't have to remember that. All you need to know is that Wikipedia provides a conversion chart at http://en.wikipedia.org/wiki/ISO_3166-1. I copied and pasted the table into Excel and then saved the important bits as a text file. It has one column for the alpha 2 and another for the alpha 3. Download it here: http://book.flowingdata.com/ch08/worldmap/country-codes.txt. Use this chart to switch between the two codes.

As for styling each country, take a slightly different route to do that, too. Instead of changing attributes directly in the path tags, use CSS *outside* of the paths to color the regions. Now jump right in.

Create a file named generate_css.py in the same directory as the SVG and CSV files. Again, import the CSV package to load the data in the CSV files with the country codes and water access percentages.

```
import csv
codereader = csv.reader(open('country-codes.txt', 'r'), delimiter="\t")
waterreader = csv.reader(open('water-source1.txt', 'r'), delimiter="\t")
```

Then store the country codes so that it's easy to switch from alpha 3 to alpha 2.

```
alpha3to2 = {}
i = 0
next(codereader)
for row in codereader:

    alpha3to2[row[1]] = row[0]
```

This stores the codes in a Python dictionary where alpha 3 is the key and alpha 2 is the value.

Now like in your previous example, iterate through each row of the water data and assign a color based on the value for the current country.

```
i = 0
next(waterreader)
for row in waterreader:

    if row[1] in alpha3to2 and row[6]:
        alpha2 = alpha3to2[row[1]].lower()
        pct = int(row[6])
        if pct == 100:
            fill = "#08589E"
        elif pct > 90:
            fill = "#08589E"
        elif pct > 80:
            fill = "#4EB3D3"
        elif pct > 70:
            fill = "#7BCCC4"
        elif pct > 60:
            fill = "#A8DDB5"
        elif pct > 50:
            fill = "#CCEBC5"
        else:
            fill = "#EFF3FF"
        print '.' + alpha2 + ' { fill: ' + fill + ' }'

    i += 1
```

This part of the script executes the following steps:

1. Skip the header of the CSV.

2. It starts the loop to iterate over water data.

3. If there is a corresponding alpha 2 code to the alpha 3 from the CSV, and there is data available for the country in 2008, it finds the matching alpha 2.

4. Based on the percentage, an appropriate fill color is chosen.

5. A line of CSS is printed for each row of data.

Run generate_css.py and save the output as **style.css**. The first few rows of the CSS will look like this:

```
.af { fill: #7BCCC4 }
.al { fill: #08589E }
```

```
.dz { fill: #4EB3D3 }
.ad { fill: #08589E }
.ao { fill: #CCEBC5 }
.ag { fill: #08589E }
.ar { fill: #08589E }
.am { fill: #08589E }
.aw { fill: #08589E }
.au { fill: #08589E }
...
```

This is standard CSS. The first row, for example, changes the fill color of all paths with class .af to #7BCCC4.

Open style.css in your text editor and copy all the contents. Then open the SVG map and paste the contents at approximately line 135, below the brackets for *.oceanxx*. You just created a choropleth map of the world colored by the percentage of population with access to an improved water source, as shown in Figure 8-22. The darkest blue indicates 100 percent, and the lightest shades of green indicate lower percentages. Countries that are still gray indicate countries where data was not available.

FIGURE 8-22 Choropleth world map showing access to improved water source

The best part is that you can now download almost any dataset from the World Bank (and there are a lot of them) and create a choropleth map fairly quickly just by changing a few lines of code. To spruce up the graphic in Figure 8-22, again, you can open the SVG file in Illustrator and edit away. Mainly, the map needs a title and a legend to indicate what each shade means, as shown in Figure 8-23.

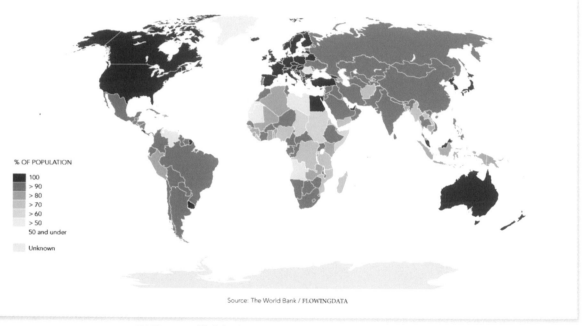

FIGURE 8-23 Finished world map

Over Space and Time

The examples so far enable you to visualize a lot of data types, whether it be qualitative or quantitative. You can vary colors, categories, and symbols to fit the story you're trying to tell; annotate your maps to highlight specific regions or features; and aggregate to zoom in on counties or countries.

But wait, there's more! You don't have to stop there. If you incorporate another dimension of data, you can see changes over both time and space.

In Chapter 4, "Visualizing Patterns over Time," you visualized time more abstractly with lines and plots, which is useful, but when location is attached to your data, it can be more intuitive to see the patterns and changes with maps. It's easier to see clustering or groups of regions that are near in physical distance.

The best part is that you can incorporate what you've already learned to visualize your data over space and time.

Small Multiples

You saw this technique in Chapter 6, "Visualizing Relationships," to visualize relationships across categories, and it can be applied to spatial data, too, as shown in Figure 8-24. Instead of small bar graphs, you can use small maps, one map for each slice of time. Line them up left to right or stack them top to bottom, and it's easy for your eyes to follow the changes.

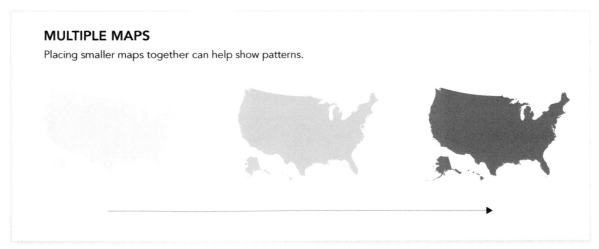

MULTIPLE MAPS
Placing smaller maps together can help show patterns.

FIGURE 8-24 Small multiples with maps

For example, in late 2009, I designed a graphic that showed unemployment rates by county (Figure 8-25). I actually used a variation of the code you just saw in the previous section, but I applied it to several slices of time.

FIGURE 8-25 Unemployment rates from 2004 to 2009

It's easy to see the changes, or lack thereof, by year, from 2004 through 2006, as shown in Figure 8-26. The national average actually went down during that time.

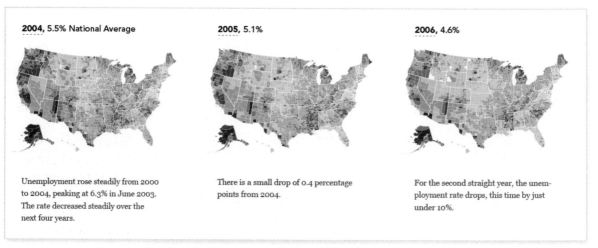

FIGURE 8-26 Unemployment rates 2004 to 2006

Then 2008 hits (Figure 8-27), and you start to see some of the increases in the unemployment rate, especially in California, Oregon, and Michigan, and some counties in the southeast.

Fast forward to 2009, and there is a clear difference, as shown in Figure 8-28. The national average increased 4 percentage points and the county colors become very dark.

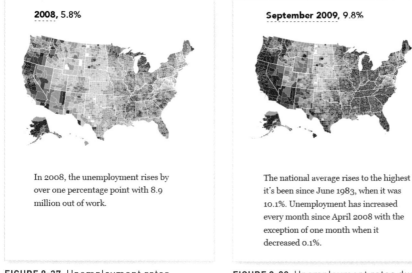

2008, 5.8%

In 2008, the unemployment rises by over one percentage point with 8.9 million out of work.

September 2009, 9.8%

The national average rises to the highest it's been since June 1983, when it was 10.1%. Unemployment has increased every month since April 2008 with the exception of one month when it decreased 0.1%.

FIGURE 8-27 Unemployment rates in 2008

FIGURE 8-28 Unemployment rates during September 2009

This was one of the most popular graphics I posted on FlowingData because it's easy to see that dramatic change after several years of relative standstill. I also used the OpenZoom Viewer, which enables you to zoom in on high-resolution images, so you can focus on your own area to see how it changed.

I could have also visualized the data as a time series plot, where each line represented a county; however, there are more than 3,000 U.S. counties. The plot would have felt cluttered, and unless it was interactive, you would not be able to tell which line represented which county.

▶ When high-resolution images are too big to display on a single monitor, it can be useful to put the image in OpenZoom Viewer (http://openzoom.org) so that you can see the picture and then zoom in on the details.

Take the Difference

You don't always need to create multiple maps to show changes. Sometimes it makes more sense to visualize actual differences in a single map. It saves space, and it highlights changes instead of single slices in time, as shown in Figure 8-29.

DIFFERENCES

Focus on changes instead of slices of time.

FIGURE 8-29 Focusing on change

If you were to download urban population counts from the World Bank, you'd have similar data to the previous example using access to improved water. Each row is a country, and each column is a year. However, the urban population data is raw counts for an estimated number of people in the country living in urban areas. A choropleth map of these counts would inevitably highlight larger countries because they of course have larger populations in general. Two maps to show the difference in urban population between 2005 and 2009 wouldn't be useful unless you changed the values to proportions. To do that, you'd have to download population data for 2005 and 2009 in all countries and then do some simple math. It's not all that hard to do that, but it's an extra step. Plus, if the changes are subtle, they'll be hard to see across multiple maps.

Instead, you can take the difference and show it in a single map. You can easily calculate this in Excel or modify the previous Python script, and then make a single map, as shown in Figure 8-30.

It's easy to see which countries changed the most and which ones changed the least when you visualize the differences. In contrast, Figure 8-31 shows the proportion of each country's total population that lived in an urban area in 2005.

FIGURE 8-30 Change in urban population from 2005 to 2009

FIGURE 8-31 Proportion of people living in an urban area in 2005

Figure 8-32 shows the same data for 2009. It looks similar to Figure 8-31, and you can barely notice a difference.

For this particular example, it's clear that the single map is more informative. You have to do a lot less work mentally to decipher the changes. It's obvious that although many countries in Africa have a relatively lower percentage of their population living in urban areas compared to the rest of the world, they have also changed the most in recent years.

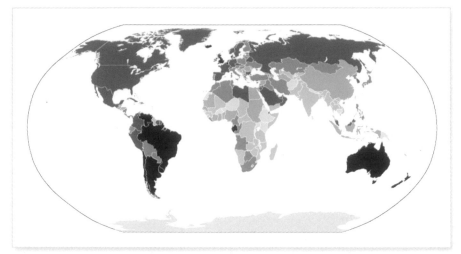

FIGURE 8-32 Proportion of people living in an urban area in 2009

Remember to add a legend, source, and title if your graphic is for a wider audience, as shown in Figure 8-33.

FIGURE 8-33 Annotated map of differences

Animation

One of the more obvious ways to visualize changes over space and time is to animate your data. Instead of showing slices in time with individual maps, you can show the changes as they happen on a single interactive map. This keeps the intuitiveness of the map, while allowing readers to explore the data on their own.

A few years ago, I designed a map that shows the growth of Walmart across the United States, as shown in Figure 8-34. The animation starts with the fist store that opened in 1962 in Rogers, Arkansas, and then moves through 2010. For each new store that opened up, another dot appears on the map. The growth is slow at first, and then Walmarts spread across the country almost like a virus. It keeps growing and growing, with bursts in areas where the company makes large acquisitions. Before you know it, Walmart is everywhere.

▶ View the Wal-mart map in its entirety at http:// datafl.ws/197.

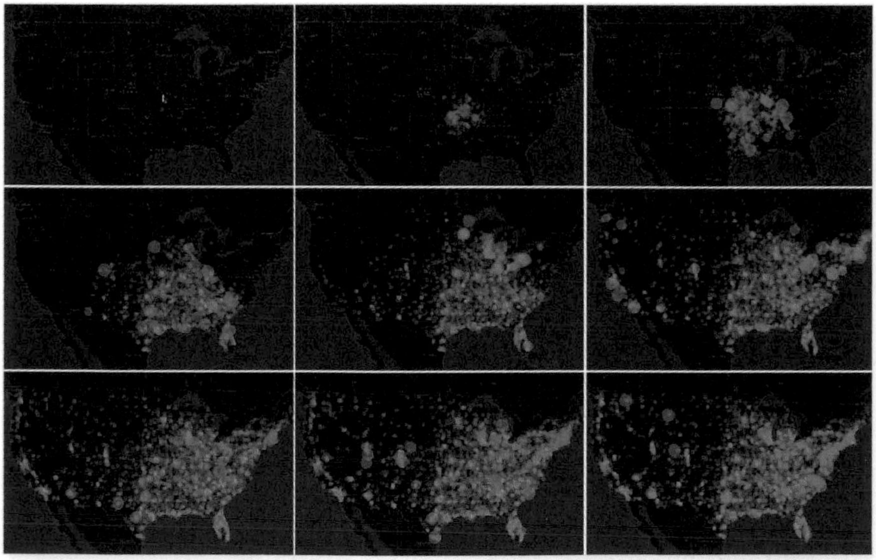

FIGURE 8-34 Animated map showing growth of Walmart stores

At the time, I was just trying to learn Flash and ActionScript, but the map was shared across the web and has been viewed millions of times. I later created a similar map showing the growth of Target (Figure 8-35), and it was equally well spread.

▶ You can watch the growth of Target stores at http://datafl .ws/198.

FIGURE 8-35 Animated map showing growth of Target stores

People have been so interested for two main reasons. The first is that the animated map enables you to see patterns that you wouldn't see with a time series plot. A regular plot would show only the number of store openings per year, which is fine if that's the story you want to tell, but the animated maps show growth that's more organic, especially with the Walmart one.

The second reason is that the map is immediately understandable to a general audience. When the animation starts, you know what you're seeing. I'm not saying there isn't value in visualization that takes time to interpret; it's often the opposite. However, there's a low time threshold for the web, so because the map is intuitive (and that people can zoom in on their own local areas) certainly helped the eager sharing.

CREATE AN ANIMATED GROWTH MAP

▶ Download Modest Maps at http:// modestmaps.com.

In this example, you create the Walmart growth map in ActionScript. You use Modest Maps, an ActionScript mapping library to provide interaction and the base map. The rest you code yourself. Download the complete source code at http://book.flowingdata.com/ch08/Openings_src.zip. Instead of going through every line and file, you'll look at just the important bits in this section.

As in Chapter 5, "Visualizing Proportions," when you create a stacked area chart with ActionScript and the Flare visualization toolkit, I highly recommend you use Adobe Flex Builder. It makes ActionScript a lot easier and keeps your code organized. You can of course still code everything in a standard text editor, but Flex Builder wraps up the editor, debugging, and compiling into one package. This example assumes you do have Flex Builder, but you are of course welcome to grab an ActionScript 3 compiler from the Adobe site.

To begin, open Flex Builder 3, and right-click the left sidebar, which shows the current list of projects. Select Import, as shown in Figure 8-36.

NOTE

Adobe Flex Builder was recently changed to Adobe Flash Builder. There are small differences between the two, but you can use either.

▶ Download the growth map code in its entirety at http://book .flowingdata.com/ ch08/Openings_src .zip to follow along in this example.

FIGURE 8-36 Import ActionScript project

Select Existing Projects Into Workspace, as shown in Figure 8-37.

Then, as shown in Figure 8-38, browse to the directory in which you saved the code. The Openings project should appear after selecting the root directory.

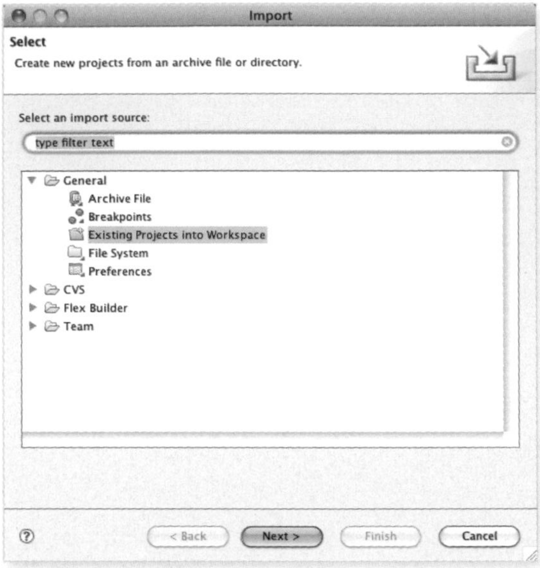

FIGURE 8-37 Existing project

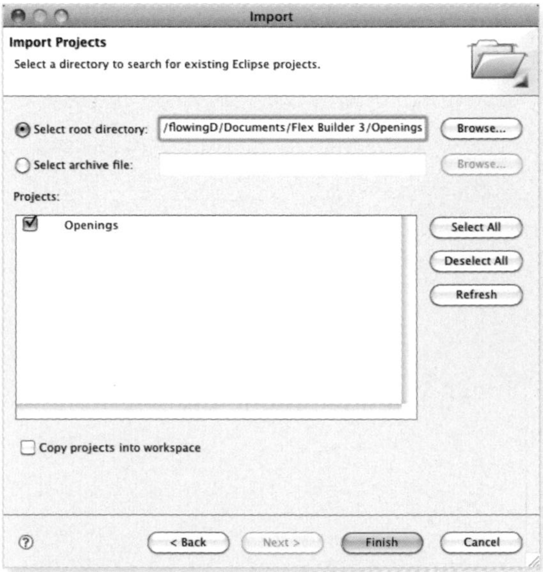

FIGURE 8-38 Import Openings project

Your workspace in Flex Builder should look similar to Figure 8-39.

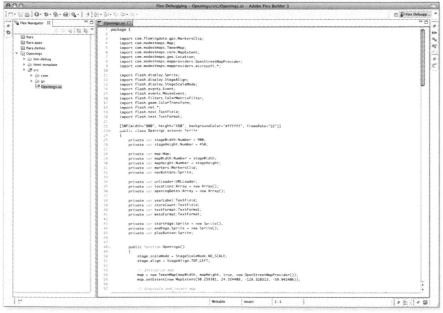

FIGURE 8-39 Workspace after importing project

All of the code is in the src folder. This includes Modest Maps in the com folder and TweenFilterLite in the gs folder, which help with transitions.

With the Openings project imported, you're ready to start building the map. Do this in two parts. In the first part create an interactive base map. In the second add the markers.

Add the Interactive Base Map

In Openings.as, the first lines of code import the necessary packages.

```
import com.modestmaps.Map;
import com.modestmaps.TweenMap;
import com.modestmaps.core.MapExtent;
import com.modestmaps.geo.Location;
import com.modestmaps.mapproviders.OpenStreetMapProvider;

import flash.display.Sprite;
import flash.display.StageAlign;
import flash.display.StageScaleMode;
```

```
import flash.events.Event;
import flash.events.MouseEvent;
import flash.filters.ColorMatrixFilter;
import flash.geom.ColorTransform;
import flash.text.TextField;
import flash.net.*;
```

The first section imports classes from the Modest Maps package, whereas the second section imports display objects and event classes provided by Flash. The name of each class isn't important right now. That becomes clear as you use them. However, the naming pattern for the first section matches the directory structure, starting with com, then modestmaps, and ending with Map. This is how you import classes most of the time when you write your own ActionScript.

Above public class Openings extends Sprite, several variables—width, height, background color, and frame rate—of the compiled Flash file are initialized.

```
[SWF(width="900", height="450", backgroundColor="#ffffff",
frameRate="32")]
```

Then after the class declaration, you need to specify some variables and initialize a Map object.

```
private var stageWidth:Number = 900;
private var stageHeight:Number = 450;
private var map:Map;
private var mapWidth:Number = stageWidth;
private var mapHeight:Number = stageHeight;
```

In between the brackets of the Openings() function, you can now create your first interactive map with Modest Maps.

```
stage.scaleMode = StageScaleMode.NO_SCALE;
stage.align = StageAlign.TOP_LEFT;

// Initialize map
map = new TweenMap(mapWidth, mapHeight, true, new
OpenStreetMapProvider());
map.setExtent(new MapExtent(50.259381, 24.324408, -128.320313,
-59.941406));
addChild(map);
```

Like in Illustrator, you can think of the full interactive as a bunch of layers. In ActionScript and Flash, the first layer is the stage. You set it to not scale objects when you zoom in on it, and you align the stage in the top left. Next you initialize the map with the *mapWidth* and *mapHeight* that you specified in the variables, turn on interaction, and use map tiles from OpenStreetMap. By setting the map extent to the preceding code, you frame the map around the United States.

The coordinates in MapExtent() are latitude and longitude which set the bounding box for what areas of the world to show. The first and third numbers are latitude and longitude for the top left corner, and the second and fourth numbers are latitude and longitude for the bottom right.

Finally, add the map (with addChild()) to the stage. Figure 8-40 shows the result when you compile the code without adding any filters to the map. You can either press the Play button in the top left of Flex Builder, or from the main menu, you can select Run ➪ Run Openings.

FIGURE 8-40 Plain map using OpenStreetMap tiles

When you run Openings, the result should pop up in your default browser. There's nothing on it yet, but you can click-and-drag, which is kind of cool. Also if you prefer a different set of map tiles, you can use the Microsoft road map (Figure 8-41) or Yahoo! hybrid map (Figure 8-42).

FIGURE 8-41 Plain map with Microsoft road map

► You can also use your own tiles if you want. There's a good tutorial on the Modest Maps site.

FIGURE 8-42 Plain map with Yahoo! hybrid map

► See the Adobe reference for more on how to use color matrices to customize objects in ActionScript at `http://livedocs .adobe.com/flash/ 9.0/ActionScript LangRefV3/flash/ filters/Color MatrixFilter .html`.

You can also experiment with the colors of the map by applying filters. You could for example, change the map to grayscale by placing the following under the code you just wrote. The mat array is of length 20 and takes values from 0 to 1. Each value represents how much red, green, blue and alpha each pixel gets.

```
var mat:Array = [0.24688,0.48752,0.0656,0,44.7,0.24688,0.48752,
    0.0656,0,44.7,0.24688,0.48752,0.0656,0,44.7,0,0,0,1,0];
var colorMat:ColorMatrixFilter = new ColorMatrixFilter(mat);
map.grid.filters = [colorMat];
```

As shown in Figure 8-43, the map is all gray, which can be useful to high-light the data that you plan to overlay on top of the map. The map serves as background instead of battling for attention.

FIGURE 8-43 Grayscale map after applying filter

You can also invert the colors with a color transform.

```
map.grid.transform.colorTransform =
    new ColorTransform(-1,-1,-1,1,255,255,255,0);
```

This turns white to black and black to white, as shown in Figure 8-44.

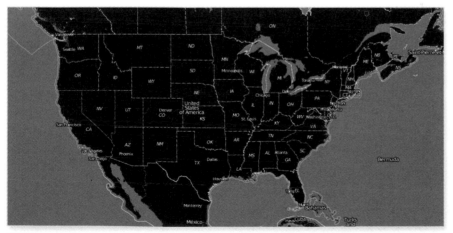

FIGURE 8-44 Black and white map after inverting colors with transform

To create zooming buttons, first write a function to make buttons. You'd think that there would be a quick default way to do this by now, but it still takes a handful of code to get the job done. The function definition of makeButton() is at the bottom of the Openings class.

```
public function makeButton(clip:Sprite, name:String, labelText:String,
action:Function):Sprite
{
    var button:Sprite = new Sprite();
    button.name = name;
    clip.addChild(button);

    var label:TextField = new TextField();
    label.name = 'label';
    label.selectable = false;
    label.textColor = 0xffffff;
    label.text = labelText;
    label.width = label.textWidth + 4;
    label.height = label.textHeight + 3;
    button.addChild(label);

    button.graphics.moveTo(0, 0);
    button.graphics.beginFill(0xFDBB30, 1);
    button.graphics.drawRect(0, 0, label.width, label.height);
    button.graphics.endFill();

    button.addEventListener(MouseEvent.CLICK, action);
    button.useHandCursor = true;
    button.mouseChildren = false;
    button.buttonMode = true;

    return button;
}
```

Then create another function that makes use of the function and draws the buttons you want. The following code creates two buttons using makeButton()—one for zooming in and the other for zooming out. It puts them at the bottom left of your map.

```
// Draw navigation buttons
private function drawNavigation():void
{
    // Navigation buttons (zooming)
```

```
    var buttons:Array = new Array();
    navButtons = new Sprite();
    addChild(navButtons);
    buttons.push(makeButton(navButtons, 'plus', '+', map.zoomIn));
    buttons.push(makeButton(navButtons, 'minus', '-', map.zoomOut));
    var nextX:Number = 0;
    for(var i:Number = 0; i < buttons.length; i++) {
        var currButton:Sprite = buttons[i];
        Sprite(buttons[i]).scaleX = 3;
        Sprite(buttons[i]).scaleY = 3;
        Sprite(buttons[i]).x = nextX;
        nextX += 3*Sprite(buttons[i]).getChildByName('label').width;
    }
    navButtons.x = 2; navButtons.y = map.height-navButtons.height-2;
}
```

However, because it's a function, the code won't execute until you call it. In the Openings() function, also known as the constructor, under the filters, add drawNavigation(). Now you can zoom in to locations of interest, as shown in Figure 8-45.

FIGURE 8-45 Map with zooming enabled

That's all you need for the base map. You pick your tiles, set your variables, and enable interaction.

Add the Markers

The next steps are to load the Walmart location data and create markers for each store opening. In the constructor, the following code loads an XML file from a URL. When the file finishes loading, a function named onLoadLocations() is called.

```
var urlRequest:URLRequest =
    new URLRequest('http://projects.flowingdata.com/walmart/walmarts_
new.xml');
urlLoader = new URLLoader();
urlLoader.addEventListener(Event.COMPLETE, onLoadLocations);
urlLoader.load(urlRequest);
```

The obvious next step is to create the onLoadLocations() function. It reads the XML file and stores the data in arrays for easier use later. Before you do that though, you need to initialize a few more variables after *navButtons*.

```
private var urlLoader:URLLoader;
private var locations:Array = new Array();
private var openingDates:Array = new Array();
```

These variables are used in onLoadLocations(). Latitude and longitude are stored in *locations*, and opening dates, in year format, are stored in *openingDates*.

```
private function onLoadLocations(e:Event):void {
    var xml:XML = new XML(e.target.data);
    for each(var w:* in xml.walmart) {
        locations.push(new Location(w.latitude, w.longitude));
        openingDates.push(String(w.opening_date));
    }
    markers = new MarkersClip(map, locations, openingDates);
    map.addChild(markers);
}
```

The next step is to create the MarkersClip class. Following the same directory structure discussed earlier, there is a directory named flowingdata in the com directory. A gps directory is in the flowingdata directory. Finally, in com ⇨ flowingdata ⇨ gps is the MarkersClip class. This is the container that will hold all the Walmart markers, or rather, the data layer of your interactive map.

As before, you need to import the classes that you will use. Usually, you add these as you need them in the code, but for the sake of simplicity, you can add all of them at once.

```
import com.modestmaps.Map;
import com.modestmaps.events.MapEvent;

import flash.display.Sprite;
import flash.events.TimerEvent;
import flash.geom.Point;
import flash.utils.Timer;
```

The first two are from Modest Maps, whereas the last four are native classes. Then you set variables right before the MarkersClip() function. Again, you would add these as you need them, but you can add them all now to get to the meat of this class—the functions.

```
protected var map:Map;           // Base map
public var markers:Array;        // Holder for markers
public var isStationary:Boolean;

public var locations:Array;
private var openingDates:Array;

private var storesPerYear:Array = new Array();
private var spyIndex:Number = 0;  // Stores per year index
private var currentYearCount:Number = 0; //  Stores shown so far
private var currentRate:Number;   // Number of stores to show
private var totalTime:Number = 90000;  // Approx. 1.5 minutes
private var timePerYear:Number;
public var currentYear:Number = 1962;  // Start with initial year

private var xpoints:Array = new Array(); // Transformed longitude
private var ypoints:Array = new Array(); // Transformed latitude

public var markerIndex:Number = 0;
private var starting:Point;
private var pause:Boolean = false;
public var scaleZoom:Boolean = false;
```

In the `MarkersClip()` constructor, store the variables that will be passed to the class and compute a few things such as time per year and coordinates for stores. You can think of this as the setup.

The storesPerYear variable stores how many stores opened during a given year. For example, one store opened the first year, and no stores opened the next. When you use this code with your own data, you need to update *storesPerYear* appropriately. You could also write a function that computes stores or location openings per year to increase the reusability of your code. A hard-coded array is specified in this example for the sake of simplicity.

```
this.map = map;

this.x = map.getWidth() / 2;
this.y = map.getHeight() / 2;

this.locations = locations;
setPoints();
setMarkers();

this.openingDates = openingDates;

var tempIndex:int = 0;

storesPerYear = [1,0,1,1,0,2,5,5,5,15,17,19,25,19,27,
        39,34,43,54,150,63,87,99,110,121,142,125,131,178,
        163,138,156,107,129,53,60,66,80,105,106,114,96,
        130,118,37];
timePerYear = totalTime / storesPerYear.length;
```

There are two other functions in the MarkersClip class: `setPoints()` and `setMarkers()`. The first one translates latitude and longitude coordinates to x- and y-coordinates, and the second function places the markers on the map without actually showing them. Following is the definition for `setPoints()`. It uses a built-in function provided by Modest Maps to calculate x and y and then stores the new coordinates in *xpoints* and *ypoints*.

```
public function setPoints():void {
    if (locations == null) {
        return;
    }
}
```

```
        var p:Point;
        for (var i:int = 0; i < locations.length; i++) {
            p = map.locationPoint(locations[i], this);
            xpoints[i] = p.x;
            ypoints[i] = p.y;
        }
    }
```

The second function, setMarkers(), uses the points that setPoints() stores and places markers accordingly.

```
    protected function setMarkers():void
    {
        markers = new Array();
        for (var i:int = 0; i < locations.length; i++)
        {
            var marker:Marker = new Marker();
            addChild(marker);
            marker.x = xpoints[i]; marker.y = ypoints[i];
            markers.push(marker);
        }
    }
```

The function also uses a custom Marker class, which you can find in com ⇨ flowingdata ⇨ gps ⇨ Marker.as, assuming you have downloaded the complete source code. It's basically a holder, and when you call its play() function, it "lights up."

Now you have location and markers loaded on the map. However, if you compiled the code now and played the file, you would still see a blank map. The next step is to cycle through the markers to make them light up at the right time.

The playNextStore() function simply calls play() of the next marker and then gets ready to play the one after that. The startAnimation() and onNextYear() functions use timers to incrementally display each store.

```
    private function playNextStore(e:TimerEvent):void
    {
        Marker(markers[markerIndex]).play();
        markerIndex++;
    }
```

If you were to compile and run the animation now, you'd get dots, but it doesn't work with the map's zoom and pan, as shown in Figure 8-46. As you drag the map back and forth or zoom in and out, the bubbles for each store are stationary.

FIGURE 8-46 Growth map with incorrect pan and zoom

Listeners are added in the constructor so that the dots move whenever the map moves. Whenever a MapEvent is triggered by Modest Maps, a corresponding function defined in MarkersClip.as is called. For example in the first line below, onMapStartZooming() is called when a user clicks on the map's zoom button.

```
this.map.addEventListener(MapEvent.START_ZOOMING,
  onMapStartZooming);
this.map.addEventListener(MapEvent.STOP_ZOOMING,
  onMapStopZooming);
this.map.addEventListener(MapEvent.ZOOMED_BY, onMapZoomedBy);
this.map.addEventListener(MapEvent.START_PANNING,
  onMapStartPanning);
this.map.addEventListener(MapEvent.STOP_PANNING,
  onMapStopPanning);
this.map.addEventListener(MapEvent.PANNED, onMapPanned);
```

This gives you the final map, as shown in Figure 8-47.

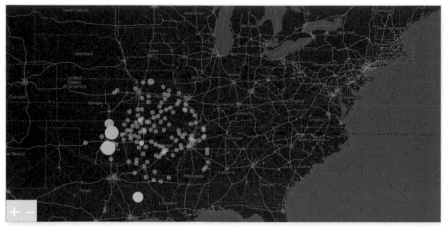

FIGURE 8-47 Fully interactive growth map showing Wal-Mart openings

The story with Walmart store openings is the organic growth. The company started in a single location and slowly spread outward. Obviously, this isn't always the case. For example, Target's growth doesn't look so calculated. Costco's growth is less dramatic because there are fewer locations, but its strategy seems to be growth on the coasts and then a move inward.

In any case, it's a fun and interesting way to view your data. The growth maps seem to spur people's imaginations, and they can wonder about the spread of McDonald's or Starbucks. Now that you have the code, it's a lot easier to implement. The hard part is finding the data.

Wrapping Up

Maps are a tricky visualization type because in addition to your own data, you have to handle the dimension of geography. However, because of how intuitive they are, maps can also be rewarding, both in how you can present data to others and how you can explore your data deeper than you could with a statistical plot.

As seen from the examples in this chapter, there are a lot of possibilities for what you can do with spatial data. With just a few basic skills, you can visualize a lot of datasets and tell all sorts of interesting stories. This is just the tip of the iceberg. I mean, people go to college and beyond to earn degrees in cartography and geography, so you can imagine what else is out there. You can play with cartograms, which size geographic regions according to a metric; add more interaction in Flash; or combine maps with graphs for more detailed and exploratory views of your data.

Online maps have become especially prevalent, and their popularity is only going to grow as browsers and tools advance. For the growth map example, ActionScript and Flash were used, but it could have also been implemented in JavaScript. Which tool you use depends on the purpose. If it doesn't matter what tool you use, then go with the one you're more comfortable with. The main thing, regardless of software, is the logic. The syntax might change, but you do the same with your data, and you look for the same flow in your storytelling.

Designing with a Purpose

9

When you explore your own data, you don't need to do much in terms of storytelling. You are, after all, the storyteller. However, the moment you use your graphic to present information—whether it's to one person, several thousand, or millions—a standalone chart is no longer good enough.

Sure, you want others to interpret results and perhaps form their own stories, but it's hard for readers to know what questions to ask when they don't know anything about the data in front of them. It's your job and responsibility to set the stage. How you design your graphics affects how readers interpret the underlying data.

Prepare Yourself

You need to know your source material to tell good stories with data. This is an often overlooked part of designing data graphics. When you start, it's easy to get excited about your end result. You want something amazing, beautiful, and interesting to look at, and this is great; but you can't do any of that if you have no idea what you're visualizing. You'll just end up with something like Figure 9-1. How can you explain interesting points in a dataset when you don't know the data?

Learn about the numbers and metrics. Figure out where they came from and how they were estimated, and see if they even make sense. This early data gathering process is what makes graphics in *The New York Times* so good. You see the end results in the paper and on the web, but you miss all the work that goes into the graphics before a single shape is drawn. A lot of the time, it takes longer to get all the data in order than it does to design a graphic.

So the next time you have a dataset in front of you, try not to jump right into design. That's the lazy person's way out, and it always shows in the end. Take the time to get to know your data and learn the context of the numbers.

Punch some numbers into R, read any accompanying documentation so that you know what each metric represents, and see if there's anything that looks weird. If there is something that looks weird, and you can't figure out why, you can always contact the source. People are usually happy to hear that someone is making use of the data they published and are eager to fix mistakes if there are any.

After you learn all you can about your data, you are ready to design your graphics. Think of it like this. Remember that part in *The Karate Kid* when Daniel is just starting to learn martial arts? Mister Miyagi tells him to wax a bunch of cars, sand a wooden floor, and refinish a fence, and then Daniel is frustrated because he feels like these are useless tasks. Then of course, it turns out that blocking and punching all of a sudden come natural to him because he's been working on all the right motions. It's the same thing with data. Learn all you can about the data, and the visual storytelling will come natural. If you haven't seen the movie, just nod your head in agreement. And then go add *The Karate Kid* to your Netflix queue.

TIP

Visualization is about communicating data, so take the time to learn about what makes the base of your graphic, or you'll just end up spouting numbers.

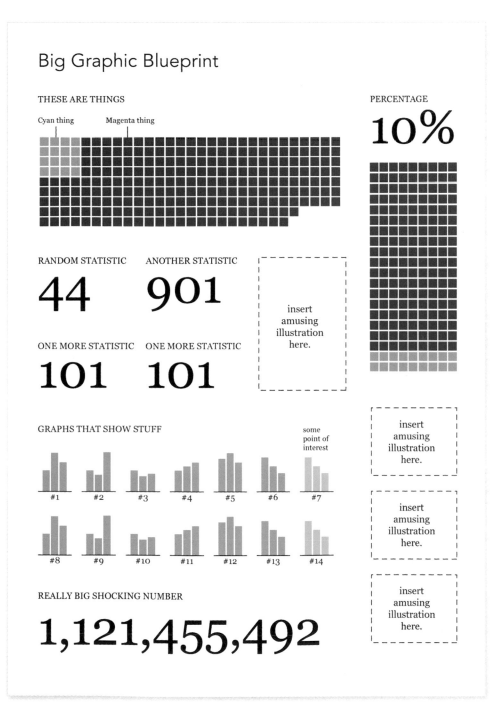

FIGURE 9-1 Big graphic blueprint. Go big or go home.

Prepare Your Readers

Your job as a data designer is to communicate what you know to your audience. They most likely didn't look at the data, so they might not see the same thing that you see if there's no explanation or setup. My rule of thumb is to assume that people are showing up to my graphics blindly, and with sharing via Facebook and Twitter and links from other blogs, that's not all that far off.

For example, Figure 9-2 shows a screenshot of an animated map I made. If you haven't seen this graphic before, you probably have no clue what you're looking at. Given the examples in Chapter 8, "Visualizing Spatial Relationships," your best guess might be openings for some store.

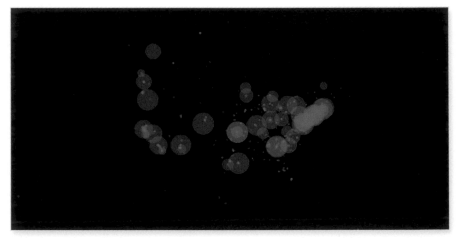

▶ Watch the full map animation at http://datafl .ws/19n.

FIGURE 9-2 Map without a title or context

The map actually shows geotagged tweets that were posted around the world during the inauguration of President Barack Obama on Tuesday, January 20, 2009, at noon Eastern Standard Time. The animation starts early Monday morning, and as the day moves on, more people wake and tweet at a steady rate. The number of tweets per hour increases as the event nears, and Europe gets in on some of the action as the United States sleeps. Then Tuesday morning starts, and then boom—there's huge excitement as the event actually happens. You can easily see this progression in Figure 9-3. Had I provided this context for Figure 9-2, it probably would've made a lot more sense.

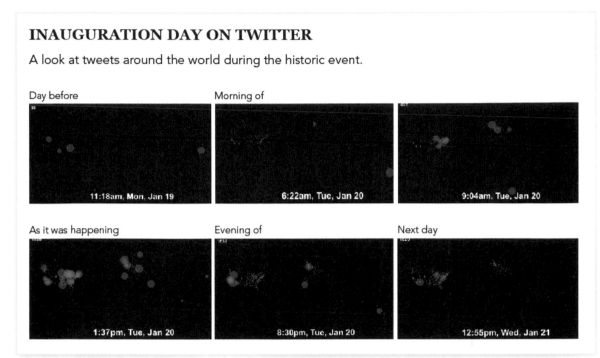

INAUGURATION DAY ON TWITTER

A look at tweets around the world during the historic event.

| Day before | Morning of | |
| 11:18am, Mon, Jan 19 | 6:22am, Tue, Jan 20 | 9:04am, Tue, Jan 20 |

| As it was happening | Evening of | Next day |
| 1:37pm, Tue, Jan 20 | 8:30pm, Tue, Jan 20 | 12:55pm, Wed, Jan 21 |

FIGURE 9-3 Tweets during the inauguration of President Barack Obama

You don't have to write an essay to accompany every graphic, but a title and a little bit of explanation via a lead-in are always helpful. It's often good to include a link somewhere on your graphic so that people can still find your words even if the graphic is shared on another site. Otherwise, it can quickly become like a game of Telephone, and before you know it, the graphic you carefully designed is explained with the opposite meaning you intended. The web is weird like that.

As another example, the graphic in Figure 9-4 is a simple timeline that shows the top ten data breaches at the time.

It's basic with only ten data points, but when I posted it on FlowingData, I brought up how the breaches grow higher in frequency as you move from 2000 to 2008. The graphic ended up getting shared quite a bit, with a variant even ending up in *Forbes* magazine. Almost everyone brought up that last bit. I don't think people would've given the graphic much thought had I not provided that simple observation.

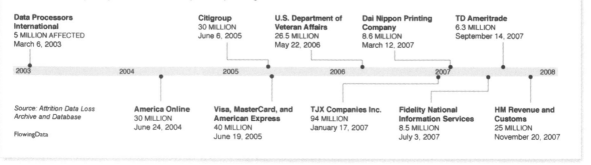

FIGURE 9-4 Major data breaches since 2000

The lesson: Don't assume your readers know everything or that they can spot features in your graphic. This is especially true with the web because people are used to clicking to the next thing.

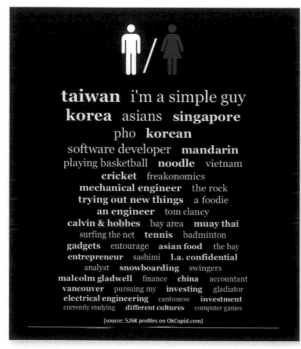

FIGURE 9-5 What Asian guys like based on OkCupid online dating profiles

That's not to say that people won't spend time looking at data. As you might have seen, the OkCupid blog has been writing relatively long posts presenting results from thorough analyses of its online dating dataset. Titles include "The Best Questions for a First Date" and "The Mathematics of Beauty."

Posts on the blog have been viewed millions of times, and people love what the OkCupid folks have to say. In addition to the tons of context in the actual post, people also come to the blog with a bit of context of their own. Because it is data and findings about dating and the opposite sex, people can easily relate with their own experiences. Figure 9-5, for example, is a graphic that shows what Asian guys typically like, which is from an OkCupid post on what people like, categorized by race and gender. Hey, I'm Asian *and* a guy. Instant connection.

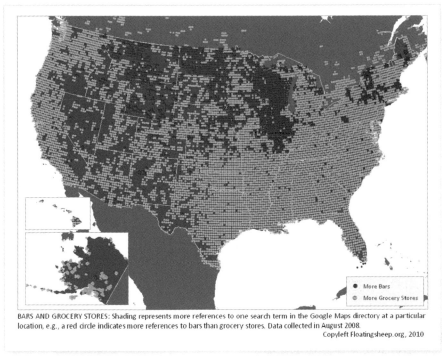

BARS AND GROCERY STORES: Shading represents more references to one search term in the Google Maps directory at a particular location, e.g., a red circle indicates more references to bars than grocery stores. Data collected in August 2008.

Copyleft Floatingsheep.org., 2010

FIGURE 9-6 Where bars outnumber grocery stores in the United States

On the other hand, when your graphic's topic is pollution levels or global debt, it can be a tough sell to a general audience if you don't do a good job of explaining.

Sometimes, no matter how much you explain, people simply don't like to read online, and they'll just skim. For example, I posted a map by FloatingSheep that compares number of bars to number of grocery stores in the United States, as shown in Figure 9-6. Red indicates areas where there are more bars than grocery stores, and orange indicates vice versa. The FloatingSheep guys called it the "beer belly of America."

Toward the end of the post, I wondered about the accuracy of the map and then finished up with, "Anyone who lives in the area care to confirm? I expect your comment to be filled with typos and make very little sense. And maybe smell like garbage." The lesson? Dry humor and sarcasm doesn't translate very well online, especially when people aren't used to reading your writing. I didn't actually expect comments to smell like garbage. Most people got the joke, but there were also a good number of insulted Wisconsinites. Like I said, the web is an interesting place (in a good way).

Visual Cues

In Chapter 1, "Telling Stories with Data," you saw how encodings work. Basically, you have data, and that data is encoded by geometry, color, or animation. Readers then decode those shapes, shades, and movement, mapping them back to numbers. This is the foundation of visualization. Encoding is a visual translation. Decoding helps you see data from a different angle and find patterns that you otherwise would not have seen if you looked only at the data in a table or a spreadsheet.

These encodings are usually straightforward because they are based on mathematical rules. Longer bars represent higher values, and smaller circles represent smaller values. Although your computer makes a lot of decisions during this process, it's still up to you to pick encodings appropriate for the dataset at hand.

Through all the examples in previous chapters, you've seen how good design not only lends to aesthetics, but also makes graphics easier to read and can change how readers actually feel about the data or the story you tell. Graphics with default settings from R or Excel feel raw and mechanical. This isn't necessarily a bad thing. Maybe that's all you want to show for an academic report. Or if your graphic is just a supplement to a more important body of writing, it could be better to not detract from what you want people to focus on. Figure 9-7 shows a generic bar plot that is about as plain as plain can be.

If, however, you do want to display your graphic prominently, a quick color change can make all the difference. Figure 9-8 is just Figure 9-7 with different background and foreground colors.

A darker color scheme might be used for a somber topic, whereas a brighter color scheme can feel more happy-go-lucky (Figure 9-9).

Of course, you don't always need a theme. You can use a neutral color palette if you like, as shown in Figure 9-10.

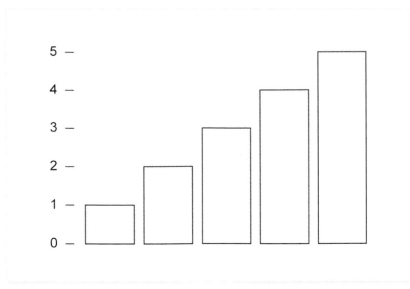

FIGURE 9-7 Plain bar plot

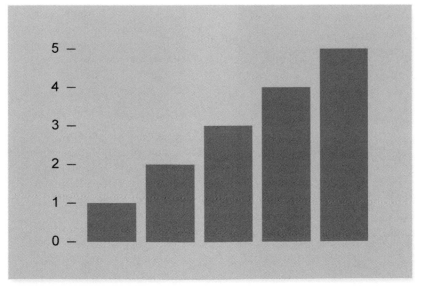

FIGURE 9-8 Default graph with dark color scheme

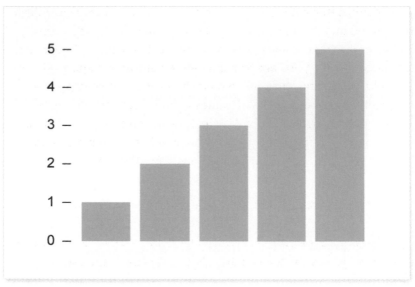

FIGURE 9-9 Default graph with light color scheme

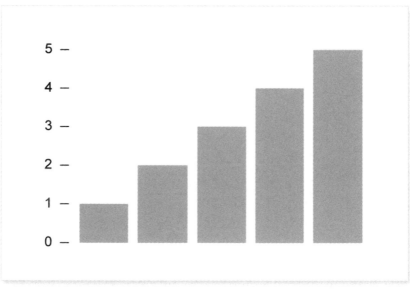

FIGURE 9-10 Default graph with neutral color scheme

The main point is that color choice can play a major role in data graphics. It can evoke emotions (or not) and help provide context. It's your responsibility to choose colors that represent an accurate message. Your colors should match the story you are trying to tell. As shown in Figure 9-11, a simple color change can change the meaning of your data completely. The graphic by designer David McCandless and design duo Always With Honor, explores the meaning of colors in different cultures. For example, black and white are often used to represent death; however, blue and green are more commonly used in Muslim and South American cultures, respectively.

Similarly, you can change geometry for a different look, feel, and meaning. For example, Figure 9-12 shows a randomly generated stacked bar chart with visualization researcher Mike Bostock's Data-Driven Documents. It has straight edges and distinct points, along with peaks and valleys.

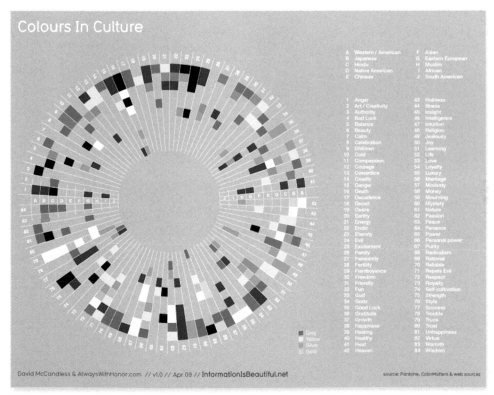

FIGURE 9-11 Colours In Culture by David McCandless and Always With Honor

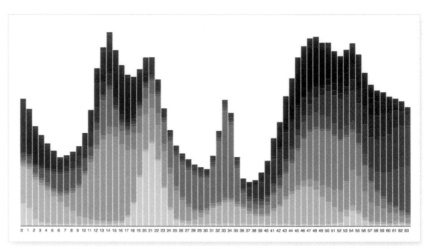

FIGURE 9-12 Randomly generated stacked bar chart

▶ Check out Lee Byron and Martin Wattenberg's paper, "Stacked Graphs— Geometry and Aesthetics" for more information on streamgraphs. Several packages are also available, such as Protovis and D3, that enable you to design your own.

If instead you used a streamgraph to show similar data, as shown in Figure 9-13, you clearly get a different feel. It's more free-flowing and continuous, and instead of peaks and valleys, you have tightening and swelling. At the same time though, the geometry between the two chart types is similar. The streamgraph is basically a smoothed stacked bar chart with the horizontal axis in the center instead of on the bottom.

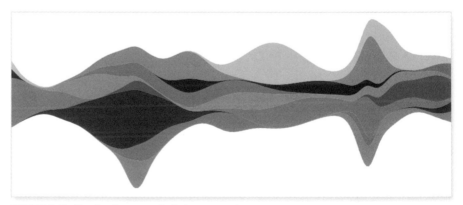

FIGURE 9-13 Randomly generated streamgraph

Sometimes context can simply come from how you organize shapes and colors. Figure 9-14 shows a graphic that I made for fun to celebrate the holidays. The top part shows the ingredients that go into brining your turkey, and on the bottom is what goes into the turkey when you roast it in the oven.

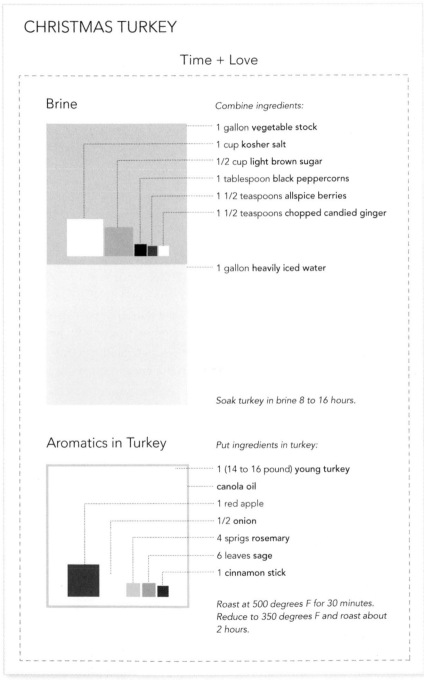

CHRISTMAS TURKEY

Time + Love

Brine

Combine ingredients:

1 gallon **vegetable stock**

1 cup **kosher salt**

1/2 cup **light brown sugar**

1 tablespoon **black peppercorns**

1 1/2 teaspoons **allspice berries**

1 1/2 teaspoons **chopped candied ginger**

1 gallon **heavily iced water**

Soak turkey in brine 8 to 16 hours.

Aromatics in Turkey

Put ingredients in turkey:

1 (14 to 16 pound) **young turkey**

canola oil

1 **red apple**

1/2 **onion**

4 sprigs **rosemary**

6 leaves **sage**

1 **cinnamon stick**

Roast at 500 degrees F for 30 minutes. Reduce to 350 degrees F and roast about 2 hours.

FIGURE 9-14 Recipe for Christmas turkey

The bottom line: At its most basic level, visualization is turning data, which can be numbers, text, categories, or any variety of things, into visual elements. Some visual cues work better than others, but applicability also varies by dataset. A method that's completely wrong for one dataset could fit perfectly for another. With practice, you can quickly decide what fits your purpose best.

Good Visualization

Although people have been charting and graphing data for centuries, only in the past few decades have researchers been studying what works and what doesn't. In that respect, visualization is a relatively new field. There still isn't a consensus on what visualization actually is. Is visualization something that has been generated by a computer following a set of rules? If a person has a hand in the design process, does that make it not a visualization? Are information graphics visualization, or do they belong in their own category?

Look online, and you can find lots of threads discussing differences and similarities between information graphics and visualization or essays that try to define what visualization is. It always leads to a never-ending back and forth without resolution. These opposing opinions lead to varied criteria for what makes a data graphic good or bad.

Statisticians and analysts, for example, generally think of visualization as traditional statistical graphics that they can use in their analyses. If a graphic or interactive doesn't help in analysis, then it's not useful. It's a failure. On the other hand, if you talk to graphic designers about the same graphic, they might think the work is a success because it displays the data of interest fairly and presents the data in an engaging way.

What you need to do is smush them all together, or at least get them in the same room together more often. The analytically minded can learn a lot from designers about making data more relatable and understandable, whereas design types can learn to dig deeper into data from their analytic counterparts.

I don't try to define what visualization is because the definition doesn't affect how I work. I consider the audience, the data in front of me, and ask myself whether the final graphic makes sense. Does it tell me what I want to know? If yes, then great. If no, I go back to the drawing board and figure out what would make the graphic better so that it answers the questions I have about the data. Ultimately, it's all about your goals for the graphic, what story you want to tell, and who you tell it to. Take all of the above into account—and you're golden.

Wrapping Up

A lot of data people see design as just a way to make your graphics look pretty. That's certainly part of it, but design is also about making your graphics readable, understandable, and usable. You can help people understand your data better than if they were to look at a default graph. You can clear clutter, highlight important points in your data, or even evoke an emotional response. Data graphics can be entertaining, fun, and informative. Sometimes it'll just be the former, depending on your goal, but no matter what you try to design—visualization, information graphic, or data art—let the data guide your work.

When you have a big dataset, and you don't know where to begin, the best place to start is with a question. What do you want to know? Are you looking for seasonal patterns? Relationships between multiple variables? Outliers? Spatial relationships? Then look back to your data to see if you can answer your question. If you don't have the data you need, then look for more.

When you have your data, you can use the skills you learned from the examples in this book to tell an interesting story. Don't stop here, though. Think of the material you worked through as a foundation. At the core of all your favorite data graphics is a data type and a visualization method that you now know how to work with. You can build on these for more advanced and complex graphics. Add interactions, combine plots, or complement your graphics with photographs and words to add more context.

Remember: Data is simply a representation of real life. When you visualize data, you visualize what's going on around you and in the world. You can see what's going on at a micro-level with individuals or on a much larger scale spanning the universe. Learn data, and you can tell stories that most people don't even know about yet but are eager to hear. There's more data to play with than ever before, and people want to know what it all means. Now you can tell them. Have fun.

Index